Dante
A Critical Reappraisal

Unn Falkeid (ed.)

Unipub 2008

©Unipub AS 2008

ISBN 978-82-7477-347-9

Contact info Unipub:
T: + 47 22 85 33 00
F: + 47 22 85 30 39
E-mail: post@unipub.no
www.unipub.no

Publisher: Oslo Academic Press, Unipub Norway
Cover and book design by Unipub AS
Cover: Portrait of Dante by Raphael. Detail from *La disputa del Sacramento* (1509), Rome, Stanza della Segnatura.
Printed in Norway: AIT e-dit AS, Oslo 2008

This book has been produced with economical support from the Department of Literature, Area Studies and European Languages and the Faculty of Humanities at the University of Oslo.

All rights reserved. No part of this publication may be reproduced or transmitted, in any form or by any means, without permission

Preface

As one of the dominating names in Western literature, Dante Alighieri (1265–1321) has also been read and studied with great enthusiasm in the Nordic countries since the early 20th century. The *Divine Comedy* has been translated into Nordic languages on several occasions and, over the last few decades, many introductions and popular monographs have been published. Equally important: interest seems to be on the increase. Dante's works are studied across different disciplines – within Italian and comparative literature; theology; philosophy and the history of ideas – to the extent that we can now refer to a new generation of *dantisti* among Nordic scholars.

The first initiative to gather Nordic Dante scholars into an organised society was taken in 1998; the Nordic Dante Network was established shortly after by Christian Kaatmann and Ole Meyer of The Royal Library in Copenhagen. The concept was to coordinate the on-going scholarly work on Dante in the Nordic countries, to incite further interest in Dante at Nordic universities and, above all, to stimulate younger generations at doctoral and post-graduate level.

The central activity of the network is the organisation of open, three-day conferences that rotate between the different countries every other year. The first conference was held in Copenhagen during the official opening of The Royal Library of Denmark in 1999 and the second at the University of Stockholm in 2001. The proceedings from these two conferences have been presented in the following publications: *Perspektiv på Dante I* (Perspectives on Dante I, edited by Christian Kaatmann and Ole Meyer, Copenhagen, 1999) and *Perspektiv på Dante II* (Perspectives on Dante II, edited by Anders Cullhed, Copenhagen, 2006).

The third conference was held at the University of Oslo in September 2006. Although the language of the previous conferences had been Scandinavian, a wish was expressed to open the network up to a broader international public, which led to the conference in

Oslo being predominantly conducted in English. This made it possible to invite a Dante scholar from abroad. An obvious choice was Giuseppe Mazzotta, Sterling Professor of Italian Literature at Yale University, and current President of the Dante Society of America. His groundbreaking works on Dante, *Dante, Poet of the Desert: History and Allegory in the Divine Comedy* (1979) and *Dante's Vision and the Circle of Knowledge* (1993) and several influential articles, have been widely read, acclaimed and discussed by Nordic scholars. It was an honour and a true inspiration when Giuseppe Mazzotta accepted our invitation. He was the keynote-speaker of the conference and his contribution forms the opening chapter of this book.

The anthology consists of proceedings from this third conference of the Nordic Dante Network. The book aims to present a picture of current developments within Dante studies in the Nordic countries; to demonstrate how domestic readings are the result of a fruitful dialogue within international scholarship, while still retaining their own individual characteristics. As such the book is a "critical reappraisal" of one of the main figures in the Western canon by Nordic scholars.

To conclude, I wish to thank the Faculty of Humanities and the Department of Literature, Area Studies and European Languages at the University of Oslo, for their generous financial support of both the conference and this publication. I also wish to thank the institution Fritt Ord [the Freedom of Expression Foundation] and the Dante Society of America for their contributions in realisation of the conference.

Unn Falkeid
University of Oslo
June 2008

Contents

Dante's poetics of births and foundations *Giuseppe Mazzotta*	7
Dante and King David *Trond Berg Eriksen*	27
Dicendo questo. A note on Dante's writing of Paradise *Anders Cullhed*	35
Aspects of negativity. Veridictory figures in the Comedy *Hanne Roer*	47
Ranking types of reading. Descriptive and epic readings in Dante studies *Jesper Hede*	69
The problem of double reception. On the dialectic of simple and complex apprehensio in the Divine comedy *Ülar Ploom*	91
Galeotto fu il libro e chi lo scrisse. Some remarks about intertextuality in Inferno V *Leonardo Cecchini*	111
Dante and the Bible. A reading of central passages in the Vita nuova and the Commedia *Asbjørn Bjornes*	121
The domestication of vernacular poetry. Measuring authority in the De vulgari eloquentia *Espen Grønlie*	145
Dante's avant-gardism reinvented. Past and present vernaculars in the 1920s *P.M. Mehtonen*	177
Petrarch in the footsteps of Dante *Unn Falkeid*	187

Vandringsmandens identitet i Den guddommelige komedie *Jørn Moestrup*	197
Hvorfor sådan? Om Komedien på italiensk og andre sprog *Ole Meyer*	205
Melodien der blev væk. Dante på dansk *Conni-Kay Jørgensen*	219
Contributors	239
Literature	243

Dante's poetics of births and foundations

Giuseppe Mazzotta

Throughout the *Divine Comedy* there runs a motif centred on the metaphor of "birth" and its political extension, "foundation". The poem deploys fully this thematic pattern and elevates it to its primary conceptual framework. It unveils "birthing" (by which I mean the individual event of being born, the foundation of a city, the conception of poetry etc.) as the radical perspective that penetrates beyond all habits of thought, right to the roots of historical experiences. Textual examples of this thematic web abound, and I shall first list some of them. I shall then probe some of the implications of the question of "birth" as both origin and foundation, what might be called the physics and metaphysics of birth.

At the beginning of the poem, Virgil, who will be acknowledged by the pilgrim variously as the father and "source" of his poetic eloquence, states: "Nacqui *sub Julio*" (*Inf.* I, 79) (I was born *sub Julio*). Francesca echoes the detail: "Siede la terra dov'io nata fui [...]" (*Inf.* V, 92) (The city where I was born lies [...]). Ciacco refers to his death in terms of the pilgrim's own birth: "Tu fosti, prima ch'io disfatto, fatto" (*Inf.* VI, 42) (You were made before I was unmade). Farinata, for whom Florence is endangered by his own aristocratic virtues and whose role exemplifies the rift between ethics and politics, describes Dante, and indirectly himself, as "[...] di quella nobile patria natio" (*Inf.* X, 26) (native of that noble fatherland). Guido da Montefeltro, while relating the changes in his moral life, speaks of the "[...] forma fui d'ossa e di polpe/ che la madre mi diè" (*Inf.* XXVII, 73–74) (form of the flesh and bones my mother gave me).

A list of this recurrent figure is by no means limited to the Inferno. Think of the epitaph Pia de' Tolomei inscribes for herself: "Siena mi fè, disfecemi Maremma" (*Purg.* V, 134) (Siena made me, Maremma unmade me) – a line that picks up and reverses Ciacco's self-definition. We might mention Sordello, who in greeting Virgil, breaks off what most likely was meant to echo Virgil's "Mantua me genuit [...]" (cf. *Purg.* VI, 72). The references to the Annunciation, to Statius's birth in Toulose, to St. Francis' birth in Assisi and St. Dominic's in Calaroga (respectively *Par.* XI, 50 and XII, 52–55) are well-known. Cacciaguida's account of his own and other great Florentine families' roots, ranging from "O sanguis meus" (*Par.* XV, 28), through the dynastic stocks of some Florentines (*Par.* XVI) to the recognition of the pilgrim as "O cara piota mia" (*Par.* XVII, 13) (O my dear seed-pot) and Dante's own horoscope, whereby the planetary arrangement signals the singularity of his birth (*Par.* XXII, 112–17), stresses the importance of the metaphor for the pilgrim's own history. Finally, at the end of the poem, the prayer to the Virgin Mary, daughter of her son, comes to focus on the most intimate receptacle of her body: the womb of Mary as the flowerpot where "[...] è germinato questo fiore" (*Par.* XXXIII, 9) (this flower has bloomed). The verb "germinare" refers back to *germen* (spore or semen) and thus it describes the receptacle where the germinal cell of redemption was deposited. The seminal causes of Neo-Platonism are embodied here.

The prayer to Mary, with its emphasis on the double, reciprocal conception of mother and son, plainly re-enacts the centrality of the Nativity event in Dante's poetry and theology. In this sense, it acknowledges Christianity as the religion making birth (and rebirth or the resurrection) the heart of its being. In the other cases, the reference to birth may function as a principle of individuation, an index of a character's identity, social standing, and origin. A birth, in its distinctive corporeality, always evokes a material fact of history: the specifics of place and time, neither of which are either directly known or willed by the figures involved. But as a physical fact, it always marks a beginning and an "event", a concrete point of departure towards an as yet nonexisting future, even when a life ends up achieving nothing and folds back into nothing. As far as the lives of the "founders" celebrated in Paradiso go, Francis, Dominic, Benedict, and Bernard, births turn into unpredictable historical events, actions breaking the chain of natural causality, bearing and giving origin to unintended consequences that touch other lives. We could provisionally generalize by saying that in a birth Dante captures the process through which nature becomes history, a fact turns into a metaphor, and ordinary occurrences take on the colour of significant actions. For every birth combines a paradoxically commonplace singularity and familiar everydayness. Adam, who is called "l'uom che non nacque" (*Par.* VII, 26) (the man who was never born) is an exception. But the rest of us share the fact of being born. Yet each birth is unique. In this sense, a birth represents a break with the past, changes it (and thus reverses the view that the past alone conditions the present), and forces on us the thought of a possible new beginning as well as the anticipation of one's mortality.

This concern with "birthing" goes beyond the biological event and biographical descriptions. It even figures outside the *Divine Comedy*. In Purgatorio XXV, in a lecture on medieval embryology, Statius (and we shall see why it is significant that it should be he) recounts the origin of the soul and its powers by charting the processes of refinement of the blood, the conjunction with the sperm, and the coagulation of the blood into a foetus in the mother's body. Further, metaphorical births describe cities' origins and foundations. After some discreet references to Semiramis and Dido as founders (cf. *Inf.* V), in Inferno XX Virgil recalls his birthplace in Mantua ("dove nacqu'io) (56) (where I was born). This recollection ushers in the revised tale of the foundation of his city – the "[...] originar de la mia terra" (98) (the origin given to my birth) on the swamps around Lake Benaco on the River Mencius (74–75). The foundation of Rome on the other hand is often cited, for instance in Inferno XXVI, where Virgil, pointing out the shades of Ulysses and Diomedes, calls the fall of Troy the catastrophe from which the "gentil seme" (60), the noble seed of the Romans, develops. Florence's origin from Fiesole and from Rome ('la nobilissima figlia di Roma") is also recorded.

Because Dante links together births, seeds, origins, and foundations with Roman poets (Virgil and Statius) and Roman history (as opposed to the Greek myth embodied by Oedipus, Ulysses and Diomedes), one cannot but ask what is Dante's sense of the origin of history or, which roughly amounts to the same thing, what precise understanding of birth, origins, and foundations does Dante inherit from the classical Roman tradition. He never refers, to be sure, to Rome's celebration of its own origin, as is displayed by its civic ritual: to this day it celebrates its *dies natalis* on April 21. As medieval numismatics attests, the ancient formula SPQR accompanies the image of the she-wolf nursing the twins Romulus and Remus. But doubtless he knows that the question of birth and foundation lies at the heart of Rome's own self-understanding and quest for a new kind of history. A couple of examples will suffice.

Livy chronicles the history of Rome not with an abstract, transcendent chronology or with a myth of sacred origin (such as one finds in Bede and Peter Comestor), but with the concrete foundation of the city, *Ab urbe condita*. The *Aeneid* retrieves the myth of the city's origin through the narrative of Aeneas, who has first suffered the loss of Troy. Unlike Ulysses, whose contrivance of the wooden horse destroys Troy, Aeneas builds one city after the other along the stages of his journeying and watches Dido's edification of Carthage on the symbolic ashes of Troy. An extension of this classical, pagan preoccupation with foundations is available in the *City of God*. St Augustine, who in this sense is the greatest Roman philosopher, finds the wellspring of the Church in the Roman ideology of foundations and binds it to the Jewish account of Creation. In the tradition stretching from Aeneas to Augustine, foundations primarily entail the experience of the will and the thought of the future (since the will is powerless vis-à-vis the past).

The web of political births and foundations described above is a far cry from both *Convivio*, where the link between birth and nobility is pondered, and from the *Vita nuova*, which posits a double riddle of birth and origination, the birth of poetry and of love. The *Vita nuova* places us from the start within the horizon of time, time in the subjective dimension of memory. The text literally begins at the beginning: "In quella parte del libro de la mia memoria, dinanzi a la quale poco si potrebbe leggere, si trova una rubrica la quale dice: *Incipit vita nova*.: (In my book of Memory, in the early part where there is little to be read, there comes a chapter with the rubric: *Incipit vita nova*). The poet will reproduce memory's inscriptions, but throughout he records what he views as the spontaneous origin of his poetry (chapter XIX); he acknowledges his descent from Guinizelli as his poetic father, and at the end of the book he discovers the singularity of poetry within the pattern of origins: the work of art gives origin to the poet as much as the work originates from him. Above all, he solves the double riddle shaping his text: he discovers that his poetry is rooted in the heart of love, which nourishes the lover, and that what makes things new, what imparts a new beginning to one's life, is love.

This topic of births and beginnings has received little or no attention from scholars (Singleton, Charity, Freccero, Harrison), who, by and large, have chosen to highlight the structure of retrospection, the typology of death, and the perspective of the end (in their Augustinian, Hegelian, and Heideggerian articulations) as the principle of Dante's representation of the afterlife. As St Augustine has it (*Confessions* XI, 28), a man's life is extended in two directions, towards memory and towards the future, and it becomes intelligible when it has passed into memory. By the same token, so it is argued, Dante's focus on death freezes life into an unalterable, permanently fixed totality. When we die, time is suspended and death reduces us to frozen appearances. Only then do we finally become what we are and, in retrospect, the ultimate meaning of our lives surfaces.

Such an understanding of the revelatory, foundational power of death depends logically on the temporal priority of birth. It says nothing about the fact that the meaning of a life, although it is revealed at the end, is implicit in its origin. Nor does this understanding tackle the textual detail that Augustine's reflection on memory's inner spaces occurs in the context of his exegesis of Genesis' "In the beginning" (*Confessions* XII, 9). In his theology of beginnings, Biblical creation – as much as the Roman practice of political foundations for Livy and Virgil – offers the open-ended conditions both to imagine the future out of some dead past and to anticipate all possible actions in the world. Indeed, because a birth in its uniqueness presupposes a singular responsibility and obligation, Augustine ties birth with the emergence of a historical action and choice. For Dante, birth and death (though different from each other in that in a physical death all is done) belong together as sacramental gifts implicating and enveloping each other: he submits to death's sovereignty as far as it brings about not an end, since there is no end, but a new beginning.

How some of these issues raised here are clustered together emerges from Virgil's autobiographical self-portrait in Inferno:

Rispuosemi: 'Non omo, omo già fui,
e li parenti miei furon lombardi,

mantoani per patria ambedui.
Nacqui *sub Iulio*, ancor che fosse tardi,
e vissi a Roma sotto 'l buon Augusto
nel tempo de li dei falsi e bugiardi.
Poeta fui, e cantai di quell giusto
figliuol d'Anchise che venne di Troia
poi che 'l superbo Ilion fu combusto.
(*Inf.* I, 67–75)

("No, not a living man, though once I was," he answered me, "and my parents were lombards, both Mantuans by birth. I was born *sub Iulio*, although late and I lived at Rome under the good Augustus in the time of the false and lying gods. I was a poet and sang of the just son of Anchises who came from Troy after proud Ilium was burned").

The lines collapse the distinction between biography and history and draw the framework of Virgil's historical circumstances and roots: family background, the place, and time of his birth. They also imaginatively connect his birth, his parents, and the birth of Aeneas, which, in turn, relates the line of Caesar's genealogy. In point of fact, the burden of the passage rests on Virgil's self-identity and origination. Biblical narrative genealogy (the dynastic line of, say, the prophet Samuel or the Book of the generation of Jesus, from Abraham through David to his birth in Judea, in Matthew's prologue) records lines of descent as a tool to vindicate the legitimacy of the claims made on behalf of the respectively prophetic and messianic voices. In Virgil's self-identification, genealogy celebrates, on the one hand, the sacredness of tradition, the Roman cult of the ancients and reverence for the authority of the past, and, on the other hand, it unveils the thread binding each figure (Virgil, Aeneas, Caesar, Augustus, Rome, and the *Aeneid*). The peculiarity of each birth consists of this: a birth is not really our own or of our choosing any more than are one's parents or time, nor is a figure its own foundation. As a point of origin, a birth, in its raw, biological facticity, sends us back to previous origins, but out of this regression into the past springs the idea of the future. As Rome does with Troy, each historical figure encompasses within itself the seeds of the past and the future realities it generates. In this sense, each birth uniquely embodies a project for the future and thus breaks the molds of the past (as, say,

Bonconte does with his father Guido da Montefeltro or Francis does with his merchant father).

We would thus be mistaken if we were to see in Dante's insistence on births and foundations merely the vestiges of a longing for recapturing pure, lost origins. In Dante's thought there is no nostalgia for an archaic mythical order (not even in his encounter with Cacciaguida and their musings on Florence's genealogy). If anything, origins necessarily entail the future. A couple of examples will clarify what I mean. The theory of language in *De Vulgari Eloquentia*, which stems from the dream of the lost Edenic language, acknowledges the unfolding of history as the locus of permutations, differences, and linguistic scraps to be forged in a language of the future not yet engendered. The second example concerns politics.

I have been arguing that every event of birth is significant because it alters the web of existing relations and changes each of us into potentially historical agents capable of willing and shaping both the past (though, in fact, the past makes the will powerless) and the future. It follows that there is a politics of beginnings, the conviction of a wilful action and choice to be realized and made. Virgil, who is thoroughly steeped in history as genealogy, envisions the future as a new historical beginning. After identifying himself when he appears to the lost pilgrim, he predicts the imminent cleansing of the world's greed by the action of the "Veltro", whose "nazion sarà tra feltro e feltro" (*Inf.* I, 105) (his birth shall be between felt and felt). The enigmatic prophecy, which stresses once again Virgil's sense of the bond between birth and history, discloses the inner connection between new beginnings and the future: it suggests that the possibility of the future presumes the idea of a beginning and vice versa.

Nowhere else does the poem explore the implications of this temporal dimension of birth than in Purgatorio. The canticle begins at dawn on Easter Sunday, the liturgical time of the Resurrection or new creation, but the new beginning for the souls cannot be construed as a second chance. Their purification, on the contrary, means that they bring to completion the spiritual renewal started on Earth. At any rate, as the process of renewal is thematized throughout the canticle, time is uncovered in its future dimension. The poet announces his poetic argument by adopting the future tense: "[...] e canterò di quell secondo regno / ove l'umano spirito si purga / e di salire al cielo diventa degno" (*Purg.* I, 4–6) (and I will sing of that second realm where the human spirit is purged and becomes fit to ascend to Heaven). In Hell the souls live in the fixed circle of immanent time. By contrast, the first soul we meet in Purgatorio, Cato, is poised between the past and future and in his juridical role he forces the penitents to resist the lure of the past and look instead towards the future.

Cato comes into view after the reader has caught sight of Caesar's murderers, Brutus and Cassius, in the mouths of Lucifer. In Purgatorio I he watches over the edicts of this new spiritual order and appears later as an ethical voice censuring the pilgrim's aesthetic self-absorption as he listens to Casella's song just as a little earlier Cato had resisted the temptations of Marcia's memory. The rejection of the ghosts of the past entails the view of time as future and introduces a notion that underlies the deepest question of beginnings: freedom.

The primary ethical implication of beginnings and foundations is freedom (for the very notion of beginning is inconceivable without an idea of freedom just as freedom is inconceivable without the notion of beginning) which emerges from the figuration of Cato's suicide as an act of and a quest for freedom: "Libertà che sì cara va cercando / come sa chi per lei vita rifiuta" (*Purg.* I, 72) (He goes seeking liberty, which is so dear, as he knows who gives his life for it). Cato sought a political and moral freedom from the tyranny of Caesar and Pompey, and, more generally, from the tyranny of the civil war, which in Lucan's *Pharsalia* encapsulated the monotonously tragic paradigm of Roman history, the dark side of its imperial claims. Dante subsumes Cato's (and his own liberty) within a theology of freedom and yet he preserves the autonomy which political and secular values warrant. In Purgatorio II, as the penitents prepare for their moral ascent, they hear the opening words of Psalm 113, "In exitu Israel de Aegypto" (46), the song of the Jews' freedom from their house of bondage in Egypt. Theology is here politics and, by the same token, politics is theology, and the two traditions (Roman and Jewish) constituting the grid of Dante's moral imagination shed a revealing light on each other as well as on the representation of Statius.

Statius' appearance in Purgatorio is introduced by the Nativity matin "*Gloria in excelsis ...Deo*" (*Purg.* XX, 136), which echoes Luke ii, 9. The motif is followed by a direct reference to Luke's account of the apparition of the risen Christ at Emmaus (*Purg.* XXI, 7 ff) (cf. Luke xxiv, 13 ff.). The Christological background prepares the further story of Statius' conversion in reaction to the Emperor Domitian's persecution of Christians (*Purg.* XXII, 81 ff.). The process of his conversion is told through Statius' poetic apprenticeship (as if writing were an ascetic labour of the soul), through his reading of Virgil's *Eclogues* and *Aeneid* to his writing about the "double sorrow" of Jocasta, namely the *Thebaid*, a task which is figured as a journey. As with Cato, here too political and moral liberty is at the forefront of Dante's concerns: he confronts and redefines the insights of the two Roman poets, Lucan and Statius.

Historically, roughly 50 years separate Statius from Lucan. Statius, actually, composes in his *Silvae* (II, 7) a "Genethliacon Lucani". In fact, they both live and write at a time of great crisis in the history of Rome and both recount the bankruptcy of freedom. Lucan, who against Nero's Caesarism casts himself as the witness of the events he narrates, focuses on the civil war between Caesar and Pompey as the battle not of two opposed visions but of the same passion for power. The antagonists are a pair of mirrors reflecting each other. Together, they bring about the catastrophe of the Roman Republic. Between them stands Cato, and Lucan shows how the curtain falls on this last incarnation of Stoic virtues. For Cato Rome's name is *libertas* (*Pharsalia* II, 301 ff). The poem, however, achieves more than that. Written between 59 and 65 AD, the *Pharsalia* comes across as a compendium of Roman history, and Roman history unfolds as an unchanging, fatal concatenation of civil wars (between Marius and Sulla, Caesar and Pompey, and Octavian and Antony). The scandal of the civil war is for Lucan an insoluble enigma shadowing all rationality and his history writing, which bypasses and questions Virgil's resolution. Virgil himself focuses on the "civil war" between Turnus and Aeneas (who by coming to Latium is in a sense returning to the place of his ancestors). Against the spectre of the civil war he retrieves Rome's foundational myths. Over and against Virgil, Lucan seeks to leave out the traditional mythical machinery of the epic in favour of a realistic, historical narrative, and he sinks into a world of hallucinations and madness: reality is indistinguishable from diabolical magical operations.

The myths of Thebes and the events and characters of Statius' *Thebaid* so litter the world of Inferno (cf., for instance, the references to the Furies, Capaneus, Jason's betrayal of Hypsipile, Eteocles and Polynice, Pisa a "novella Tebe" in Inferno XXXIII etc.) that Thebes can be envisaged as the radical emblem of the fallen earthly city. Conceived in conversation with Lucan's poem, the *Thebaid* dispels from the start the illusion of a rational understanding and exorcism of Thebes' mythical history. The night of madness hangs forever over the house of Oedipus and Jocasta. Statius keeps repeating the ancient myth's truth: the serpents of the Furies – madness of power, lust for revenge, monster of pride, the nightmare of fratricidal wars etc. – are always ready to be unleashed again. If Lucan spins out the interplay between history and literature (in the intuitive recognition that political life finds its best look-alike in fiction), Statius plunges us into the dark fantasies engulfing historical existence: politics comes across as psychology and, as such, this unveils the fatality we know but cannot change: the steady human transgression of divine laws.

The insight into history as a phantasmatic, mythical repetition organizes the narrative of the *Thebaid*. Quite at odds with this insight, Statius, who at the start describes his own mind as beclouded by madness, casts writing as the undertaking of a solitary journey ("whence, heavenly ones, am I to take the road?") (*Theb*. I, 4–5). This metaphor of poetry as a journey or spiritual adventure, which Dante picks up in the representation of Statius, begins in the shadow of both Lucan (I, I, 19) and Virgil, who is celebrated as the "magnus magister" (XII, 810ff.) Through the references to the Roman literary tradition, Statius self-consciously inscribes himself in that tradition. The awareness of the singularity of his poetry, however, counters the repetitive thematic pattern of the poem. Dante will exploit, as will be shown, this complication in Statius' poetic self-consciousness.

After a nod in the direction of Rome's political theology, the 'divina domus" of the Flavii and of Domitian as 'dominus et deus", the poet descends into the mind of Oedipus, who has plucked out his eyes to punish his guilty shame. Oedipus is blind, and his blindness appears at the opening of the text as he curses his sons, Eteocles and Polynice, who were conceived in his mother's bed. In Virgil the fact of birth, say in the Fourth Eclogue, is a cause for celebration. In the *Thebaid*, the birth of Eteocles and Polynice is a tragic event, for they repeat the old curse and, by being born, introduce nothing new to history. They will destroy each other, and this thematic kernel reproduces itself in an endless series of variations to confirm the hold of the past on them. Accordingly, Statius presents the vicissitudes of his tale through a "baroque" rhetoric in which the language ceaselessly turns inwards and curves in sinuous deadends like the incestuous plot it makes its subject matter and excludes all alternatives.

In Purgatorio Dante deliberately erases or re-interprets the literal traces of both the *Pharsalia* and the *Thebaid*. Yet these two epics of the Roman civil wars constitute the preamble to Dante's own representation of the Florentine civil wars. On Florence's political stage we watch the hallucinatory spectacle of empty bodies, "persone" (*Inf.* VI, 36), a word etymologically denoting both the language of histrionics, the actors' empty masks through which sounds are emitted and, ironically, the substantiality of what theological discourse understands as "persons". A look at the canto of punished gluttony ("la dannosa colpa de la gola"), (*Inf.* VI, 53) (the ruinous fault of gluttony) will show Dante's understanding of naturalistic history, of a politics of bodies. At stake is the general sense of Nature, a term (from *nascor*) encompassing all that is born. He filters such an understanding through Epicurean philosophy, classical political theories, and the city's idolatry of power.

Here Dante meets Ciacco, a shade who explains his death in terms of Dante's birth: "Tu fosti prima ch'io disfatto fatto." From his perspective, life comes forth for everybody as a natural cycle of deaths and births, although, for all their temporal proximity, the two occurrences remain unrelated to each other and without any necessary link between them. For Ciacco these two facts scan the biological succession/continuity in the city. To emphasize the naturalistic burden of the canto, Dante frames it with a reference to the Resurrection, the event radically transfiguring the biological conception of bodies (*Inf.* VI, 94 ff), but without any impact on Ciacco's condition. In effect, Ciacco casts himself as an outsider in the city's values and power play, as one who, driven from the social fabric, claims no history and no redemption for himself. From his viewpoint, however, his gluttony pales in relation to what he perceives as the real voraciousness and gluttony of the body politic.

Ciacco's name means "pig". From the standpoint of the citizens to whom he refers in his speech ("Voi cittadini mi chiamaste [...]") (52) (You citizens called me), he has violated the city's image of decorum and purity and is thus banished from it. The presiding figure of the canto is Cerberus, the three-mouthed dog flaying the empty shades. To the pilgrim who inquires about the future of their divided city ("la città partita") (61), Ciacco predicts the violence of an imminent blood bath. The sense of the prophecy is specific: over the years, from 1300 to 1302, the Whites and Blacks will destroy each other till Boniface VIII, with the help of Charles of Valois, brings about the defeat of the Whites.

In drawing together politics and gluttony and in deploying gluttony as a mirror for the realm of human affairs, Dante argues that Florentine local politics is a politics of bodies, rooted in the blind desires of bodies, and these desires are symbolized by the materiality of food, its ingestion and elimination. The central conceit binding the two themes of the narrative, the bloated body of the gluttons and the sick body politic of the city, derives from the classical fable of Menenius Agrippa as told by Livy in his *Ab urbe condita* (II, 32, 2–33). To heal the dissension between patricians and plebeians, Menenius draws an analogy between the food, the belly, and the corporate structure of the state. Livy's parable aims at the harmony of the city by arguing that an organic corporate model underlies the structure of the city. The belly gives back to each part of the body what it needs and divides among the veins of the body the blood fashioned by digesting the food. By virtue of the analogy, the city's order depends on the organic interdependence of all its parts.

But Dante does not believe in the validity of the corporate political analogy. The belly takes in everything endlessly. And he sees neither a way out of this contingent hell of political hatreds nor any possible cohesion in his native city. Minds – a word that ironically and contrapuntally recurs with high frequency in the space where the body's sovereignty is both celebrated and damned – are divided from bodies and are split within themselves. The anatomy of the body, hideously dismembered and diligently enumerated, litters the canto: "gole", "occhi", "barba", "ventre", "unghiose mani", "bocche", "sanne", "spanne", "canne", "facce", "gola", "sangue", "fronti", "cuori", "occhi", "carne", "figura". The body parts mock any effort to reconstitute them into a harmonious whole. The very heart of the city is ruled by injustice:

> [...] Ciacco, il tuo affanno
> mi pesa sì ch'a lagrimar m'invita;
> ma dimmi, se tu sai, a che verranno
> li cittadini de la città partita;
> s'alcun v'è giusto; e dimmi la cagion
> per che l'ha tanta discordia assalita."
> E quelli a me: 'Dopo lunga tencione
> verranno al sangue, e la parte selvaggia
> caccerà l'altra con molta offensione.
> Poi appresso convien che questa caggia
> infra tre soli, e che l'altra sormonti
> con la forza di tal che testè piaggia.
> Alte terrà lungo tempo le fronti,
> tenendo l'altra sotto gravi pesi,
> come di ciò pianga o che n'aonti.
> Giusti son due, e non vi sono intesi;
> superbia, invidia, e avarizia
> son le tre faville c'hanno i cuori accesi.
> (*Inf.* VI, 58–75)

("Ciacco, your distress weighs on my heart and summons me to tears. But tell me, if you know, where they will end, our party-riven city and its people. Have we a single man of justice there? Say why such discord has assailed the town." And he: "After a struggle long and tense they'll come to bloodshed, and the backwoods side will chase the other out with great offence. Then by his force who waits his chance to strike, that party will collapse within three years. The other one then climbs to power again, and long they hold their foreheads high for pride, and despite all the cries and accusations, they heap great burdens on the other side. Two men are just, but no one heeds their words. Avarice, pride, and envy are the three principal flames that set their hearts on fire.")

"Discordia" evokes etymologically the dissonance of the heart, the receptacle where the condensation of evil gathers. Ciacco's description of the moral disease infesting Florence echoes St Augustine's view of the earthly city "[...] divided against itself by litigations, by wars, by battles" (*City of God* XV, 4). Its founder was Cain, a perpetrator of fratricide, who "[...] overcome by envy [...] slew his own brother"

(XV, 5). We are bound to overhear in the description an allusion to Rome's foundation in Romulus' murder of Remus.

This perspective on current Florentine history belongs to Ciacco, who sheds a lurid, surreal light on the city's going from war to war. The factions, he say, "verranno al sangue". The phrase literally refers to the bloodshed caused by one of the party of the Cerchi family. But in Ciacco's mind, who thus views his own gluttony as the lesser of two evils, there glowers a hallucination enveloping the savages of either party: a taste for blood, a haemorrhage of violence in which they tear each other to pieces and which constitutes a literal political vampirism. The horrific scene (made of reticent allusions, as if to both suggest and elude any possible literalism) is prefigured by Cerberus' cannibalization of the shades / corpses and ingestion of waste. The civil war as self-cannibalization offers a glimpse of the sinister, foul face of gluttony: in the reciprocity of violence trapping the bloodthirsty sinners, there is no sacramental bread to break or share nor is there any cup they bless.

This sort of politics as desecration arouses disgust in the pilgrim as if he had gazed at the leftovers of a macabre meal. But the canto does not stop here. It unfolds by highlighting both the aesthetics and the philosophical assumptions of gluttony. *Gula*, we are told by St Thomas Aquinas, concerns the pleasures of touch and taste, the "judicium saporum", the "gustus" as well as the inordinate pleasure in food and drink (*Quaestiones Disputatae de Malo*, XIII, art. 3, resp. 4). Going beyond Aquinas, Dante focuses on the privy, as it were, on the private other side of the rituals of the gourmet who now sits in his own excrement and whose food turns into waste he will most likely consume. The glamour and excesses of refined pleasures have vanished altogether as we witness the melancholy spectacle of their disagreeableness: the stench of the earth drenched by foul rain, the mud, and Cerberus eating it. Words denoting the subtleties of the palate punctuate the text: on the one hand, we find the adjective "dolce" used twice (84, 88), to designate the sweet quality of taste, and, on the other, "attosca" (84) (bitterness) and "spiacente" (48) (unpleasant). Their contrast conveys, firstly, the discrepancy between the allure and the consequences of the sin.

There are also other implications about a politics of taste. If Ciacco fancied himself as an aesthete (he was probably a court jester, a banker, or an actor) cultivating in his "serene life" the pleasures of the body and food and a loathing of the city's wolfish appetites, he now bears no resemblance to the two mildly Goliardic poets and gluttons of Dante's youth, Forese and Bonagiunta, who in *Purgatorio* are enchanted by the inner sweetness of style and the tongue. If anything, Ciacco has literalized the impulses of the Goliards' drinking bouts and belly worship. Through his aesthetic deformation Dante gauges the "place" pleasure occupies in the economy of the city. Two strains of classical philosophy are discreetly evoked for the city's decay: Cynicism and the vulgar version of Epicureanism. The Cynics, says St Augustine, are "canine philosophers" (*City of God* XIV). Isidore of Seville, in his wake, calls them "dogs in the street," who blur the boundaries between private and public morality, and who in their "filth of impudence" violate all public decency (*Etymologies* VIII, 14). At the same time, gluttons are called "hogs of Epicurus", distinct from the Epicurean philosophers, such as Epicurus himself, who deny the immortality of the soul. To the gluttons knowledge is mere taste and, as the verb "savere" (83) shows, they make the palate their organ of knowledge and thereby reduce philosophy to a question of elegant savouring.

This prophetic-political rhetoric binding the canto echoes the accounts of two contemporary Florentine chronicles, Dino Compagni and Giovanni Villani. Dino Compagni comments on the mimetic rivalry of the factions: "La città, retta con poca giustizia, cadde in nuovo pericolo, perchè i cittadini si cominciarono a dividere per gara di uffici, abominando l'un l'altro" (*Cronaca*, I, 20). (The city, ruled with little justice, fell into a new danger, because the citizens began to divide themselves competing for government positions). And Giovanni Villani, using the same words as Ciacco (and, later, Brunetto Latini), attributes to pride, envy, and avarice the cause of the city's discord (*Cronica* VIII, 68–96).

By aligning his stance with the views of the Florentine chroniclers, Dante roots his reading of the city's political turmoil in the documentary evidence of contemporary witnesses. By adopting the rhetoric of the chroniclers, moreover, he steers clear of the grandiose claims of the classical epics of the civil war. For Lucan and Statius civil war embroils Rome in insoluble moral and political problems: it dismantles the myths of law and order that justify the existence of the empire. The stakes in Florence – though a pawn in the Pope's manoeuvres – are not that high. Unlike these epics, finally, a chronicle is wedded to the particulars of the city's personalities and concrete power play. Yet the division in ancient Rome and the wars in contemporary Florence share in the view of history as a blind fatality inherent to and governing naturalistic doctrines.

The chroniclers, moreover, give a hard edge to Ciacco's mix of monstrous fantasies and facts as well as to his self-deception in not wishing to see the link between his gluttony and political vampirism. When the pilgrim confesses his desire to know the fate of some worthy Florentines – Farinata, Tegghiaio, Jacopo Rusticucci, Arrigo, and Mosca – and those others who set their minds on "ben fare" (*Inf.* VI, 79–81), he answers that they have sunk under the heavier weight of their corruption: "[...] Ei son tra l'anime più nere;/ diverse colpe giù li grava a fondo" (85–86) (They dwell among the blackest souls below weighed to the pit by different faults). The phrase, "ben fare" (which picks up Ciacco's words on birth and death – "fecemi"-"disfecemi") highlights the realm of doing and making – in a word, work – as the main ingredient of the city's existence. To do and to make are both acts of the will, and as such they imply action and purposes. The phrase, however, simultaneously carries two contradictory senses: to do well and to do good. Ciacco's response, in effect, focuses on the discrepancy between contingent, human judgements and the divine perspective on human actions. Dante thereby exposes the hollowness in the city's cult of its local pantheon and thus dismantles its political idolatry. Finally, civic *gravitas* and political ordering by rank appear as artificial values deprived of any genuine basis in nature or biology.

So satanic, so narrow is this "biology" of politics and ethics, so deep is Dante's anguish at the tribulations to which the civil war has subjected its citizens that his poetry runs the serious danger of casting politics as a vain, irretrievably senseless mythology. From this standpoint Dante's naturalistic stance goes beyond the perspective of Augustine, who in his apotheosis of the Heavenly City subverts the ideology of secularism. For all its perversions of the good, for all its different faith and different love, so he maintains, "...the earthly city ... enjoys with the heavenly one," "temporal good things." In what way, however, does Dante believe that the tragic economy of politics as a succession of civil wars can be overcome and redeemed? The answer, no doubt, lies in the sacrificial economy of redemptive history. More to the point, the *Pharsalia* and

Thebaid are so re-thought as to mark the path for an alternate, possible new beginning for history. To achieve this aim, he needs to identify a redemptive view of the natural world not imposed from the outside but from within the world's own self-understanding. In this secular light, classical theories of cycles, natural recurrences, mythical forces of fate chaining human beings can be transcended. In short, a theory of the future is needed, and Dante finds that such a theory depends on the most natural and commonplace event of all: the fact of birth.

In Purgatorio XXII, the figuration of Statius unfolds as an autobiography (starting from his birth in Toulouse (though he was actually born in Naples)) and as an account of his poetic apprenticeship. In his self-presentation of the totality of his life that pivots on his Christian conversion while writing the *Thebaid*, he ends up radically changing the sense of his life and his past. This change occurs through a reflection on poetry, Virgil's poetry, Statius's own poetry, and the Greco-Roman tradition. Statius asks about the fate of Terence, Varro, Plautus, and Caecilus (97–99) and Virgil answers that they dwell with Persius, with Homer (who drank most deeply at the muses' breast), Euripides, Antiphon, Antigone, and the sorceress Manto ((100–115). This posthumous reconciliation of Classical authors certainly shows Virgil's consciousness of the unity of tradition as well as Statius' poetic reflection on the Greek roots of his own vision. The oblique history of poetry is in turn introduced by Statius's acknowledgement of Virgil's poetry as both the "seme" (*Purg.* XXI, 94) and "mamma" and "nutrice" (97–98) (mother and nurse). Such a genetic view of poetry suggests, first of all, the radical originality of Dante's poetry. It is original in the etymological sense of the word: it brings us back to the origin. Second, it gives him grounds for confidence in the fecundity of his spiritual inheritance: voiced by the authority of Virgil, the values of that inheritance could not be wholly false. Finally, these metaphors of poetry's origins reveal to him the world's vitality and sustenance. The world is called "pregnant" (*Purg.* XXII, 70) with the beliefs disseminated by the messengers of the eternal kingdom. This understanding of poetry's harmonies stands in dramatic contrast to the tragic scenario of Thebes' civil war and of Jocasta's fratricidal children: their belief in violence and in the tyranny of fate is completely reversed.

The view of poetry as the reversal of the *Thebaid* (a story in which characters fornicate with their own fancies), continues in the canto with the "mistranslation" of two lines from the *Aeneid* (III, 56–57): "Per che non reggi tu, o sacre fame / dell'oro, l'appetito de' mortali?" (*Purg.* XXII, 40–41) (To what, O cursed hunger for gold, dost thou not drive the appetite of mortals?). "Sacre" means both profane and holy. More to the point, the Virgilian lines evoke a political context: Aeneas' first founding of a city in Thracia, which he calls after his own name "Aeneadas" ("meo nomen de nomine fingo" (*Aeneid* III, 18). The foundation is marked by sacrificial offerings, "sacra", to Venus and the building of an altar in the belief that the city's beginning occurs by an act of consecration. But a sacrilege had been perpetrated by the violent death inflicted on Polydorus. The phrase about the theft of the gold, "auri sacra fames", which Statius' lines echo and "appropriate", enjoins Aeneas to leave the place of profanation: political beginnings require a consecration to the gods but not the sacrilege of founding violence.

It is not in death but in birth that origins are found. Statius, showing how he was transformed by the reading of Virgil's text, cites the central passage of the Fourth Eclogue "Secol si rinova; / torna giustizia e primo tempo umano, / e progenïe scende da ciel nova.") (*Purg.* XXII, 70–71) (The age turns new again; justice comes back and the primal years of men, and a new race descends from heaven). The poem is a *genethliacon*, a poem celebrating the birth of Asinius Pollio's son, and through the omen of his birth, Virgil announces the rebirth of the world. The advent of the "novus ordo saeclorum," in truly Pythagorean fashion, is presented as a return of Justice or Astraea, a return by which, as in an endless circle of becoming, the past coincides with the future. For this is what a birth means to Virgil: the most repetitive physical fact in nature can break the chain of events, be free or unlike all that has come before, and, more generally, redefine nature in terms of a grace that perfects but does not erase nature.

From this standpoint we grasp the sense of Cato waiting for the day of the resurrection of the body (*Purg.* I, 73–75) and why the appearance of Statius is also described in terms of the risen Christ. What the two scenes share is that bodies are not circumscribed within a natural, realistic principle of materiality. They are spiritualized, and yet, they would be inconceivable without that materiality. This is to say that the values of naturalism and secularism generally are unavoidably coextensive with theology: each needs the other and each caricatures the other. Taken together they end up resembling each other. Undoubtedly, the generation of Oedipus' family may even look like a variant of the Trinitarian conception. The resemblance between the myth and the mystery, however, simply suggests that human monstrosity bears the ineradicable sign of its proximity to the sacred. By virtue of this proximity between nature and grace, theology both recognizes nature's irreplaceable role in its discourse and signals a necessary transfiguration of nature.

One final, basic point must be made about beginnings and sacredness. Aeneas discovers, when Anchises dies in Sicily, that death hallows the ground: by burying the dead human beings reclaim the ground. But so does a birth. The fact of birth inaugurates the sacredness and mystery of all beginnings, and it posits a new beginning and stakes out a future on that ground. As such, it turns into the central figuration in Dante's moral and poetic experience. Morally, the event of birth ends up clashing with the reality of sinners, such as Ciacco, who refuse to take guilt upon themselves, they cling to the habits in the persuasion that this world is the source of their worth, and obliterate the differences between past, present and future. Sin, for Dante, comes through as the habit of sin, which reflects the understanding of life in terms of the physical cycles of bodies. Poetically, as Statius had intuited, the journey of poetry asks that we venture out of the familiar, purely natural imaginings.

One hero from the classical world, Ulysses, undertakes such a journey and leaves behind his natural world – his father, son, and wife Penelope. His willed voyage – which is a voyage of the mind – bears an uncanny affinity to Dante's exile and journey in the beyond. There is, however, a difference between them, just as there is a difference between Aeneas and Ulysses in their respective classical epics. Ulysses' journey comes across as a circular journey home (from Ithaca back to Ithaca) with all the poignancy nostalgia entails. Aeneas, instead, has no home to return to, and he cannot but venture into an open-ended quest, at times aimlessly, and mistaking every new city he builds along the route as if it were the destined one. In Inferno XXVI, Ulysses comes across as a figure of both Aeneas and Dante: he leaves home, as if he were Aeneas, but he plunges into the abyss as his gaze rends the night of the world.

By contrast, Dante manages to see God face to face. The difference between them depends on the pilgrim's ability to kick the habit, to see the new in the old, and to grasp the mystery and sense of the beginning.

All this talk about beginning is bound to jar with the obvious detail that the *Divine Comedy* begins *in medias res*, in the "middle" of life's parabola: "Nel mezzo del cammin di nostra vita" (*Inf.* I, 1) (midway upon the journey of our life). The poem begins indeed "nel mezzo" with the pilgrim taking stock of what is at hand, his irreducible existential situatedness here and now. But this is not the real beginning of the pilgrim's spiritual predicament, which in fact is rooted in distant causes. In the wild woodland where he comes to, the pilgrim repeatedly tries to climb the hill to the light, only to be driven back to the dark valley. "[...] i' fui per ritornar più volte volto" (*Inf.* I, 36) (I often turned to go the way I came). The repeated, circular action, as much as the repeated sounds in the line, conveys his impasse: he goes around in a vicious circle and gets nowhere. The lines that immediately follow, however, evoke the time of the day, the hour of the morning when the sun was in the constellation of Aries right there and then at the moment of Creation.

> Temp'era dal principio del mattino,
> e 'l sol montava 'n sù con quelle stelle
> ch'eran con lui quando l'amor divino
> mosse di prima quelle cose belle
> (*Inf.* I, 37–40)

(The hour was morning at the break of dawn. The sun was mounting higher with those stars that stand beside him where the Love Divine in the beginning made their beauty move).

Whereas Ulysses willfully follows the movement of the sun in its repetitive pattern, Dante goes to the "beginning," to "birth", and back to love, to what makes things new. He calls on us to think anew and differently.

Dante and King David

Trond Berg Eriksen

I have chosen this subject not because I have found anything new or sensational about it, but because I am still trying to find some answers. Many years ago, when I was intensely occupied with studying the *Comedy*, there was one problem I never could solve: what was Dante really doing? If it is anachronistic to call the *Comedy* "literature", what sort of text was it? What was it intended to be? If calling Dante a "poet" is too modern, what was then his role? What did he wish to be?

Ernst Robert Curtius helps us to some extent understand the poetry and poets of the Middle Ages and the manner in which they perceived what they were doing, but he generally ignores the biblical and ecclesiastical tradition. He associates the self-understanding of the poets and their literature too closely with the legacy of Classical Antiquity. King David provides – as we shall see – the model for the Christian singer, as Orpheus provided the model for the classical singer. Yet Curtius does not mention David. He treats the poetry of the Middle Ages as if it survived on the fringes of the ecclesiastical tradition and in spite of it.

Many readers and critics of Dante have gone in the same direction and ignored Dante's dependency on the biblical tradition in his self-interpretation as a poet. As I read the *Comedy*, it is as heavily indebted to the ritual texts of the Mass, as it is to the Book of Psalms which has always been the main biblical poetry. Volumes and volumes have been written about the relation of Dante to Vergil, but hardly anyone has studied the relation of Dante to David and the Book of Psalms. In my opinion every citation and every reference to the Book of Psalms in the *Comedy* is also a reference to David the singer who was also a priest and king.

Dante himself, of course, points to Vergil as a source of inspiration for the *Comedy* by choosing Vergil as his travelling companion. When they meet their professional colleagues in Inferno 4, they are the Classical ones: Homer, Horace, Lucan and Ovid. At first glance we could think that Dante wished to belong to this circle of poets. He gives us the impression of being flattered by the invitation, but in fact he never intended to stop in Limbo. Classicistic scholars and readers have seldom had a feeling for Dante's *Comedy*. Within a historical perspective relatively few readers have appreciated both the *Aeneid* and the *Comedy*. Vergil's supporters have never been impressed by Dante as the classicism of the *Comedy* is limited at best.

If we look more closely at the figure of Vergil in Dante, he is a peculiar sort. He is not the Vergil of modern literary history or Classical philology. He is a seer, a prophet, a god-sent counsellor in moral and political problems. Comparetti (1872) understood that *Vergilio nel Medioevo* was a figure who had been absorbed into a strange tradition and therefore had very little in common with the Vergil of the humanists in the fifteenth century. Vergil was transformed by Dante, but he was transformed according to the principles of the biblical legacy.

With Homer, the case is similar. The only more comprehensive use of Homeric matters in the *Comedy* is the tale of Ulysses in Inferno 26, which provides a curious image of the Greek singer. Besides being an inspiration for Vergil, is it Homer's role as the supposed originator of the legend of Ulysses which qualifies him for the title of the prince of poets in Inferno 4? If both Vergil and Homer are transformed nearly beyond recognition in the *Comedy*, what principles, what models and ideals have been effective in this transformation? We cannot blame the distortion of these figures on the Middle Ages in general, as Comparetti does. The figures of Greece and Rome were not transformed by the invasions of the barbarians alone. The portraits Dante provides of Homer and Vergil are not due to a lack of information, but result from a quite different set of ideals than those which were to guide the humanists in their attitude to the legacy of Antiquity.

The Book of Psalms is among the parts of the Bible that Dante cites most often – there are about 40 citations from it in the *Comedy*, and a long list of allusions to them. King David is the biblical figure of the Old Testament that Dante refers to most frequently. In addition to that, parts of the Book of Psalms are not only cited 9 times, but also sung by the characters of the *Comedy* at crossroads of strategic importance. *Salmista* in Dante always means David (*Purg.* X, 65; Con 2,3,11; Mon 1,15,5).

The Psalms were used as a book of hymns throughout the Middle Ages. Not one Mass was celebrated without a recitation from the Book in prayers, hymns or lamentations. The gamut of emotions in the Book is considerable. There are psalms of malediction (Sal 108 and 136) besides psalms of thanksgiving, prayer and praise. Moreover, in Dante's day, the Book was used as a reading book to learn Latin in Florentine ecclesiastical schools. Everybody, including Dante, with a command of Latin beyond the elementary also knew the Book of Psalms by heart.

Poetry has a central position in the biblical and ecclesiastical landscape. If the development of Christian poetry in late Antiquity and the early Middle Ages may seem slight and hesitant, it was not due to a contempt for art or literature. The reason was rather that the Christians were, thanks to the Bible, already well supplied with poetry. Any person wanting to write poetry had to compete with King David, who wrote the Book of Psalms; as King Solomon had written the Proverbs, the Song of Songs, the Wisdom, the Ecclesiasticus and the Ecclesiastes, as Moses had written the books bearing his name (Mon 3,4,11) and John had written a gospel, his epistles and the last book of the Bible. This was common knowledge at the time of Dante.

David was not only a singer. He was a king and priest, a clear-sighted man of power, a prophet (Mon 3,3,12). He also belonged to the tree of Jesse and was an ancestor of the Saviour. After Moses, David was the one who united Israel and selected Jerusalem as the capital city.

In Dante, the presence of King David is like a shadow wandering throughout the *Comedy*. David is present both in person – when he actually appears – and as an image. In addition his presence is conjured up by the citations from and allusions to the Book of Psalms. Even in *De Monarchia* and *Convivio* David is present. In the *Comedy* he appears with the very first words of Dante the traveller, "Miserere di me" (*Inf.* I, 65), taken from Psalm 50. This exclamation makes David an invisible travelling companion from the very moment the two main travellers meet. Dante turns away from the sinful journey of the *selva oscura* by citing the repentant, deep sigh of King David.

When Vergil and Dante meet the other poets in Limbo, we hear that Vergil and David were once there at the same time before David was taken away by Christ on Easter Eve when he was harrowing in Hell (*Inf.* IV, 58). Limbo provides Dante with an opportunity to remind the reader about an important poet who does not belong to the circle of Vergil and Homer.

Sometimes David is first and foremost a king, at other times a singer, as in Purgatorio X, 55–72 where he dances about the Ark of the Covenant. He always retains, however, the special combination of singer, king and priest. Dante associates him with a notable doctrine of inspiration when he calls David *cantor dello Spirito Santo* (*Par.* XXVIII, 38) or *tuba Spiritus Sancti* (Mon 1,16,5). David is God's own singer: *sommo cantor del Sommo Duce* (*Par.* XXV, 72). With reference to his dancing naked dancing about the Ark, he is also called *umile salmista* (*Purg.* X, 65). In this foolishness – which his wife of course did not appreciate – David was "both more and less than king" (*Purg.* X, 66). Dante finds qualities in David which he is anxious to imitate. King David is evidently a *figura Christi*, but he is also a *figura Dantis*. David prefigures both characters – the one in his real humility, the other in the humility he wished for.

Teodolinda Barolini associates the title of the *Comedy* to Dante's wish to imitate the humility of David. As with the Book of Psalms, the *Comedy* is a *poema sacro* (*Par.* XXV, 1–2) – an expression Macrobius uses about the *Aeneid* (*sacrum poema*). But the *Comedy* reminds us also of the incarnation through its *umiltà*. For in the biblical tale God made himself less than He actually was. He became a man to serve His own creatures. In Dante humility always has something to do with truth. The high literary styles of the tragic poets, such as Vergil's *Aeneid*, are lies disguised as truths. The Comedy, however, is *bassa* in the sense that it – for instance in the tale about Geryon – offers a truth that seems to be a lie (*Inf.* XVI, 124–136).

Vergil and David are connected in Dante's view because the one started his career as a shepherd in Bethlehem, and the other sings bucolic songs (*Purg.* XXII, 61). King David was the first to instil the hope of salvation into Dante's heart (*Par.* XXV, 71–74; Psalm 9,11), as Vergil was the one who led Statius to faith (*Purg.* XXI, 97). Incarnation, song and the instilling of hope are tied together in a pattern in which David is the main figure. He communicates hope, humility and penance.

In Paradiso XXXII, 12 – near the end of the *Comedy* – we find a reference to the first exclamation of the journey. Dante tells us that it was David who originally said "Miserere di me". David is the *cantor che per doglia del fallo disse: Miserere mei*. In this way a connection is established with Inferno I, thereby implicitly completing the identification of Dante with David. The *Comedy* as a whole is presented as a psalm of penance. Dante escaped from the same dark wood as David, and found his way to the same heaven. The relation between Dante and David commands the final verses of the *Comedy*, as the relation between Vergil and Dante dominates the beginning of the story.

This can already be noticed in Purgatorio X, 49, where the humility of Mary in the tale of the incarnation is connected to David the singer – *Ecce ancilla Dei* (v. 44). Dante there "went past Vergil" (v. 53) to take a closer look (*e fe' mi presso*) at David dancing about the Ark of the Covenant. The subject in this image is "humility" (v. 98), and David is the *umile salmista* (v. 65). In this way Dante indicates a decisive gulf between Vergil and David. Later on Dante establishes a connection between his own exile and the mobility of David. The king, priest and singer carried the Ark of the Covenant from village to village – *di villa in villa* (*Par.* XX, 39). It is difficult to read this as anything else but a reference to the poet Dante himself who, at this very moment, is travelling from place to place.

David and Vergil are, however, also intertwined. For "David was born when Rome was born," as Dante says in *Convivio* (4, 6). And Rome was born when Aeneas came from Troy to Italy. This is expressly stated in the same place. Dante is the one who brings the legacy of David and the legacy of Aeneas together. The two lines appeared at the same time in history, but independently of each other. We can discern the domain of the emperor (Aeneas) and the domain of the pope (David). The two traditions discovered each other and have converged gradually. Vergil's prophecy about a new prince and David's establishment of Jerusalem as the capital city of Israel show that the first had a presentiment of Christ and the second a presentiment of Rome. In Dante the two traditions are connected and correctly understood for the first time.

Finally, Dante meets David the singer in the centre of the eye of the Roman eagle in Paradiso (XX, 37–42). David belongs in the heaven of Jupiter among the righteous. He is the heavenly eye of power. His humility connects him once again to Emperor Trajan. The singer and the emperor had met already in *the intagli nel marmo* in Purgatorio X where we find them side by side with Mary. Emperor Trajan was saved by Pope Gregory who is thought to have brought the emperor back to life and baptized him – 500 years after his death – due to the legend of his mercy and humility towards the widow who had lost her son. St Thomas relates this quite seriously.

Dante intends his *Comedy* to have the same function as the Bible. He is himself a sort of *scriba Dei*. In the *Comedy scriba* is only used to characterize Dante himself and the biblical authors (*Par.* X, 27; XXIX, 41). In the earthly Paradise the traveller Dante marches behind the books of the Bible (*Purg.* XXIX). The poet Dante is the new *salmista*. His poem represents what is lacking in the poets the travellers have met in Purgatorio. With the exception of Statius, Dante and Vergil only met singers of private and erotic sensations. The *Comedy* rehabilitates the priestly, prophetic and political view of poetry. Love has been given a cosmic quality and is seen in a universal perspective. It is no longer *folle amore*, but is understood correctly as *caritas*. When we later meet poetry in the Heaven of Venus, it is this very concept of Love which has been transformed (*Par.* VIII and IX).

Not long ago Dante was himself like the singers Cassella and Sordello. Therefore Purgatorio contains so much elaborate self-criticism. The Roman Cato appears as a literary critic in his castigation of Cassella in Purgatorio II. Cato's criticism is of course a critique of the poetry of Dante's youth. Dante conjures up the contrasting image of David when he lets the flock of the dead sing the psalm "In exitu Israel de Egypto" just before meeting an entertainer who lacks all interest in priestly, prophetic or political matters. Dante has himself progressed from *dolci rime* to *sacro poema*, from the private to the public, from entertainment to education, from an aesthetic and flimsy attitude – to a political and responsible attitude. At least that is what he wants us to believe.

Teodolinda Barolini has shown (*Dante's Poets*, 1984) that Dante is writing a personal literary history. In placing himself among his ancient and contemporary colleagues, he provides an elaborate interpretation of himself by implicitly and explicitly referring to various phases of his own development as well as to his competitors. Dante argues for his own central position in history from Homer, Vergil, Lucan and Statius – and he shows the necessity of the development he himself has undergone during his lifetime. Dante is certainly "Vergil reborn", as Giovanni di Virgilio calls him. But his relation to the Roman poet is far more problematic and a great deal more reserved than is implied by a superficial reading.

Barolini underscores that Dante surpasses and transcends Vergil. Dante the traveller leaves Vergil behind and makes him superfluous. In the bigger picture, even Statius surpasses Vergil. Compared with the lyric poets, Vergil is *maestro* and *savio*. Dante employs, however, both Statius, Folco (*Par.* IX) and, least but not last, King David to make it perfectly clear that Vergil cannot be the final model in the landscape which is opened up in the Comedy.

Barolini also underestimates the presence of David in the *Comedy*, because she does not grasp fully the consequences implied by David being a poet, or the fact that the citations from the Book of Psalms are as much citations of poetry as citations from the Scriptures. If we exclude the image of David, we distort, in my opinion, Dante's conception of poetry and the poet.

When she pulls David from the line of poets and treats him as mainly a biblical figure, Barolini maintains the existence of a gulf between the Bible and literature which Dante himself did not recognize, or rather: which he exerted himself to eliminate. Barolini falls, in short, into the same trap as Curtius, because she does not understand how central the position of poetry within the biblical and ecclesiastical tradition really is. You don't have to be a Greek, a Roman or a Provençal to be a poet.

Part of the paradox of King David in the *Comedy* is that he is structurally and systematically placed at the summit of all human poetry. Only God himself is a better poet. He is the only "true author" (*verace autore, Par.* XXVI, 40). David is not only a *poeta*, but *cantore*. At the same time Dante does not elaborate any further on David's position. David is present from the first to the last verse as a model and a pattern for the combination of poet, king and priest. In the fifth circle of Purgatorio, among the greedy and the wasteful, we first meet an angel

(*Purg.* 19–21), then a pope (Hadrian 5), a king (Hugo Capet) and a poet (Statius), before we finally meet an angel again. Here Dante discloses some of his most encompassing ambitions on behalf of poetry. We remember David being "both more and less than king" (*Purg.* X, 66).

The poet has a vocation and an office which is no less important than the offices of pope or king. The pope and king are left behind in the circle as the poet Statius travels along in the company of Vergil and Dante. The poet has evidently found a way to serve his fellow human beings and God's plan – a way that the king and the pope have not yet discovered. No lyric poet is ever called *poeta* or *savio* in the *Comedy*. Those are epithets used exclusively for Vergil, Statius and Dante. Behind them and above them stands David the singer and king. Dante is here advertising his own biblical and literary version of Plato's philosopher-king.

A poet of the right sort can be a stand-in for both king and pope. The poet Sordello, we remember (*Purg.* VI), talks more willingly about politics than about literature. Therefore he has reached far higher than Cassella and the youthful poetry of Dante. After meeting Statius (*Purg.* XXI), Dante only meets poets in Purgatorio: Forese Donati (*Purg.* XXIII), Bonagiunta da Lucca (*Purg.* XXIV), Guido Guinizelli and Arnaut Daniel (*Purg.* XXVI). Poetry and poets are obviously meant for the process of cleansing and purifying.

Through the line of poets that Dante meets on his journey, he manages to comment on his own development and justify the *Comedy* as a proper work of art. When the pope or the king fails, the poet is the best counsellor of mankind. The poet Dante wants to be his own *rettore e pastore*, his own master and shepherd, his own king and pope, as Vergil declares at the moment Dante leaves him (*Purg.* XXVII, 130). With such an ambition, Vergil and his poem cannot possibly provide a sufficient exemplary model. Since the *Comedy* contributes both to good order on earth, as the emperor should do, and actually opens the gates of heaven, as the pope should do, the *sacro poema* is a continuation of the psalms of David, and so the poet would be the rightful heir and successor to the biblical king.

Finally, I have only one question: whatever happened to humility?

Dicendo questo.
A note on Dante's writing of Paradise

Anders Cullhed

In the fourth song of Paradiso, the final and most daring part of the *Comedy*, Dante sketches out an answer to this fundamental question of the work: how can we know anything about God? More precisely: how shall I, a mortal man, a Florentine and a sinner, express the ineffable in words? How shall I write of Paradise?

The scene of Paradiso IV is the following: Dante and Beatrice are in the lunar heaven, the first of the seven planetary spheres, proceeding up through Paradise. Dante marvels at this brave new world at which he has arrived, replete with its glittering constellations and glaring reflections everywhere (in the new translation by Jean and Robert Hollander 2007, my source for the English text of the *Comedy* throughout this paper):

> I kept silent, but my longing
> and my questions all were painted on my face
> more ardently than words could have expressed.

For the Italian original, I shall follow Natalino Sapegno's edition from 1957:

> Io mi tacea, ma 'l mio disir dipinto
> m'era nel viso, e 'l dimandar con ello,
> più caldo assai che per parlar distinto.
> (IV, 10–12)

Dante's perplexity chiefly concerns the abode of the blessed. One of them, Picarda Donati, once upon a time a nun in earthly Florence, has just explained to him how the blessed are arranged by degree, "from height to height" (*di soglia in soglia*) in this heavenly realm (III, 82–83). Consequently, Dante realizes that the blessed are to be found in all the seven planetary spheres of Paradise: on the Moon, Mercury, Venus, the Sun, Mars, Jupiter and Saturn. This means, or should mean, that the ancient philosophers such as Plato were right in their assumptions that certain elect souls after their earthly existence enjoyed the privilege of returning to the stars. But – Dante has to ask himself – how can this antique theory agree with orthodox Catholic doctrine, according to which the blessed are together with God, in the Empyrean, beyond all heavens?

Classical philosophy seems to contrast with Christian faith here. Nevertheless, Dante's perplexity will soon disappear and the conflict will be resolved. Beatrice knows the answer to this problem, as she does to everything else. She explains that Piccarda and the other torch-lights in the lunar heaven are in fact to be found in God's vicinity, just like the seraphim or the Virgin Mary herself. But though all these souls reside in the Empyrean, they "enjoy sweet life in different measure, / as they sense less or more of God's eternal breath" (*differentemente han dolce vita / per sentir più e men l'etterno spiro*, IV, 35–36). This, of course, is typical of the *Comedy* as a whole. In its Catholic universe, everything has to observe degree, priority and place, and merits are never to be despised, not even in the closeness of divinity.

In other words, right through celestial equality appears a hierarchical pattern, and this has to be emphasized in the work, as the very structure of Paradise depends on it. Beatrice deals with this phenomenon in some (admittedly famous) lines, which – as I see it – provide us with one of the clues to the poetics of Paradise. Piccarda and the Norman Queen Constantia, she says (IV, 37–48):

> put themselves on view here
> not because they are allotted to this sphere
> but as a sign of less exalted rank in Heaven.
>
> It is necessary thus to address your faculties,

since only in perceiving through the senses can they grasp
that which they then make fit for intellect.

For this reason Scripture condescends
to your capacity when it attributes hands and feet
To God, but has another meaning,

and for your sake Holy Church portrays
Gabriel and Michael with the faces of men
and that other angel who made Tobit well again.

Qui si mostraro, non perché sortita
sia questa spera lor, ma per far segno
de la spiritual c'ha men salita.
Così parlar conviensi al vostro ingegno,
però che solo da sensato apprende
ciò che fa poscia d'intelletto degno.
Per questo la Scrittura condescende
a vostra facultate, e piedi e mano
attribuisce a Dio, e altro intende;
e Santa Chiesa con aspetto umano
Gabriel e Michel vi rappresenta,
e l'altro che Tobia rifece sano.

The key words here are to be found in the first lines: to make a sign (*far segno*). Beatrice speaks of a heavenly reality, a world full of enigmatic and often dazzling signs, which confuses Dante and, as a result, constantly requires interpretation. The story of Paradise is to a great extent the story of Dante step-by-step acquiring the hermeneutic competence necessary to understand the Book of the universe, that all-encompassing *volume* he mentions in the final song of the work (XXXIII, 86). All in all, this amounts to an extended lesson in divine semiotics. To elucidate its workings, Beatrice hints at Piccarda and Constantia: these two souls enjoy their eternal existence close to God, beyond physical space, but they appear down in the Moon's sphere to *far segno* – to make a sign – of their peculiar degree of blessedness.

The very same semiotic concept characterizes Dante's idea of language or, on closer inspection, Beatrice's analysis of the Bible's manner of signifying. Since people, according to venerable Aristotelian tradition, assimilated into contemporary Scholasticism, can only apprehend what they themselves have experienced with their senses (*da sensato*), the Bible has to "condescend" or adapt to their naturally limited faculties of understanding. In other words, the Bible relies on rhetoric, as St Augustine was one of the first to admit, most scrupulously in his groundbreaking treatise on Christian hermeneutics, semiotics and eloquence from the late fourth century, *De doctrina christiana*. The Holy Writ makes frequent use of metaphors, personifications, and other figures. It can, as in Beatrice's example, represent in human shape God and the Archangels Gabriel, Michael and (the unnamed) Raphael so that we may recognize them, even though they do not resemble human beings at all.

At this point in Beatrice's argument, Dante reveals a split between representation (*rappresentare*) and the meaning or significance (*intendere*) of Biblical discourse, a tension which is just as typical of his own allegorical poetics in Paradise. This part of the *Comedy* deals with an adventure which surpasses human understanding, and Dante is keen to emphasize the consequences of this enterprise on his authorial persona in the very first lines of the work: he will be, or is already from the start, *changed* in Paradise. He is endowed with supernatural or unearthly powers, such as being able to look straight into the sun, a capacity which traditionally in mythology and poetry since ancient times was restricted to the eagle. Accordingly, in the prelude to this third part of the *Comedy*, Dante outlines a form of understanding, or even of existence, which could be labelled superhuman, though it is neither angelic nor divine. It is made possible for him by Beatrice's presence:

and I now fixed
my sight on her, withdrawing it from above.

As I gazed on her, I was changed within,
as Glaucus was on tasting of the grass
that made him consort of the gods in the sea.

To soar beyond the human cannot be described
in words. Let the example be enough to one
for whom grace holds this experience in store.

e io in lei
le luci fissi, di là sù rimote.
Nel suo aspetto tal dentro mi fei,
qual si fé Glauco nel gustar de l'erba
che 'l fé consorto in mar de li altri dei.
Trasumanar significar per verba
non si poría; però l'essemplo basti
a cui esperienza grazia serba.
(I, 65–72)

At the mere sight of Beatrice, Dante is transformed like old Glaucus, the mythical fisherman from Boeotia – portrayed in Ovid's *Metamorphoses* – who became a sea-god after having tasted some life-giving herbs. Here as always, the Roman poet was fascinated by the effects of metamorphosis upon the soul: at the moment of his irreversible change, Glaucus remembers that "I felt my heart beating fast within me, seized with a passionate desire for this other element" (*subito trepidare intus praecordia sensi / Alteriusque rapi naturae pectus amore*, XIII, 945–46). On the whole, the passage from Paradise referred to is characteristic of Dante's recycling of the Classics: he exploits them to his heart's content as rough patterns or 'types' of the episodes in his *Comedy*, interpreted in the light of true Catholic faith. If Ovid's fisherman was changed into a god in the material element of water, Dante enters into the divine dimension of being, located in the superlunary ether, both imitating and transcending his pagan model. The poet in his turn enters into the truly allegorical mode of Paradise.

What he will experience in this holy realm cannot be adequately rendered in ordinary language. It is impossible to signify in words, *per verba*, what in fact exceeds human understanding. This is of course an application of the well tried and tested rhetorical device Ernst Robert Curtius labelled *Unsagbarkeitstopoi* in his great work on the European literature of the Middle Ages (pp. 168 ff.), but Dante goes far beyond the usual conventions. At this point he relies on a linguistic neologism, *trasumanar*, which testifies to his delight in experiments, so typical of Paradiso. To "transhumanize", to move beyond the human predicament, is an act unfeasible to render in ordinary language. From now on, Dante's audience must remember that the words they shall read on the pages of his work are only poor efforts to suggest what no words can tell, some shadowy approximations to the divine reality which the poet has been allowed to perceive.

But if that is the case, how can we trust him? From which precise source does Dante draw authority for his work? One answer to this question is obvious: from divinity, as is well known from the poet's surprisingly syncretistic invocations of both the Catholic God and the pagan gods in the *Comedy*, such as "O buono Appollo" in Paradiso I, 13. Nevertheless, I would like to emphasize an even more astounding aspect to Dante's legitimizing strategy, also apparent from the quotation above: his appeal to the enlightened recipients of his work, reminiscent of the manifold addresses to the reader in the *Comedy*, analyzed by Leo Spitzer, William Franke and others, but more oblique, referring to his audience as an indeterminate third person singular. Therefore, when human language shows itself incapable of communicating the poet's overwhelming vision (of Paradise), he can still appeal to the readers' personal experience: "Let the example be enough to one / for whom grace holds this experience in store."

Those people on whom God has bestowed His grace, more precisely the truly Catholic readers, will thus be able to understand. Dante uses the Italian word for experience here, the particular *esperienza* (perhaps some premonition of the state of the blessed) which Grace grants us. This concept was quite important in the *Comedy*, most famously in Inferno XXVI, the Ulysses episode, in which it denotes a hunger for new discoveries: another bold adventure, another transgression of boundaries, though reserved for an altogether earthly and at least morally ambiguous enterprise (98, 116). Here in Paradiso Dante substitutes the Greek seafarer's Atlantic waves with the believer's divine cosmos: it has to be experienced to be understood. In his own way, then, he recycles a famous idea from the *Sermons* (43;4) of St Augustine, updated for medieval use by Anselm of Canterbury: *credo, ut intelligam* (I believe so that I may understand, *PL* 38.255, 158.227c).

Dicendo questo

This strategy presupposes precisely an Augustinian linguistic scepticism: at the very moment when words are produced by our tongue or pen, or in fact even before that – when they become manifest as signs in our mind – their meanings run the risk of being distorted.¹ That is why, after all, words are frequently considered superfluous in Paradise. Much more frequently than in Hell or Purgatory, the blessed communicate through gestures, expressions (often smiles) and gazes. Beatrice illustrates constantly how this non-verbal interchange occurs: she does not need to wait for any sounds from Dante's lips. Instead she reads his face or eyes, the proverbial mirrors of his soul, mystically – or angelically – neglecting the detours of his discourse (I, 85–87, II, 13–15, VII, 16–18 etc). The theme of Paradiso is to a great extent Dante's becoming used (or disposed, *disposto*, XXX, 54) to this non-discursive world of signs governed by divine love, which also includes singing and dancing. In contrast to life on earth, where a Babylonic confusion of tongues seems omnipresent – what Baudelaire was to call "le malentendu universel" (universal misunderstanding) – heavenly bliss is regulated by a transcendent, scrupulously planned semiotics or choreography.²

If that is the case, we might well repeat Juliet's old question: what's in a name? An approximate hint, at best, according to this powerful tradition imbued by Platonic Cratylism and an Augustinian distrust of language. Dante recycles the same scepticism, but he converts it remarkably into something entirely different: into a source of joy. Though all verbal expression seems insufficient in this context, Dante *feels* – intuitively, self-confidently, and happily – that his words not

---

1 The most important Augustinian document about language, or more precisely the shortcomings of language, is surely *De catechizandis rudibus* (PL 40.309-48). It should not be isolated from the wider context of apophatic theology, inherent to Platonic thought throughout the Middle Ages, from Plato's own *Timaios* to the thirteenth-century Franciscan St Bonaventure. Zygmunt G. Barański emphasizes Dante's adhesion to this "symbolic" tradition, as opposed to Aristotelian rationalism, in his 1995 essay on medieval semiotics and Dante, pp. 149 ff. Peter S. Hawkins analyzes the Florentine poet's "dialectic of ineffability" in an interesting article from 1984; I compare the same phenomenon to related (albeit dissimilar) apophatic tendencies in Dante's precursor Alan of Lille and his successor Petrarch in a contribution to a *Festschrift* for my colleague at Stockholm University, Professor Gunilla Iversen (forthcoming).
2 V. Baudelaire's *journal intime* "Mon cœur mis à nu", *Œuvres complètes*, p. 1297 ("C'est par le malentendu universel que tout le monde s'accorde").

only hit the right note but also the correct targets, and he urges those of his readers whom Grace has granted divine experience to feel the same: to trust the "example" of his poetry. This joyful self-assurance is perhaps most evident in some lines at the very end of Paradiso, containing another reference to ancient pagan mythology. There, in the final song of the *Comedy*, the wanderer enjoys at last an all-embracing cosmic vision, suggested in the famous lines about the scattered leaves of the universe bound in one single volume, referred to above. However, of interest to me here is the poet's commentary to these verses which follows right afterwards:

> as though they were conflated in such ways
> that what I tell is but a simple light.
>
> I believe I understood the universal form
> of this dense knot because I feel my joy expand,
> rejoicing as I speak of it.
>
> My memory of that moment is more lost
> than five and twenty centuries make dim that enterprise
> when, in wonder, Neptune at the *Argo*'s shadow stared.
>
> quasi conflati insieme, per tal modo
> che ciò ch'i' dico è un semplice lume.
> La forma universal di questo nodo
> credo ch'i' vidi, perché più di largo,
> dicendo questo, mi sento ch'i' godo.
> Un punto solo m'è maggior letargo
> che venticinque secoli a la 'mpresa,
> che fé Nettuno ammirar l'ombra d'Argo.
> (XXXIII, 89–96)

From the beginning and the end of this quotation, which involves one of the most complex and disputed concepts of the whole work, we may understand that the words of the poet only reflect a faint reflection, *un semplice lume*, or even a "shadow" of his vision's original source. This is, once again, the sceptical side of Dante's hermeneutics. It makes itself felt all through Paradiso, whose images and figurations in another well-known line are called "shadowy prefaces", *umbriferi prefazi*, of their own truth (XXX, 78). The metaphor impregnates this linguistic or semiotic deficiency with a mystical or perhaps apocalyptic *telos*: human words are like shadows, indeed, but they point forwards to an angelic state of communicative transparency which shall dispel them. Such a pattern of thought is quite common in medieval symbolism based on Pauline typology, for example in St Bonaventure's *Itinerarium mentis in Deum*, in which all signs – those of language as well as of creation – appear as "shadows, echoes and pictures, as traces, phantoms, and representations" of divine reality.[3]

But Dante's ensuing, highly rhetorical representation of this split between vision and expression is quite original. The old Greek myth of Jason and his quest for the Golden Fleece on the Argo indicates extreme pastness; according to many ancient and medieval commentaries, it dealt with the origin of the art of shipbuilding. Argo was the first ship ever built, hence Dante's snapshot of how Neptune, the sea-god, was amazed by that hitherto unknown shadow crossing the surface of his waters. The *Comedy's* dating of this event to a point in time twenty-five centuries ago refers to a popular belief according to which Jason should have set sail in 1223 BC. But surely it is best understood as a classical metonymy for innumerable time. Now, when Dante is trying to reproduce his final vision, one second only, *un punto solo*, inevitably eclipses such an enormous space of time. This sole moment, then, signifies the insurmountable distance or oblivion, *letargo*, which separates the poet's vision from his words, experience from writing. Im modern times it was to be recalled by TS Eliot, one of Dante's best 20th century readers: "Between the conception / And the creation / Between the emotion / And the response / Falls the Shadow".[4]

Perhaps even the mythological scene twenty-five centuries ago reflects this sense of poetic shortcoming mixed with proud confidence. The sea-god is confronted with something he has never seen before, Jason and the Argonauts' bold "enterprise" which not only anticipates Ulysses' *sperienza* of the unknown but also Dante's own venturing into

---

[3] *sunt umbrae, resonantiae et picturae, sunt vestigia, simulacra et spectacula nobis ad contuendum Deum* (II.11).
[4] From "The Hollow Men", *Collected Poems 1909–1962*, p. 92.

the Christian beyond.[5] Pagan Neptune admires this *impresa*, but he can only glimpse a fleeting shadow of it, much as the poet himself in the following verses "Thus all my mind, absorbed, / was gazing, fixed" (*Così la mente mia, tutta sospesa, / mirava fissa*, 97–98) prepares to look into the abundant light which will make his speech, in comparison, sound like baby-talk (106–08).

But even though Neptune is that amazed, even though the oblivion that precedes writing seems immense, even though it is impossible to recall and communicate mystic vision, Dante holds an unshakeable belief in his words. This becomes evident from lines 91–93 from the final song of Paradiso, and the reason for the poet's confidence is the "joy" he "feels" when he speaks of these things: "I believe I understood the universal form / of this dense knot because I feel my joy expand, / rejoicing as I speak of it." At this crucial moment of the work, perhaps Longfellow's nineteenth-century translation is more literal: "The universal fashion of this knot / Methinks I saw, since more abundantly / In saying this I feel that I rejoice." The key word here is the subordinate conjunction "since", corresponding to the Hollanders' "because", indicating an explanation of the preceding clause, just like the Italian original's *perché*. The poet is confident that he saw the divine pattern of creation – the Aristotelian *forma universalis* theologized in Scholastic philosophy – and he believes in his all-encompassing vision *because* of the joy he feels while, however inadequately, talking about it.

This might be Dante's final paradox in the *Comedy*. This work, which remains so distrustful of language, draws its authority from the happiness the poet feels at the moment of writing, here typically translated into the more immediate mode of speech, "saying this" (*dicendo questo*). The passage is slightly reminiscent of a quite different but just as conspicuously self-authorizing declaration from the first part of the work in which Dante is confronted with Geryon, the guardian of Malebolge, the eighth of the infernal circles. To make us

---

5 The contrast and parallels between Ulysses' "mad flight" beyond the Pillars of Hercules (*folle volo*, *Inf*. XXVI, 125) and Dante's own "high flight" beyond the Moon (*alto volo*, *Par*. XV, 54, cf. XXV, 50) constitute a commonplace in modern Dante research. Jason, for his part, is punished among the seducers in Hell (*Inf*. XVIII, 83-99) but is nevertheless obliquely referred to as a distant precursor to Dante's heavenly journey in Paradiso (II, 16-18, XXV, 7-9).

believe he really saw this hideous monster combining three natures (of man, lion and snake) in one body, he can do nothing better than refer us to his own words. His amazing experience is authenticated by "the strains / of this Comedy" (*le note / di questa Comedia*, *Inf.* XVI, 127–28). There is no sense of triumph here, of course, on the threshold of Malebolge, but the demonstrative *questa*, pointing to the poet's own work, vaguely anticipates the *questo* of Paradiso XXXIII: in both cases, the text's source of truth tautologically appears to be the text itself.

As for the last case: even if the words come too late, and even if they prove insufficient, it is they – not doctrine, not personal conviction, not allegorical schemes of signification, but the words of poetry – that provide Dante with the assurance he needs. The seemingly insurmountable distance between jubilant vision and insufficient expression could only be cancelled out by virtue of this authorial "feeling" which extends the concept of experience from the former (the poet's *Erlebnis*) to the latter (the poet's writing). To all appearances, it was this verbal bliss rather than old Apollo that permitted Dante to write Paradiso.

Aspects of negativity.
Veridictory figures in the Comedy

Hanne Roer

La divina Commedia is known as the sublime, epic poem of the later Middle Ages in which Dante depicts the universe seen from the realms of the dead. During his travelling, the Dante pilgrim describes the physical features as well as the inhabitants of the three realms of the afterlife. Throughout the poem we hear the comments of the voice of the narrator, a Dante speaking from a safe point beyond the journey and back on earth. The *Comedy* as a whole with its mixed narrative layers gives us a sublime version of medieval cosmology while also being a personal *summa* of Dante's views of theology, love poetry and ethics. How then is it possible to characterize this unique, captivating universe as negative?

Dante represents the world of the dead from an impossible position, the *Comedy* being the memories of a traveller in the realms of the dead, now returned to the land of the living. However vivid and graphic Dante's world may seem it is written from the perspective of death, a state of negativity. The world of the living is reflected in the world of the dead, most evidently in the speeches of the dead souls and in the many similitudes. The classification of the poem as an allegory might seem an obvious explanation of these narrative paradoxes. That the *Comedy* is an allegory is beyond doubt, but there is very little agreement among critics as to the interpretation of Dante's allegorical writing. Allegory is a kind of representation involving two layers, hence closely related to irony as Quintilian points out. This ambiguity is what characterizes allegory in the *Comedy*: it can be read positively as referring to a metaphysical reality or negatively as exhibiting its own textuality. Accordingly a central question in modern

Dante criticism has been whether the allegory in the *Comedy* represents divine or moral truths, or rather demonstrates the literary and fictional character of the text.

Charles S. Singleton suggested in 1954 that Dante's letter to Cangrande della Scala offered a key to the interpretation of the *Comedy*. As a result Dante's use of the allegory of the theologians meant that the *Comedy* was to be understood as true in the literal sense, like the Bible. Choosing between the allegory of the theologians and that of the poets has since seemed a compelling issue that has cast its spell on Dante criticism. It has resulted in an idiosyncratic discourse that seems strange to other literary critics, as pointed out by Teodolinda Barolini in *The Undivine Comedy* from 1992. Barolini actually believes that Singleton was right in declaring about the *Comedy* that "the fiction is that it is not a fiction" (Singleton 1954, 62). She also agrees with Bruno Nardi who argued in favour of reading the poem as an example of visionary literature, expressing Dante's personal, visionary experience. Her book offers us impressive close readings of narrative structures of the *Comedy* which leave aside the abstract discussions of allegory in favour of stringent, textual analyses. Barolini's special interest is the rhetorical strategies used by Dante in representing his vision in what is basically a literary genre. She refers to Augustine's rhetorical prescriptions in *De doctrina Christiana* as an early example of rhetorical and linguistic self-consciousness in medieval, religious texts. In fact medieval, visionary texts are often full of explicit metaliterary comments. She objects to the naive belief in the referentiality of the allegory and emphasizes the rhetorical, secular texture of the poem. Since the *Comedy* creates divine truths, she focuses on the way in which Dante involves his readers and tricks them into believing in the text.

It is some of these veridictory aspects that I wish to discuss in more depth in this paper. Barolini, apparently, has been criticized for naively accepting Dante's belief in a metaphysical background for his literary representation. She claims that she does not argue in favour of the truth of the poem, but shows how Dante makes us believe that it is true. But here she reveals her understanding of Dante as a rhetorician who cleverly exploits the persuasive techniques of language to seduce his reader. She talks throughout her book about Dante's intentions that she apparently wants to uncover. In spite of her subtle readings, Barolini turns Dante into a technician because she does not distinguish between literature and rhetoric, or between literary and rhetorical criticism. Literary criticism does not have the uncovering of authentic, authorial intentions as its main goal for the very good reason that literary works are multilayered and polysemous, to use Dante's own word from the letter to Cangrande. Barolini's focus on Dante's rhetorical intentions has the unfortunate side-effect that she neglects the many enunciatory dimensions of the poem. This is rather strange as structural and narrative analysis has been most occupied with enunciation, implied authors and readers.[1]

By adding the concept of negativity I hope to show that some of Dante's narrative structures and figures have an aesthetic aspect. Negativity is a term that has both theological and poetico-rhetorical dimensions as well as a modern, aesthetic dimension. While these dimensions should be separated in close readings of the *Comedy* I believe that the term unites some of these notions. Hence it offers a way into the *Comedy* and out of the false dilemmas connected with allegorical exegesis. I shall start with the medieval connotations, i.e. the concept of negativity in medieval mysticism and in the *Comedy*. Since I am not the first to introduce this idea I shall paraphrase some important texts on the subject, such as Angelo Jacomuzzi's structural reading of the topoi of ineffability in the *Comedy*. I shall then turn to a structural analysis of some extraordinary similitudes, the most important being Inferno XXX, 136–141 and Paradiso XXX, 91–96.

Via negationis

The problem of representing the divine in human language is formulated in terms of negativity in the mystical tradition. I shall only take up some major points as a background for my analysis of the veridictory figures. The medieval problem of negative representation is posed in the *The Celestial Hierarchy* ascribed to a certain Pseudo-Dionysius. As the name indicates, we do not know the author of these early Greek works from the fifth or sixth century that seem to have exerted a major influence on medieval thinking including poetics. The later

---

1 She does not discuss her own method, and just refers to Conte.

Latin translations of *The Divine Names*, *The Mystical Theology*, *The Celestial Hierarchy* and *The Ecclesiastical Hierarchy* were widely diffused in the Middle Ages. From the ninth century onwards they exert a deep impact on mystical theology and literature. In the *Comedy* we find Dionysius among the wise in the heaven of the Sun (*Par*. X).

In *The Celestial Hierarchy* the author reflects on the deficiency of human language to represent the angels and the heavens. He points to the Bible that abounds in naive or grotesque images, providing us with examples to be imitated: "The word of God makes use of poetic imagery when discussing these formless intelligences but, as I have already said, it does so not for the sake of art, but as a concession to the nature of our mind." Two ways of symbolizing are possible, according to *The Celestial Hierarchiy*: "– firstly, by proceeding naturally through sacred images in which like represents like, while also using formations which are dissimilar and even entirely inadequate and ridiculous."

"Similar" images designating God may for example be Word, Mind and Deity. Though they may seem more respectful, rationality and wisdom being necessary attributes of God, such names are not better than the dissimilar images. The author of *The Celestial Hierarchy* concludes that the second way, the way of negation, is the better one: "Then there is the scriptural device of praising the deity by presenting it in utterly dissimilar revelations. He is described as invisible, infinite, ungraspable, and other things which show not what he is but what in fact he is not. This second way of talking about him seems to me much more appropriate, for, as the secret and sacred tradition has instructed, God is in no way like the things that have being and we have no knowledge at all of his incomprehensible and ineffable transcendence and invisibility. Since the way of negation appears to be more suitable to the realm of the divine and since positive affirmations are always unfitting to the hiddenness of the inexpressible a manifestation through dissimilar shapes is more correctly to be applied to the invisible" (149–150).

In the short text *The Mystical Theology* the deficiencies of language in representing divine revelation are further emphasized:

> What has actually to be said about the Cause of everything is this. Since it is the Cause of all beings, we should posit and ascribe to it all the affirmations we make in regard to beings, and, more appropriately, we should negate all these affirmations, since it surpasses all being. Now we should not conclude that the negations are simply the opposites of the affirmations, but rather that the cause of all is considerably prior to this, beyond privations, beyond every denial, beyond every assertion (136).

The author is arguing against the Aristotelian notion of negations as the opposite of affirmations and opens up for a wide range of rhetorical and stylistic experiments (Pseudo-Dionysius 1987, 136).

Negative theology and later mystical writing is clearly the cultural background for the *Comedy*. Inferno in particular abounds in grotesque imagery such as Lucifer with his three heads, a perverted image of the triune god. Barolini interprets the infernal monster of Geryon as a grotesque representation with such metaliterary implications. In the *Comedy* the topos of the ineffability of the divine is turned into a new kind of literature, but with many explicit references to the negative theology of Pseudo-Dionysius.

Negation in Inferno. The privation of the divine

In all of the three canticles negativity is a theme that pushes the question of linguistic and poetic representation to the fore. I shall mainly concentrate on Inferno and Paradiso though it should not be forgotten that the problem of representation runs as an explicit theme throughout the poem. The Inferno is characterized by the absence of the divine, as seen in the fact that the name of Christ is never mentioned, but alluded to by periphrases. Christ is called *possente* in Inferno IV, 53; *nol* (*s'altri nol niega*) in Inferno V, 81; *il nimica podesta* in Inferno VI, 96; *tal* in Inferno VIII, 105; *colui* in Inferno XII, 38, and *l'uom* in Inferno XXXIV, 115. This discretion extends to Beatrice who is called *tal* in Inferno XII, 88. It is the place where the sun is silent, *là dove 'l sole tace*, Inferno I, 60. The sinners long for escape from their eternal punishments, sentenced according to *la legge del contrapasso*, but they are forever deprived of divine grace: "Nulla speranza li conforta mai, / non che di posa, ma di minor pena", Inferno V, 44–5, and "Regola e qualità mai non l'è nova" Inferno VI, 9. In the speech proffered by Francesca, the negativity of her love and the hopelessness of freeing herself from it are stressed by the imprisoning *non*:

> Amor, ch'a nullo amato amar perdona,
> Mi prese del costui piacer sì forte,
> Che, come vedi, ancor non m'abbandona
> (*Inf.* V, 103)

The absence of the divine is underlined by the countless neologisms starting with the prefixes *dis-* and *ex-*. In an excellent reading Luigi Scorrano points out that the beginning of Inf. XIII hammers out the infernal horizon of negativity with an unusual force. The intensity is due to the fact that the suicides have denied the divine gifts of life and freedom of will. Pier della Vigna has chosen suicide for egoistical reasons, in contrast to Cato who is set up as an exemplum in Purgatorio I. It is the only canto in Inferno beginning with a negation: "Non era ancor di là Nesso arrivato". This first verse anticipates the opening *non* of each of the verses 4–7. In fact it is the only canto starting with a negation in the poem since Purgatorio XIII, which opens with *Né il dir, né l'andar* […], is in quite another hopeful atmosphere. The *non* pervading the first and second terzina and extending into the third seals the negativity that is the essence of Inferno and especially of canto XIII. Scorrano analyzes the structure of vv, 4–6:

> Non fronda vede, ma di color fosco;
> Non rami schietti, ma nodosi e 'nvolti;
> Non pomi v'eran, ma stecchi con tosco.

He concludes that though the second part of each verse seems to weaken the opening *non*, the sad content of it actually reinforces the negativity: *il color fosco delle fronde, i rami nodosi e 'nvolti, gli stecchi con tosco inverano in imagine ciò che la negazione ha già, per la sua forza stessa,* communicato" (Scorrano 1998, 101).[2] Scorrano's verb *inverano* points to the essential theme of the poetics of the *Comedy*: how is it possible to represent the world of the dead as true and, more importantly, how is it possible to convey the truth of Christian faith? Scorrano basically asks the same question as Barolini and in this light some of the more confusing constructions make sense. Scorrano analyzes the following verse: "Cred'io ch'ei credette ch'io credesse" (I believe that he believed that I believed [...], v. 25): the verse gives an adequate form to the doubts and perplexity of Dante.[3] The artificial rhetorical figure actually emphasizes the hollowness of rhetoric that is a major theme in the following speech by Pier della Vigna. This speech is, Scorrano concludes, an example of how rhetoric turns into destructivity if it is not informed by divine light, the *verbum dei* (p. 114). Pier della Vigna is punished by the deprivation of the body: "ché non è giusto aver ciò ch'om si toglie", v. 105. This shows that *la legge del contrapasso* is in itself a principle of negativity. To conclude, negativity is an important theme in Inferno, referring to a theological concept as well as a stylistic and rhetorical problem, i.e. the question of representing evil as privation. The famous opening of Inferno XXXII states the infernal problem of representation: "S'io avessi le rime aspre e chiocce / come si converebbe al tristo buco".

Negation in Paradiso. The topoi of ineffability

The metaphysical problem of linguistic deficiency vis-à-vis the divine is combined in medieval literature with the rhetorical topos of ineffability. E. R. Curtius has sharply distinguished between the metaphysical topos of ineffability and the rhetorical *Unsagbarheitstopos* (*recusatio*). That this distinction expresses a modern dichotomy between theology and rhetoric is one of many important points made by Angelo Jacomuzzi in his essay "Il 'topos' dell' ineffabile nel 'Paradiso'". In his article, he convincingly argues that these topoi in the *Comedy* are

---

2 Scorrano lists another nine instances of negated clauses and five verbs denoting absence (p. 101).
3 Scorrano quotes the condemnations of critics such as Lana ("uno scherzo poco degno d'imitazione") and Petrocchi ("chi bisticcia entro di sé un po' più del lecito, è il nostro poeta"), p. 106.

not extraordinary additions or rhetorical ornaments. This has been the view of many critics since Bruno Croce defined the recurring exclamations regarding the shortcomings of language as *iperboli negative*. On the contrary, they are essential for the structure of the *Comedy* where Dante transforms these traditional topoi into a writing of his own. The question is not how the poet may verbalize his vision or how he technically construes a vision, but how the text of the *Comedy* becomes poetry in its own, superior right.

Jacomuzzi points to the fact that though we find topoi of ineffability in the first two canticles, they appear in abundance in the Paradiso. The numerous critical essays about them fall into two categories, according to Jacomuzzi. Either they look at the topoi *a parte obiecti*, regarding them as exclamations of deficiency vis-à-vis a given supernatural, mystical reality. It is a philosophical, abstract perspective that has nothing to do with literary criticism. Or they look at the topoi of ineffability *a parte subiecti*, i.e. as expressions of the doubts of the poet confronted with his great task, no different from similar exclamations by poets such as Leopardi or Carducci. Whether the point of departure is the abstract philosophical or the aesthetic they both seem to claim that Dante takes language to its limits in the *Comedy*. Either the topoi of ineffability are explained as figures of an unusual efficiency in light of the disproportion between human instruments and the quality of the mystical vision, or they are explained as an instance of the poetic exploitations of the word taken to its limits, privileged but essentially no different from what other poets do.

Both perspectives are based on a *premessa astrattamente contenutistica* (p. 80), i.e. an axiom claiming an intrinsic ineffability in the Paradiso of which the topoi of ineffability are but traces and verifications. Jacomuzzi instead proposes a structural approach that analyzes these topoi as immanent signs, decisive for the structure of Paradiso and revealing the writing (*scrittura*) of the *Comedy* in the passage from lyrical and doctrinal poetry to that of the *Comedy*. Since the *Comedy* is a *fictio rhetorica* (according to *De vulgari eloquentia*) the topoi of ineffability emerge as essential moments, internal limits or negations of the structure. They linger in the ambiguity between invention and vision, between the allegory of the poets and that of the theologians,

Aspects of negativity

between mythopoiesis and vision, spreading light one on the other and on the nature of their relations.

Jacomuzzi then turns to the passage in the letter to Cangrande della Scala in which Dante interprets the first verses of Paradiso I (28–30). He emphasizes that Dante talks about *phantasia*, a "virtù organica" that functions as an intermediary between sensation and intellect, as capable of articulating the word, "rationale signum et sensuale". The exegesis in the letter suggests that poetic enunciation is impossible, and Dante points to Plato who had to turn to metaphors to represent his ideas. Jacomuzzi concludes his reading of the passage with the idea that the *proprietas* of language is contrasted with figurative language – metaphorical, allegorical, or in other words characterized by essentially negative connotations. The passage shows how Dante transforms the simple topos of ineffability into critical awareness, leading to the definition of the poem as *poeticus, fictivus, transumptivus* (p. 84).

I shall leave aside the many subtle points of Jacomuzzi's reading of the topoi of ineffability in Paradiso and restrict myself to paraphrasing some of his conclusions. Instead of looking at isolated topoi he suggests that a structural approach may lead to a better understanding of their function. There are two basic movements forming the relation between the sacred vision and invention, between the mystical experience and the poem, between *il fatto* and *il dir*. This duplicity verifies that the internal ambiguity in these relations is not overcome *a priori* but eternally reconfigures itself as a critical, qualifying constant.

The first of these two opposed movements characterizing the relationship between the poet-person and the material of the vision is the ascension of Dante through the heavens which is accompanied by topoi of ineffability ("transumanar significar per verba / non si porria; però l'essemplo basti/a cui esperienza grazia serba", *Par.* I, 71–72). The other, opposite movement is the paradisiacal material moving down towards the poet-person in series of metamorphoses, most eminently in Paradiso XXX. This latter movement is similar to accounts of mystical visions but Jacomuzzi rejects a mystical reading as well as a traditional, four-fold allegorical exegesis. Instead he sees the two movements as a double presence, with the story as vision divinely authorized and the vision as a story, the fruit of human genius and linguistic technique. This double presence is a high, unresolved tension inherent in the structure of Paradiso. The topoi of ineffability distance themselves from the rhetorical and the theological-mystical tradition not only in intensity and efficiency but because their function is different. Jacomuzzi analyzes the prolonged apostrophes of ineffability in Paradiso XXIII, 46–49 and XXX, 16–33 that explicitly refer to literary antecedents ("Se mo sonasser tutte le lingue / che Polimnïa; figurando il paradiso / conviene saltar lo sacrato poema; poetando"). The audience is no longer the spectator of a mystical experience but becomes conscious of the exceptional character of the poem. A dialectical relationship between the poet and the reader is another result of the topoi of ineffability. Dante locates such topoi between the mystical and literary traditions, but they are not identical with either of them (but a critical condition, p. 93).

The traditional, literary function of the topoi of ineffability is the praise of a fact or person and the less striking topoi of ineffability in Paradiso are of this kind (*Par.* X, 40–45, 70–75; XIV, 79–81; XXIII, 22–24). But the major part of the topoi of ineffability points to the exceptionally metaphorical and fictive character of the poem. The poem is not a mystical ascension with a clear moral because at the end it dissolves into figures and metaphors. The final vision is constructed on the ambiguity of the moments of *letargo* and *vedere*. The verse "All'alta phantasia mancò possa" shows this duplicity since *phantasia* both refers to the imaginative power that has become impregnated with intuitive visions and to the instrument that determines the whole edifice of the poem (p. 97). Jacomuzzi quotes some of the ancient commentators who interpret *phantasia* in this way.

The pseudo-Dionysian and the rhetorical topoi of ineffability form a tension that cannot be resolved, but which is turned into a critical attitude (p. 101). There is no doubt that Dante knows the mystical traditions of which he prefers the Pauline version of the *raptus*, but the poem is first poem, secondly holy (*il sacrato poema*). Jacomuzzi often refers to the heritage of Croce who regarded the philosophical and theological structure as essentially unpoetic. The misconstrued philosophical approaches mixed with "mystical" theology tend to obscure many "analyses" of the *Comedy* (106). Hinting at Nardi, Jacomuzzi says that the *Comedy* read retrospectively from the final vision can be seen as the highest form of vision, an ineffability transgressing the words of the prophet. But the allusions to the Pauline descent emphasizes that

Aspects of negativity

this is a corporal journey. Not just a body in the allegorical sense, but body in the ultimate sense which is only realized at the final judgement with the resurrection of the bodies. The allegory of the theologians is applied to a past story whereas the story of the *Comedy* takes place in a single moment and a single space. The story is linked to the body of the poet that still carries the memories of past experiences (p. 109). There is no other reality than the one that the poet carries with him; the final vision is not the climax but encloses the whole text.

The *sonno* of the first canto of Inferno forms a circle with the *assonna* of Paradiso XXXIII, the former being an instance of the typical, didactic kind of allegory, whereas the latter is ambiguously realistic and literary. The allegory has become allegorical writing: the *Comedy* does not contain "another" reality that justifies the words spoken by the earthy poet. This allegorical writing is perhaps most fully realized in Paradiso XXX in the living sparkling and lights of the heavenly river – a metamorphosis beyond metaphor and allegory. Jacomuzzi concludes: "Il rapporto che si viene, così, a stabilire nella struttura tipica dell'allegoria dantesca non è tra due realtà o avvenimenti, ma tra la rappresentazione fittizia della realtà definitiva e il significato che ontologicamente e ineffabilmente le appartiene e che si identifica con la sostanza stessa delle cose, rappresentate non alla stregua della mimesi realistica ma della visione rivelativa e giudicante" (p. 111).

He then discusses the recurring *vidi*, I saw, in the *Comedy*. One could object that the recurrent *vidi* of the *Comedy* functions as a topos that guarantees the truthfulness of the vision. But the two topoi do not function as opposites as they are stabilized on different levels. In the *vidi* the protagonist and the poet coincide; in the declarations of ineffability the poet and the awareness of the work emerge on the protagonist. The former is a moment in the representation on the level of narration; the latter is a trace of the structure on the level of the poem. The former exalts the representative function of language; the latter negates the application of words to things and opens up for the use of language for a literary process that cannot be identified with the univocal tone of the chronicle of a mystic. The *Comedy* points to a disproportion between *dir* and *fatto* that excludes mimetic representation but opens up for an epistemic and judging use of poetry. This function is assigned to the ultimate myth of the poem, Beatrice, whose beauty is metamorphosed and transformed. Her last words are a prophetical condemnation of the two popes that Dante has placed in Hell (*Par.* XXX, 145–148). The lyrical image of the beloved *donna* has become part of the violence of history which is another deviation in the *Comedy* from the literary tradition.

Veridictory puzzles

I am using a classic structuralist approach to some of the some most intriguing similitudes. Veridiction is a central concept in the structural narratology of Greimas. In an article from 1980 "The Veridiction Contract" he argues that plausibility is linked to descriptive and narrative discourse. Though plausibility might seem complementary to the idea of "fiction" it is not a term restricted to literary theory. Cultural contexts seem to determine whether the receivers of a text accept it as true (or plausible), as shown by the reception of oral, African texts and the problem connected to interpreting medieval, religious texts.[4] But cultural context is not the only explanation. Veridiction is situated in the discourse and the question is: under what conditions is what we say "true"? I quote from Greimas: "How do we lie? How do we go about hiding our secrets? To this series of questions which might be asked of a producer of discourse, there corresponds another series which concerns the receiver of that discourse. Under what conditions do we believe that the discourse of others is true? How do we recognize lies and impostures? How is it that we sometimes see them as vehicles of profound truths because of a presentiment of 'those things that are hidden behind other things'? The problem of the plausible is thus also integrated within the whole question of the veracity of discourses." (p. 653)

When religious medieval texts are read today as literature, one would expect this to be the result of the cultural context of the modern receiver. Greimas however does not want to give up the idea of textual structures and isotopies that to a great extent determine the reception. Some readings are simply not possible, because texts do have some invariants that the receiver cannot overlook. That implies that

---

4 Greimas refers to the work of Juri Lotman.

discourses define cultural contexts, not the other way round. This of course is a major hermeneutic problem in Dante criticism and linked to the question of the value of authorial intention in criticism. When we ask whether and how deeply Dante is determined by the mystical tradition and to what extent he changed that tradition, we might be seeking to expose his intentions. That is what Barolini seems to do, concluding that Dante followed tradition, while being far above his antecedents in rhetorical technique. Jacomuzzi, on the other hand, insists on the unique literary character of the *Comedy* and the way it breaks with tradition.

Greimas says that the text itself has marks indicating isotopies, what are known as veridiction marks. Barolini's analysis of Dante's persuasive strategies and Jacomuzzi's analysis of the topoi of ineffability treat many of the important veridiction marks in the *Comedy*. Barolini has analyzed the oaths of the narrator who swears on the poem that he is telling the truth. An oath is a classic mark of veridiction that in the *Comedy* is turned into poetry: when the narrator swears on the holy poem he attracts the attention to the exceptional character of the poem. This is the same function that Jacomuzzi emphasizes in relation to the topoi of ineffability. Greimas in fact calls the naive belief in an oath "Adamic innocence", an innocence that Dante clearly does not rely on. This innocence, Greimas continues, has been replaced by two discursive forms that seek the trust of the receiver, a subjectivizing strategy (his example is the secretive, psychoanalytic discourse of Lacan) and an objectivizing strategy (academic, scientific language).

Trust is established in a contract between the sender and the receiver of discourse because in a text there is always an exchange structure. There are two superimposed levels of the veridiction contract: knowing and believing, truth and certitude, knowing to be and believing to be true.

The transaction in which knowledge is exchanged can be inscribed into the semiotic square. I have copied a version exemplifying the use of the square with the pair beautiful-ugly from a fine paper published on the Internet:[5]

---

[5] The figure is from Roar Høstaker's paper on Greimas' influence on Bruno Latour: http://ansatte.hil.no/roarh/artiklar/latouroggreimas.htm. The few pages about Greimas demonstrate a superb overview of his work.

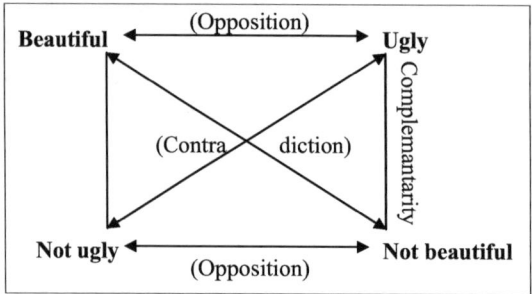

What I would propose here is that some of the most confusing similitudes install a veridictory game in the reader. There are a few of these seductive and confusing similitudes; some are perfect examples of an inherent ambiguity whereas others are more simple games with appearance and being, non-appearance and non-being.

My first example is Inferno II, 37–39: "E qual è quei che disvuol ciò che volle / E per novi pensier cangia proposta / Sì che dal cominciar tutto si tolle / Tal mi fec' ïo"(And like one who unwills what he has willed and with new thoughts changes his resolve, so that he quite gives up the thing he had begun, such was I [...], Singleton's translation). It is a rather complicated way of comparing the protagonist to someone who changed his mind due to new ideas. But the negated content (dis-vuol, tolle) and the syntactic mosaic reflect the confusing train of thought. It is the same stylistic mimesis that we have seen in Inferno XIII ("Cred'io ch'ei credette ch'io credesse"),[6] but here the superimposed levels of being and appearance, non-appearance and non-being, fit into the semiotic square:

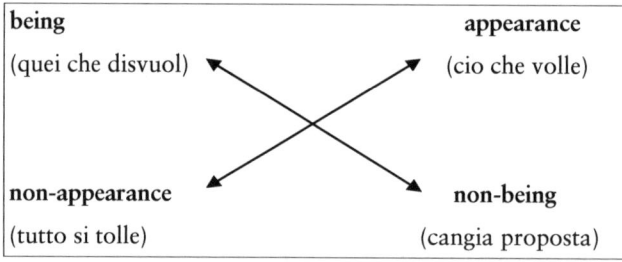

---

6 Another example of many possible is Inferno VI 42: "Tu fosti, prima ch'io disfatto, fatto." Here the syntax has been turned into a polyptoton that seems to eliminate the oppositions in the verse, forcing the reader to analyze the sentence more closely.

Aspects of negativity

What does this tell us except for that *doctor quadratus* (as Umberto Eco called Greimas in *Il nome della rosa*) has not been quite forgotten? It tells us that knowledge is being transported in a dialectical relationship with the reader in a way that exemplifies the basic, Aristotelian rules of logic. The reader is put to the test: only after an intellectual effort do the sentences make sense and the sender finally seems psychologically consistent and trustworthy. The veridictory figures act out truth and deceit, true and false impressions. Sometimes similitudes show how false impressions are removed by knowledge leading to true impressions. An example is Inferno VIII, 22–24: "Qual è colui che grande inganno ascolta / Che li sia fatto, e poi se ne rammarca, / Fecesi Flegïàs ne l'ira accolta" (As one who listens to some great deception that has been practised on him, and then pines at it, such Phlegyas became [...], Singleton's translation). In Purgatorio XV, 117 the phrase *non falsi errori* is used and it describes very well what is at stake in the narrator's games with the reader.[7]

Sometimes the negated sentences are so complicated that they are hard to translate, such as Inferno IX, 58–60: "Così disse 'l maestro; ed elli stessi / mi volse, e non si tenne a le mie mani, / Che con le sue ancor non mi chiudessi" (Thus said the master, and he himself turned me round and, not trusting to my hands, covered my face with his own hands; Singleton's translation). Though the second use of *non* is an idiomatic use expressing doubt and not negation, the negative context of Inferno stresses the use of the two *non*. Singleton's translation is correct but does not have the negative connotations of *non* in the Italian text. This chain of negations is followed by a apostrophe: "O voi ch'avete li 'intelletti sani, / mirate la dottrina che s'asconde / sotto 'l velame de li versi strain" (O you who have sound understanding, mark the doctrine that is hidden under the veil of the strange verses!). The narrator tells us that his verses are truth with the face of a lie, as is said in Inferno XVI, 124–132.

But often it is not easy for the reader to grasp the proper allegorical sense of the strange verses. A striking example is the *villanello* similitude that opens Inferno XXIV. As Barolini has shown, it is unclear whether the peasant is analogous to Dante or Virgil (p. 86–87). This long, stylistically refined similitude is loaded with ambiguity. This

---

7 See also Barolini p. 13 who takes the phrase as a point of departure for her readings.

is underlined by the extensive use of *rime equivoche*, homonymous rhymes that in spite of their apparent identity have different significations. The peasant sees the ground white with hoarfrost (called the image of his white sister), and shortly after he sees that "'l mondo aver cangiata faccia," the world has changed its face. This is a veridictory figure that fits perfectly into the semiotic square:

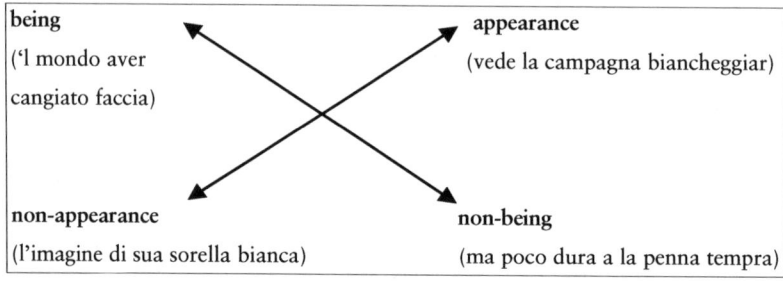

The figure illustrates that two superimposed levels of the veridiction contract, knowing/truth/knowing-to-be versus believing/certitude/believing-to-be true, have been mixed. When being is described as "having changed face", appearance and being are hard to distinguish between. This is also the case in the remarkable similitude that Barolini simply calls strange, Inferno XXX, 136–141: "Qual è colui che suo dannagio sogna / che sognando desidera sognare / sì che quel ch'è, come non fosse, agogna / al mi fec' io, non possendo parlare / che disïava scusarmi, e scusava / me tuttavia, e nol mi credea fare" (And as is he who dreams of something hurtful to him and, dreaming, wishes that it were a dream, so that he longs for that which is, as if it were not, such I became that, unable to speak, I wanted to excuse myself, and did excuse myself all the while, not thinking I was doing it; Singleton's translation):

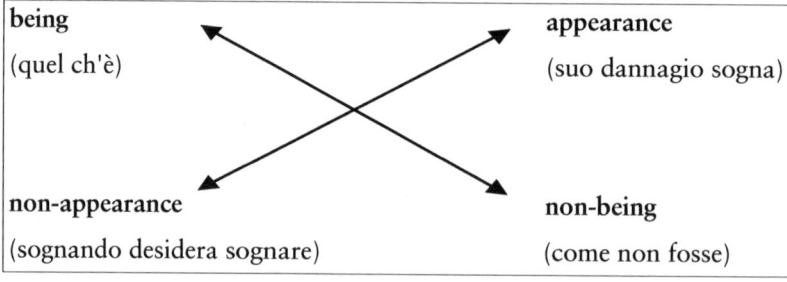

Appearance is a dream, reality is marked by something non-existent – which is the state wanted! The fiction of the dream is so cruel that the dreamer wishes that it were fiction, and so it is. This is an allusion to the allegorical character of the poem on the structural level of *The Comedy*, not on the narrative level, to use Jacomuzzi's terms. The narrative layers of the traditional visionary text form a contract with its readers making it easy to decode the allegorical isotopies. Sleep refers to well known conventions for the presentation of a vision but in the *Comedy* this contract is broken. It becomes increasingly difficult for the reader to decode the text. Singleton's "the fiction is that it is not a fiction" is contradicted by this similitude saying that this is not fiction, but unique poetry. The ironic games result in a veridictory contract between the enunciating instance and the receiver of the enunciation preparing the reader for complicated confusions of appearance and fact, lies and truths. The problems of veridiction, of telling the truth, exposed by this similitude are at least one indicator of the special contract between the narrator and the reader in the *Comedy*.

Questioning the meaning of analogy is another way in which the text puzzles the reader, giving no stable solutions. Hence the belief in the logical and literary value of the analogy is questioned. In Inferno XXXIV, 28–31 there is an analogy that at first glance seems rational, even logical but on closer scrutiny turns out to be absurd: "Lo 'mperador del doloroso regno / da mezzo 'l petto uscia fuor de la ghiaccia; / e piú con un gigante io mi convegno, / che i giganti non fan con le sue braccia / vedi oggimai quant'esser dee quell tutto/ ch'a così fatta parte si confaccia" (The emperor of the woeful realm stood forth from mid-breast out of the ice; and I in size compare better with a giant that giants with his arms: see now how huge that whole must be to correspond to such a part). This is a *reductio ad absurdum* of analogical representation. The relation between the "I" and the giant is in no way analogous to the relation between the giant and the arms of Lucifer. The negated comparison is appropriate in Lower Hell, Lucifer being the perverted mirroring of the Divine, but a closer look shows that the analogy is empty. Commentators who have tried to calculate the length of Lucifer, have arrived at very different results. Sapegno concludes in his commentary that all attempts to calculate the length of Lucifer from this analogy have been a waste of time. His example is Camilli (*Lingua nostra* XIV, 1953, 22) who reached the conclusion that Lucifer measures more than 1000 metres! The limits of the analogy are demonstrated; there is no simple compatibility between man and the universe, or between the universe and the textual universe of the *Comedy*.

The similitude in Inferno XXX seemed to say that appearance is a dream negating the real state of things. In Paradiso XXX, 91–96, the negations in the veridictory puzzle of the similitude of the unmasked masked people are even more complicated:

> Poi come gente stata sotto larve,
> che pare altro che prima, se si sveste
> la sembianza non sua in che disparve,
> così mi si cambiaro in maggior feste
> li fiori e le faville, sí ch'io vidi
> ambo le corti del ciel manifeste.

To paraphrase the similitude, it says that people who have been in disguise appear in a different way than before, if they put off the appearance not their own in which they earlier made a false appearance (*disparve*). Singleton's translation is of course correct but smoothes out some of the force of the negatives: "Then, as folk who have been under masks seem other than before, if they do off the semblances not their own wherein they were hid, so into greater festival the flowers and the sparks did change before me that I saw both the courts of Heaven made manifest."

Here, we step further out into the insolubility of representing truth in language and language as being truth: appearance is not just a dream, with the implied unreality implied, but being is appearance, and appearance is in the past tense:

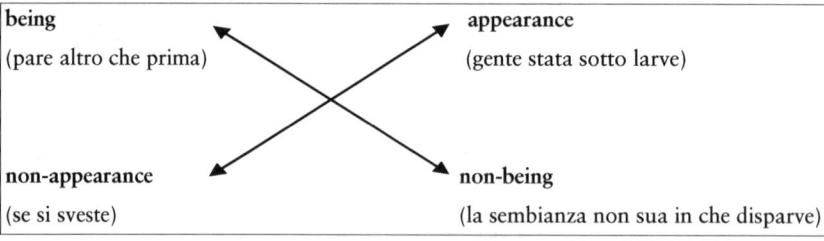

The analysis of the similitude, distributing it in the semiotic square, shows that there is actually no positive description of the people. They are being described as having been masked, e.g. in the past tense. Being is not distinguishable from non-being nor is appearance from non-appearance on the level of content. The text seems to say that it is possible to negate negations in language without anything positive coming out of it. It could be argued that the text demonstrates the pseudo-Dionysian description of negative theology that we have seen in *The Mystical Theology*: "Now we should not conclude that the negations are simply the opposites of the affirmations, but rather that the cause of all is considerably prior to this, beyond privations, beyond every denial, beyond every assertion."

The negation of the negation of the negated in the similitude alludes to the difficulty of representing the profound cause of affirmations as well as negations. But the similitude also has a veridictory aspect, insofar as it forces the reader to think about the power of language, or more specifically the power of the poem at hand. As Jacomuzzi and Barolini both emphasize, the *sonno* of Inferno I is a conventional topic from visionary literature, [8] but that in the *Comedy* it is encircled and overruled by the metapoetic *assonna* of Paradiso XXXIII. The two most striking examples of the veridictory puzzle, the similitudes analyzed above in Inferno XXX and Paradiso XXX, circle around the themes of sleep and masquerading. [9] In Purgatorio XXX there is no veridictory figure but it is the song in which Beatrice appears in the midst of an allegorical procession. And in the last canticle of Purgatorio this procession is metamorphosed into the perverted image of the Whore of Babylon flirting with the King of France. To conclude, it is no coincidence that we find the veridictory puzzles at symmetrical positions at the end of the first and of the third canticle. The theme of the first similitude is sleep, of the second masquerade, which again hints at the magnificent procession at the end of Purgatorio. These figures with their inherent instability are structural marks, like the topoi of ineffability analyzed by Jacomuzzi. They support his thesis: there are structural marks in the poem telling us that this is to be understood as original poetry. Hence it is no anachronism to talk about the aesthetic dimensions of the poem.

---

8 We should also remember the affinities between the *Comedy* and the *Roman de la Rose* in this respect.
9 There are many more related examples but the similitudes mentioned fuse the levels of veridiction to an extreme extent.

The voice of the invisible

An aesthetic approach means that the question of the relevance of authorial intentions has to be asked once again. If we, like Barolini, regard Dante as a Christian orator with an exceptional grasp of fables and good stories, then I guess that we as critics are in a position to criticize him. This normative approach is what we meet in older commentaries, such as the quoted condemnations of the more "bizarre" figures in the *Comedy*. This understanding of philology as a basically normative discipline is rare today, and in literary criticism almost taboo. It overlooks the fact that literary texts are polysemous, to use Dante's word. I shall only give one example of the multidimensionality of the enunciative structures in the *Comedy* to show that authorial intention in literary analysis is of limited values.[10]

If we return to the chain of metamorphoses in Paradiso XXX, the angelic substances are not described per se, but shown in changing apparitions. The Dante-person in what follows the analyzed similitude in Paradiso XXX sees the metamorphoses of the River of Light, with flowers and sparks of fire on the banks, which turn into the two heavenly courts. In the following *canti* the courts turn into the Celestial Rose, and finally the paradisiacal metamorphosis ends with the three circles representing the Trinity. If we remember Jacomuzzi's two opposite movements structuring the relation between vision and invention, this is the second one in which the paradisiacal material is moving towards the poet-person. In some cultures, according to Greimas, reification on the level of the signifier is understood as a guarantee of the truth of the text. The materiality of the signifier alludes to the supposed anagogical and true character of the signified (Greimas & Courtés 1988, 287). The reification of the signifier in the form of recitation, metric or rhythmic distortion gives the impression of an underlying voice, a true discourse underlying the spoken word. This is exactly what we meet in the grand paradisiacal metamorphosis:

---

10 Literary criticism may well be an anomalism in contrast to others areas of research such as historical, autobiographical and rhetorical studies in which intention is an important hermeneutic guideline.

Non fur più tosto dentro a me venute
queste parole brievi, ch'io compresi
me sormontar di sopr'a mia *v*irtute;
e di no*v*ella *v*ista *m*i raccesi
tale, che nulla *luce* è tanto mera,
che li occhi *m*iei non si fosser difesi.
E *v*idi *lume* in forma di ri*v*era
flu*v*ido di fulgore, intra due ri*v*e
dipinte di *m*irabil pri*m*a*v*era.
Di tal *fiumana* uscían fa*v*ille *v*i*v*e,
e d'ogne parte si *m*ettien ne' fiori,
quasi rubin che oro circunscri*v*e.
(*Par.* XXX, 55–66)

The dominating consonants are *l* (which I have not marked), *m* and *v*; the dominant vocals are *i* and *u*. The alliterations describe the metamorphosis of the celestial light, the letters form patterns imitating and accompanying the glide from *luce* into *lume* and then into *fiume*. The transformation was seen – *novella vista* (v. 58), *vidi* (v. 61) – by a human subject, the Dante-person, hence the insistence of the letters *m*(e) and *i*(o). The last terzina (64–66) is an image of the poetical paradox of the Dante-narrator who must describe that which transcends language, God, who circumscribes everything, including human language. The paradoxes between vision and invention are not resolved but dramatized in a visual, graphic and phonosymbolic writing. The protagonist as well as the narrator are dissolved into phonosymbolic structures culminating in the metaphoric and figurative dissolution of the final terzinas of Paradiso. Explaining phonosymbolic structures such as these as conscious rhetorical strategies hardly make sense as they are formed on a connotative level transgressing the individual who is left behind as an empty referent of the text.

Conclusion

I have suggested that a literary approach to some of the most intriguing figures in the *Comedy* might explain them as instances of a negativity that has historical aspects as well as aesthetic dimensions. My quotations from Pseudo-Dionysius have shown that the question of representation of the divine is formulated in a rather advanced way. But although the poetic potentiality of this old text is obvious, such texts should not be used as a master key to the interpretation of the *Comedy*. I quite agree with Barolini and Jacomuzzi in that a structural approach is necessary. Barolini however tends to treat Dante as a rhetorician rather than a poet. Though her approach might seem a fine way of combining a medieval and a modern narrative approach, and thus avoid extreme, anachronistic meta-readings, she does not quite escape the inherent hermeneutical traps of the *Comedy*. Jacomuzzi goes further and leaves behind the question of Dante's intention, instead focusing on structural movements and axes of the text. My analysis of the veridictory and phonosymbolic figures reinforces his interpretation of the *Comedy* as original poetry with an unusual critical awareness.

Ranking types of reading.
Descriptive and epic readings in Dante studies

Jesper Hede

In literary hermeneutics it is often maintained that whenever we argue in favour of an interpretation of a literary text, we cannot show that it is the true or correct one, and that every other interpretation is false or incorrect. This distinction is held to be untenable because literary interpretation is infected with semantic indeterminacy and based on a type of reasoning that does not permit precision and exactitude. But this does not mean that we cannot distinguish between good and bad readings or better and worse readings. Although we cannot prove a reading to be the correct one, we can render it probable that it is better than other readings. However, this is no easy task. It is difficult enough to compare only two readings and show that one of them is better than the other because there are many criteria for ranking two competing readings. Therefore it is much more difficult to show that one reading is better than all other readings. But we can use a typological approach to decide between different readings and classify the various readings into different types of reading. On this basis, we can show that one particular reading of a literary text is better in its approach to the thematic content than other types of reading. It is logistically easier to demonstrate the superiority of one type of reading over another type than to demonstrate the superiority of one particular reading over other particular readings.

This typological manner of interpretive demonstration is the issue explored in this article through a detailed study of different types of reading Dante's *Divine Comedy*. As the issue is discussed, the discussion has two premises. First, since the aim is to distinguish between the better and worse readings of the *Comedy* in typological terms, the article is an example of abductive reasoning in that it subscribes to the method of inference to the best explanation. Second, with this commitment to abductive reasoning, the article asserts that Dante's poem contains enough evidence to substantiate an argument in favour of a specific type of reading that can be defined as the most plausible or adequate one, given the generic aspects discussed in the article.

Diversity of types of reading

The fact that there are many different types of reading of any literary text is different from the fact that there can be many different particular readings of the same text. The latter can be called the diversity of particular readings, and the former the diversity of general readings, or, more precisely, the diversity of types of reading. The diversity of particular readings can apply to any text, but the diversity of types of reading rarely happens. For example, there is nothing unusual in there being many different particular readings of Shakespeare's *Hamlet*. But imagine that the play could be read either as a tragedy or as a comedy. That would be extraordinary. This is what is meant by the diversity of types of reading. If *Hamlet* can be read either as a tragedy or as a comedy, it belongs to two different literary genres. Hence the typological diversity of reading raises the question of genre.

By genre I here mean the formal and substantial features that enable us to define the distinctive character of a text and associate it with other texts with similar features. There are many different ways to define the character of a text. Let me highlight some of them to point out how the question of typology raises the question of genre. For example, we can distinguish between fiction and non-fiction. This is a substantial criterion because it is based on the content of the text. A historical novel and a historical study can have different features in common. They can both narrate a sequence of historical events and depict a specific historical setting, but the former invents the events in the form of dramatic encounters, and the latter reconstructs them by examining historical sources. In generic terms, the one should be read as a work of fiction, and the other as a work of historical documentation. In this sense, the type of reading designates the genre of the text, and vice versa.

However, just as historical studies can have different forms, depending on their focal points, objectives and intended audiences, literary texts can also have different generic characteristics in formal terms. For example, we can distinguish between epics, dramas, poetry, novels, or short stories, each of which can be divided into various sub-genres, such as the classical epic, the Renaissance drama, the sonnet, the science-fiction novel, or the postmodern short story. This type of generic demarcation involves a formal criterion in considering the diversity of texts. By this I mean that it is a criterion based on the form of the text. However, in some cases, the formal and substantial criteria overlap. For example, the epic definition can be taken to refer to the form as well as the content, based on the length and verse form of the text or on its narrative content; it may even be a short piece that does not follow metric conventions. Hence a text can lack the formal features of an epic but display an epic action – i.e., an action in which a character takes on a heroic stature.

In addition, we can speak of modes of expression that originate in the formal and substantial criteria of definition without implying definitions of genre. For example, a non-fiction text may contain epic, dramatic or poetic modes of expression, although it belongs to neither of the original genres. In a similar manner, a text may be defined as an epic or drama even though it does not seem to depict any epic or dramatic action and instead favours various poetic modes of expression. This last point is particularly important to bear in mind when considering the *Comedy*. The point is that, when the question of genre is unclear in any literary text, it can produce more than one type of reading because the text can be assigned to more than one genre. This is what has happened to the *Comedy*. Dante called it a *comedìa* (*Inf.* 16, 128), but it is not a comedy. In short, the title does not designate the genre. What kind of poem is then the *Comedy*? As an elementary hermeneutic requirement, every reading of Dante's text presupposes some answer to this question, and the answer will determine what type of reading is given to the poem.

For centuries, Dante scholars have tried to answer the question of genre in different ways. But these answers, I believe, can be classified into two basic types. The best known of these two is provided in what is presumed to be Dante's dedicatory letter to the Can Grande della Scala: the theme of the *Comedy* is *status animarum post mortem* – i.e., "the state of the souls after death" (*Epistle* XIII, § 11). In this perspective, the *Comedy* describes how all souls are punished or rewarded in accordance with their sins or virtues. If this is the thematic content of the *Comedy*, the poem is largely descriptive. The other type of reading is to read Dante's poem as an epic; it is supposed to narrate an epic action. Whatever the epic action may be is the thematic content of the *Comedy*.

The descriptive and the epic readings of the *Comedy* designate two different poetic genres which reflect two different types of thematic content. On the one hand, if the *Comedy* is taken to be a descriptive poem, its subject is the world of the dead. On the other hand, if the poem is taken to be an epic, it should be read as a book of the living. A dead person cannot perform an action. To be sure, it is possible to talk about the epic action of a dead person, as Vergil does in the *Aeneid*, but the action is described as the action of a living person. But punishments and rewards in Dante's afterworld are not given in life, but after death. The state of the souls after death cannot belong to living persons. If the *Comedy* is regarded as a descriptive poem, it belongs to the same genre as Lucretius's *De Rerum Natura*. But to take Dante's work to be a descriptive poem does not allow for only one way of reading. The same goes for the epic reading of the *Comedy*. As I shall argue, each of the two typological readings can produce different particular readings of the *Comedy*.

In textual interpretation the diversity of individual readings is common, while the typological diversity of reading is rare. To make this point clearer, let me give two examples of the typological diversity of reading. The first one is Jonathan Swift's "A Modest Proposal" (1729). It was meant to be a savagely satirical pamphlet, in which the author suggests that the problem of starving children in Ireland can be solved by using them as food for the rich. Some readers saw it as an outrageous but serious proposal on publication. Only later when the identity of the author was revealed was the true intent discovered. Hence "A Modest Proposal" was placed in two different genres at two different stages. The same is not the case with Dante's *Comedy*. The difference between the descriptive and the epic reading cannot be associated with two particular stages in Dante studies. Both types of reading are still in practice.

The other example of typological diversity of reading is Plato's *Republic*, in which Socrates constructs the ideal state. Many readers take it to be the first utopia. But in the second half of the twentieth century, Leo Strauss and his followers stressed the importance of Socratic irony in their interpretation of the *Republic* (Strauss 1964, 50–52). For example, Allan Bloom argues that the equality of women to men that Socrates advocates in book 5 should be taken as an ironic reply to Aristophanes' attacks on Socrates (Bloom 1991, 380). Bloom also says that there are two sides to the ideal city that Socrates constructs – a sincere and an ironic one (Bloom 1991, 410). The ironic side is to ignore the private and personal dimension of human beings in Socrates' proposal of the communalization of not only property, but also women and children. Unlike "A Modest Proposal," the *Republic* has never been read as a straightforward satire, only as a mixture of sincere and ironic expositions. Even this view is not universal. Many Plato scholars still take the ideal state to be a sincere proposal. Nevertheless, the *Republic* is now being situated in more than one genre. To make the matter even more complicated, it is possible to read the work as a pure irony or satire of the utopian daydream. To do so may be the best defence of Plato against Karl Popper's attack on him. In *The Open Society and Its Enemy*, Popper charges the ideal state of Plato's *Republic* with being the fountainhead of Western totalitarianism (Popper, 1971, 86–89). Plato's ideal city does look like the proto-totalitarian state since everything is controlled by the philosopher-king. If Plato truly advocated this, he deserves to be called the grandfather of totalitarianism, as Popper contends. But if the ideal state is meant to be a satire, Plato should be praised as the first critic of totalitarianism.

The question whether Plato's ideal state is a sincere proposal or a satire of such a proposal is a question of thematic content, which determines the literary genre. As pointed out, there are two ways of determining a literary genre. One is based on the literary form, and the other is based on the thematic content. The typological diversity of reading the *Comedy* reflects mainly the diversity in our understanding of its thematic content. To define the poem's theme as the spiritual conditions of the afterworld or as an epic drama, in which some character takes on the role of an epic hero, is to propose a definition of the poem's content in its entirety. But for different reasons, neither of the two definitions has been capable of encapsulating the thematic complexity of the *Comedy*. I shall examine these reasons in detail and draw readers' attention to a qualified solution to the problem of defining the poem's thematic content.

Descriptive reading of the Comedy

"The state of the souls after death", is the general theme that dictates the descriptive reading. This theme can be broken down into different levels, such as the poem's three parts: the state of the souls in damnation (Inferno), purgation (Purgatorio), and salvation (Paradiso). These designations can be regarded as three sub-themes of the general theme. Since Hell, Purgatory and Paradise constitute the three regions of Dante's afterworld, they can be said to constitute its triadic structure. In that case, the triadic structure of the afterworld provides the triadic thematic structure of the poem. The three sub-themes are distributed in accordance with the triadic structure of the afterworld. These sub-themes can be further divided. For example, the theme of damnation can be divided into the nine circles of Hell, each circle thus providing a sub-sub-theme identified with one of the infernal sins. Some circles have their own subdivisions, and each of these subdivisions has a sub-sub-sub-theme. This scheme of continuous subdivision finally reaches the episodes. This is the top-down picture of the thematic hierarchy, but there is also a bottom-up picture.

Let us begin at the bottom with the individual scenes or episodes. Each of them is often said to have its own theme, as emphasized, for instance, by Charles S. Singleton, who claims that "each scene in the *Comedy* arises from its own real center of inspiration" (Singleton 1954, 30). But we can also subsume the individual theme of an episode under a regional theme. For example, the theme of the Francesca and Paolo episode in canto 5 of Inferno can be subsumed under the theme of lust in the second circle. This theme can further be subsumed under the theme of damnation in Hell, which, in turn, can be subsumed under the general theme. The bottom-up and the top-down picture are two different ways of mapping out the same thematic order. When we read the *Comedy*

– tercet by tercet, episode by episode, canto by canto – we try to organize our reading by constructing the bottom-up picture. The top-down picture becomes available only when we have read the whole poem.

Given this thematic order, it is possible to achieve thematic unity on different levels. On the lowest level, we can recognize the thematic unity of each episode or scene. But there is one problem with this assertion: what is the demarcation of each scene? For example, what takes place on the top of Purgatorio, is that one scene or an assemblage of many scenes? Or what takes place in the heaven of the Sun, is that one scene or an assemblage of many scenes? The question of demarcating scenes can be asked of every region in Dante's afterworld. Whatever demarcation each scene or episode may be given, it can have its own thematic unity. This is the notion of thematic unity on the most basic level, but we can also move higher on the thematic hierarchy. The thematic unity of the circle of lust is higher than the thematic unity of the story of Paolo and Francesca. The thematic unity of Hell is higher than the thematic unity of the circle of lust. But what is the thematic relation of the nine circles of Hell? Their themes do not seem to have any direct thematic connection with each another. For example, the theme of lust does not seem related to the theme of violence in the seventh circle of Hell. For this reason, Dante scholars often maintain that it is possible to understand each circle without knowing anything about the circles. All themes are independent of each other in their content.

But if the themes of the nine circles are independent, what principle governs their order? Their ordering involves two elements. First, the different circles are the different segments of Hell. This element can be defined as the principle of segmentation, which gives a measure of thematic independence to all the circles of Hell. Second, the circles are ordered by the gravity of the sins represented by the different circles. The lighter sins are placed in the upper region of Hell, and the heavier sins in its lower region. These two principles constitute the segmental hierarchy of sins in Hell. The same can be said of the hierarchy of Purgatory. Because the thematic hierarchy of Hell is segmental, it provides a segmental organization for the descriptive reading. For example, the theme of lust is one segment in the theme of damnation, and the theme of damnation is one segment in the theme of the state of the souls after death. Hence the segmental hierarchy of themes corresponds to the segmental hierarchy of sins. This is the thematic structure, which corresponds to the moral structure.

The segmental thematic hierarchy provides a specific method of reading: the segmental method of reading. The notion of segment is flexible. It can refer to the whole of Hell, one of the nine circles, or one subdivision of a circle. A segmental reading should be distinguished from the episodic reading. Strictly speaking, the episodic reading takes each episode as a self-contained unit. For example, the story of Paolo and Francesca can be and has been read as a unit; there is no need even to enclose it in the circle of lust. Because the story is so gentle and different from the other stories of lust, some Dante scholars have treated it as a *sui generis* and have thought that there was nothing to be gained by relating it to the theme of lust.

A segmental reading of the *Comedy* depends on its segmental thematic hierarchy. This type of reading has been the standard method for the descriptive type of reading, which can have different results, depending on the different moral and thematic hierarchies employed. Most descriptive readers employ the moral hierarchies given by the poet himself. But there are two problems with this procedure of reading. First, Dante provides a hierarchy of negative and positive qualities for Hell and Purgatory, but none for Paradise. This problem can be defined as the problem of absence. Second, Dante provides two different hierarchies of qualities for Hell and Purgatory. This problem can be defined as the problem of difference. Let us consider how these two problems jeopardize the integrity of the segmental reading.

The problem of difference endangers the continuity between Hell and Purgatory. If the hierarchies of Hell and Purgatory do not coincide with each other, we have to assume that some of the sins in Hell cannot find a suitable place for purgation in Purgatory. Conversely, some of the sins in Purgatory cannot be the grounds for damnation in Hell, if they cannot be assigned to any circle of Hell. This is a serious theological problem because it undermines the firm belief of medieval Christians that every sin can be forgiven. For this reason alone, there should be some correspondence between the two hierarchies of sins. Once such a matching relation is established, it opens up for the possibility of a parallel reading of Inferno and Purgatorio. Without such a matching relation, we are stuck with the serial type of reading; we have to go through the two hierarchies, one after the other, as two independent entities.

The serial, segmental type of reading is the simplest and easiest way to read the *Comedy*. When we read about one circle of Hell, we need not worry about what is happening in the other circles. Likewise, when we read one part of the poem, we need not worry about what happens in the other two parts. This method of reading is the opposite of the method of parallel reading. The principle of parallel reading is connectionism. For example, when we read about the circle of lust, we have to connect it thematically to the terrace of lust and the heaven of Paradise that correspond to the circle of lust, if any such heaven can be found. Neither the serial nor the parallel type of reading is fully permitted by the hierarchies of Hell and Purgatory provided by the poet because they are not totally different. There is a partial matching relation. Some of the sins in Hell can be matched with some of the sins in Purgatory.[1] This partial overlap does not allow us to have the luxury of a complete serial reading, which can be justified only if the hierarchy of sins for Hell is totally different from the hierarchy of sins for Purgatory. But this is not the case.

Because of the partial overlap between the two hierarchies of sins, we have to conduct a serial reading only where there is no overlap between the two hierarchies, and a parallel reading where there is an overlap between the two. This way of reading produces a mixed reading: the mixture of serial and parallel reading. This way of reading is awkward and uncertain. We can never be certain when and where we should or should not look for the correspondence between Hell

---

[1] The nine circles of Inferno are commonly given the following demarcations: (1) Limbo, (2) lust, (3) gluttony, (4) avarice or prodigality, (5) wrath, (6) heresy, (7) violence, (8) fraud and (9) treachery. The seven terraces of *Purgatory* have the following demarcations: (1) pride, (2), envy, (3) wrath, (4) sloth, (5) avarice, (6) gluttony and (7) lust. There is some symmetrical correspondence between lust, gluttony and avarice in the structures of Hell and Purgatory. Wrath also appears in the two structures, but the appearances are not symmetrical. As for Limbo, prodigality, heresy, violence, fraud and treachery in Inferno, there does not seem to be any correspondence, just as pride, envy and sloth in Purgatorio do not seem to be thematised in Inferno. The structure of Purgatory is constructed according to the notion of seven capital sins, but the structure of Hell does not seem to rest on any unifying principle. Moreover, the seventh, eighth and ninth circles of Hell have different subdivisions: the seventh circle has three, the eighth has ten and the ninth has four. No similar subdivisions are found in Purgatory.

and Purgatory. To get out of this uncomfortable situation, some Dante scholars have proposed a common hierarchy of sins for the first two parts of the poem. Once we obtain a common hierarchy of sins for Hell and Purgatory, we cannot avoid the parallel reading of the two parts.

The problem of absence is more serious than the problem of difference. Since the hierarchies of sins provide the thematic structure of Hell and Purgatory, we would expect the hierarchy of virtues to provide the thematic structure of Paradise. But this expectation is denied because Dante never explicitly identifies the properties of the ten spheres of Paradiso.[2] As a result, we have to wonder whether there are any poetic devices to indicate the segmental themes for Paradiso. Some Dante scholars have turned to Classical mythology for help. For example, the association of the sphere of Venus with the myth of Venus (the symbol of lust) is an example of this approach. Other examples are the association of the sphere of Mars with the myth of Mars (the god of warfare), and the sphere of Jupiter with the myth of Jupiter (the god of justice). But these thematic guides from Classical mythology are unsatisfactory for two reasons. First, they are unreliable. The thematic matches between the Classical myths and Dante's ten heavens are only partial and superficial. Second, the thematic guides are incomplete. Beyond the three heavens of Venus, Mars, and Jupiter, Classical mythology offers no thematic clues. For these two reasons, it is best to disregard the mythological guides altogether. Moreover, it is not likely that Dante used the pagan myths as thematic indicators because they are inconsistent with his Christian outlook (Hede 2007, 171–83). Hence Dante's ten heavens stand out as nameless. We are apparently forced to discover the theme of each heaven by studying what takes place in it. Thus our reading of Paradiso becomes truly episodic; it is not even segmental. In the segmental reading of Inferno and Purgatorio, it is possible to place

---

2 The ten spheres of Paradiso follow medieval cosmology: (1) the Moon, (2) Mercury, (3) Venus, (4) the Sun, (5) Mars, (6) Jupiter, (7) Saturn, (8) Fixed Stars, (9) Prime Mover and (10) Empyreum. In various editions of the *Comedy*, these spheres are associated with different properties, such as different virtuous deficiencies as is the case with the Moon, Mercury and Venus, or the four cardinal virtues (prudence, fortitude, justice, temperance) as in the case of the Sun, Mars, Jupiter and Saturn. But these and other associations are not Dante's demarcations of the heavenly properties. They are the results of different interpretative tendencies in the tradition of Dante studies from the fourteenth century onwards.

each circle of Hell or each terrace of Purgatory as a segment in a thematic hierarchy. But this is not possible for Paradiso because the poet does not seem to provide any hierarchy of virtues.

A truly episodic reading is a truly serial reading. Different episodes follow one another without thematic connections. If so, Dante's Paradise is far less orderly than Hell and Purgatory. This problem can be defined as the increasing entropy of ascent in Dante's afterworld. As far as the segmental ordering is concerned, it operates in all three regions of Dante's afterworld. The ten heavens are the ten segments of Paradise, and they constitute a segmental hierarchy; the higher heavens display greater glory and power than the lower heavens, just as the lower circles display greater degradation and depravity than the higher circles. In this regard, Paradise follows the same principle of organization as Hell and Purgatory. But the segmental hierarchy of Paradise is not a thematic hierarchy because it does not seem to display any hierarchy of virtues. Let us assume that the ten heavens are truly nameless. In that case, we have to wonder what happens to all the works performed in Purgatory. The sins of Purgatory are different from the sins of Hell. The latter are supposed to stay in Hell, but the former are supposed to be transformed into virtues. What happens to these virtues when they are taken up to Paradise? Are they completely forgotten? These are the troublesome questions that have driven some Dante scholars to recognize a hierarchy of virtues for the ten heavens.

The difference between the segmental reading of Hell and Purgatory and the episodic reading of Paradise can be underlined by distinguishing between the thematic and the narrative frame. The nine circles of Hell constitute the thematic frame for Inferno, and the seven terraces of Purgatory constitute the thematic frame for Purgatorio – i.e., the circles and terraces are thematically distinctive in their outline of sins to be condemned and sins to be purged. But the ten heavens of Paradise do not function as a thematic frame. They provide only a narrative frame – i.e., a device for narrating a series of episodes and events. If so, Paradiso becomes comparable to Boccaccio's *Decameron*. The latter is divided into ten days, and the former into ten heavens. In the *Decameron*, none of the ten days gives any indication of the thematic content of the stories told on each of these days. The framework of ten days is no more than Boccaccio's framework for delivering one hundred stories. Likewise, the pilgrimage to Canterbury is only a narrative frame for Chaucer's *Canterbury Tales*.

Even when we extend the hierarchy of virtues and sins to Paradiso, the descriptive content of the last part of the poem is radically different from that of the first two canticles. This is an important point that has often been overlooked in the standard descriptive readings. Each circle of Hell gives the state of the souls condemned in that circle. Likewise, each terrace of Purgatory gives the state of the souls undergoing purgation on that terrace. But each of the ten heavens does not give the state of the souls happily living in that heaven. None of the blessed souls lives in any of the nine heavens below the Empyreum. All of them are supposed to live in the highest heaven. Even when Dante finally gets to the highest heaven, he does not describe the state of their happiness. He simply sees them all assembled in the Mystical Rose and does not describe the state of their souls after death. The Mystical Rose is not a mechanism of punishment or reward in the way Hell and Purgatory are. Each circle of Hell is a mechanism of punishment for the souls imprisoned in that circle, and each terrace is a mechanism of purgation for the souls situated on that terrace. But the ten heavens are not a mechanism of measuring out the reward of happiness for the blessed souls. In Hell the condemned souls talk about how they are being punished. In Purgatory the repentant souls talk about how they are being purged. In Paradise the blessed souls do not talk about what sort of happiness they enjoy. The primary object of their talking is what they did in the mortal world. Therefore, what is described in Paradiso is not the state of the souls after death. For this reason, the last canticle is not amenable to a descriptive reading.

When Dante scholars insist on reading the *Comedy* as a poem describing the state of the souls after death, this often involves a rejection of reading it as an epic because the poem is devoid of an epic hero or epic action. It is the nature of an epic hero and epic action that they cut across the different segments and sustain themselves from the beginning to the end of an epic. The episodic and the segmental readings do not allow for the existence of such overarching actions and themes. For example, the theme of lust cannot be extended beyond the circle or terrace of lust because it is restricted and contained in it. Even a bigger theme such as damnation or purgation is contained in a particular region. In short, the state of the souls after death is not a single theme. At least, it divides itself into three themes: damnation, purgation and salvation. For this reason, if the *Comedy* is read as a descriptive poem, it breaks down into three poems. At times, this consequence has been hailed as the poem's essential quality. For example, Ezra Pound claimed:

> The *Divina Commedia* is not to be considered as an epic; to compare it with epic poems is usually unprofitable. It is in a sense lyric, the tremendous lyric of the subjective Dante; but the soundest classification of the poem is Dante's own, "as a comedy which differs from tragedy in its content," for "tragedy begins admirably and tranquilly," and the end is terrible, "whereas comedy introduces some harsh complication, but brings the matter to a prosperous end." The *Commedia* is, in fact, a great mystery play, or better, a cycle of mystery plays (Pound 2001, 3)

The descriptive reading produces at least three thematic unities, one thematic unity for each of the three canticles. There is no overarching thematic unity for the poem as a whole. This is the most dissatisfactory consequence of the descriptive type of reading. Hence the most important question is whether we are content to read the *Comedy* as a descriptive poem, or whether we would rather see it as an epic poem. This is the question of literary genre.

Epic reading of the Comedy

Dissatisfied with the descriptive reading, some Dante scholars have tried to read the *Comedy* as an epic. To that end, Dante the traveller is commonly seen as the epic hero. This reading is inspired by Dante the traveller's reference to Aeneas's journey to the underworld at the beginning of the *Comedy*. When Vergil proposes a travel plan to Dante, the latter expresses his fear by comparing it to Aeneas's journey (*Inf.* II, 31–36). Since Aeneas's journey is an epic journey, Dante's proposed journey should be understood as an epic journey, too, if it resembles Aeneas's. This is the motivation or justification for the epic reading of the *Comedy*. But who is going to be the epic hero? The common answer is Dante the traveller, who is rescued from the Dark Wood. There are mainly two versions of the epic reading.

In the first version, Dante is supposed to be an everyman or every Christian (Mastrobuono 1990, 8). As such, he is an impersonal symbol. In the second version, Dante is not merely an impersonal symbol, but a concrete person. The two versions of the epic reading produce two different journeys. In the impersonal version, Dante's journey is like the journeys of Odysseus and Aeneas. The only difference is that the latter journey celebrates secular heroes, and the former journey a religious hero. However, the difficulties with this version of the epic reading are obvious. The first point against it is that Dante the traveller strikes a paltry figure as an epic hero. Some Dante scholars have used the epistle dedicated to Can Grande to support the view that Dante the traveller is the hero of his own epic. In that letter, the traveller is said to be the agent (*Epistle* XIII, § 11). But what sort of agent is he? He is surely too weak a character to play a heroic role. He cannot take a single step in the afterworld without the aid of his guides; he is totally helpless. In technical terms, he is no autonomous agent. It takes an autonomous agent to play the role of an epic hero.

When Dante scholars talk about the reward and punishment of human souls for their virtues and sins, they usually stress the free will of these souls and assume that all human souls are autonomous agents. But as T. K. Seung points out, to make such an assumption is to commit the Pelagian heresy (Seung 1982, 163–69). It implies that, according to Dante, man is given mastery over his actions; he has complete freedom to do good and evil. If so, God is outside the domain of the human free will. God's agency consists solely of rewarding or punishing man in accordance with his merit or demerit. But as Seung explains, "this doctrine is incompatible with the orthodox Christian teaching that the grace of God is indispensable for the salvation of man – that is, man can never achieve eternal bliss through his merit alone." The Pelagian heresy infringes on the sovereignty of God's will:

> If God must reward and punish man in accordance with the merit or the demerit that he earned in the exercise of his own free will, the exercise of divine will is being dictated by that

of human will. In that event, human will is the agent of action, while divine will is only the agent of response. The question of who shall be rewarded and who shall be punished will ultimately be determined by human rather than divine will. Because of this serious implication, the Pelagian heresy was consistently and emphatically condemned from Augustine through Aquinas to Martin Luther
(Seung 1982, 164)

The second point against the impersonal reading is that Dante the traveller goes through the three regions of the afterworld not as a participant, but as an observer. He does not experience the process of damnation, purgation or salvation. Instead of participating in these processes, he only observes the souls in damnation, purgation and salvation. There is nothing heroic in his role of observation. As epic heroes, Odysseus and Aeneas are not observers of other people's actions; they are the heroes of their own deeds. They are actors and participants.

To overcome this problem in Dante's role as an epic hero, some Dante scholars have proposed seeing his journey as a journey to Beatrice (Singleton 1958). This is the second version of the epic reading of the *Comedy*. In the first version, Dante the traveller is a public figure. In the second version, he is a private person, who has fallen in love with Beatrice, and fallen away from her, and now returns to her. But Dante's epic journey is not seen only as a private enterprise, it is also seen as the union of the public and private roles in Dante the traveller. But is such a union possible? If Dante's journey is an epic journey back to Beatrice, what does she stand for? Is she a private person, with whom Dante is in love, or does she stand for something bigger? This question has never been solved by Dante studies. Since the question of what Beatrice stands for remains unsettled, the epic journey back to her does not amount to much.

As long as Beatrice is taken to be a purely private person, Dante's journey back to her remains a private affair. His journey can take on a public character only by taking her to be a symbol of something greater than a human being. Hence, if Dante's journey is to have a dual character, Beatrice should also have a dual character. However, as soon as we assign a dual character to her role, we also have to assign similar dual characters to Dante's other guides, not only Vergil, but also St Bernard of Clairvaux, whose role near the end of the poem is no less important than that of Vergil and Beatrice because, without Bernard, the final vision of Empyreum would not occur. Hence the second version of the epic reading has to contend with the symbolic roles of the three guides.

However, most commonly, the second version of the epic reading assigns a special role and significance only to the second guide because the journey is seen as a journey back to Beatrice. But what is Vergil's role in this? Does it consist solely of guiding Dante the traveller to Beatrice, or does it amount to something bigger? If not, Dante's reunion with Beatrice should be the ultimate goal of his epic journey; the top of Purgatory should be his destination. But the top of Purgatory is only the launching station for Dante's flight to the ten heavens of Paradise (Hede 2007, 164–66). As the second guide, Beatrice's role is to take Dante the traveller from the top of Purgatory to the top of Paradise. Just as Vergil takes Dante to Beatrice, her role is to take him to Bernard, whose prayer to the Virgin Mary in the poem's final canto (*Par.* XXXIII, 1–39) opens up Empyreum to Dante. Hence Dante's journey cannot be only his journey back to Beatrice.

Trinitarian reading of the Comedy

In Dante's medieval Christian world, no created being is autonomous and powerful enough to play the role of an epic hero. If anyone affirms such an autonomous power for the created beings, he subscribes to the Pelagian heresy. Does this mean that the *Comedy* cannot be read as an epic? This problem, I believe, can be resolved only if we leave aside many of the traditional ways of approaching Dante's poem, including the descriptive and epic readings outlined above. We can avoid the Pelagian reading only by accepting the Creator as the epic hero because God is the only truly autonomous agent in Dante's Christian world.

This perspective on Dante's poem was originally proposed by Seung nearly half a century ago in his neglected study *The Fragile Leaves of the Sibyl: Dante's Master Plan* (1962). It was further substantiated in his *Cultural Thematics: The Formation of the Faustian Ethos* (1976) and *Semiotics and Thematics in Hermeneutics* (1982), and it has been restated in his long article "The Metaphysics of the *Commedia*" (1988). The method of reading Seung employs is a systematic, parallel reading of the poem's three parts. With this method of reading, Seung outlines various coherent connections and correspondences between the system of sins condemned in Inferno, the system of sins being transformed into virtues in Purgatorio, and the system of virtues celebrated in Paradiso. Although this Dante theory still has the character of being a proposal for understanding the poem as a whole, the thematic coherence Seung detects in the *Comedy* provides a highly qualified solution to the problem of defining the poem's thematic content.

In Seung's reading, the Trinity (the Father, the Son and the Holy Spirit) is the hero of Dante's epic in two ways: it governs the role of the three guides (Vergil, Beatrice and Bernard), and it governs the hierarchy of virtues and sins in the three realms of the afterworld.[3] To emphasize the far-reaching consequences of Seung's theory, let me here outline some of its main features. The three guides are indispensable in Dante's journey because the traveller cannot make it on his own. As mere human beings, however, the three guides cannot help Dante on his journey, either, because they are not more powerful than Dante himself. They can help Dante only as divine agents. In Dante's Christian world, God is the only truly autonomous agent. When Vergil comes to Dante lost in the Dark Wood, he declares his divine agency by telling him that he has been sent by the Virgin Mary for his succour (*Inf.* II, 85–140). If Vergil is a divine agent, the other two guides must be so, too. The number of divine agents coincides with the number of persons in the Trinity. By taking this numerical coincidence as his guide, Seung argues that the three guides represent the three persons of the Trinity.

At the outset of his journey, Dante stresses the indispensability of divine power and assistance for his journey to the afterworld. When

---

3 According to Seung's Dante reading, Hell, Purgatory and Paradise are structured according to the medieval table of seven natural virtues (humility, mercy, meekness, fortitude, liberality, temperance and chastity) and three theological virtues (faith, hope and charity) and their contraries. These ten virtues and their contraries constitute ten steps on the ladder of divine grace divided into two sections: the natural and the supernatural. The seven natural virtues and their contraries constitute the seven steps of the natural section, and the three supernatural virtues and their contraries constitute the three steps of the supernatural section. Seung combines these ten virtues and their contraries with the notions of the tripartite soul (and its powers) and the triune God.

Vergil proposes his travel plan, Dante compares it not only to Aeneas's journey to the underworld, but also to St Paul's ascent to the third heaven (II Cor. 12, 2–4). Apostle Paul did nothing on his own to make this heavenly ascent; it was totally controlled by the power of God. In *The Fragile Leaves of the Sibyl*, Seung stresses the fact that Dante the traveller never encounters St Paul in his journey in spite of his allusion to the heavenly ascent. Seung takes this point to be Dante's indication that the traveller's journey is meant to be a Pauline journey; the former is meant to re-enact the latter. Since the traveller is a sort of St Paul the traveller, the former cannot meet the latter during the journey (Seung 1962, 387–88).

The presence of guides in Dante's epic is no new invention; it follows a long tradition. Athena is the patron and guide for Odysseus and his son Telemachus, and Venus is the mother and patron of Aeneas. But, as Seung argues in *Semiotics and Thematics in Hermeneutics*, the role of guides in the Classical epics is radically different from the role of Dante's three guides (Seung 1982, 136–42). In the Classical epics, the guides and patrons do nothing to jeopardize the heroic stature of the epic heroes; Dante's three guides do the exact opposite. They demonstrate how helpless and powerless their charge is. At the same time, Dante is totally dependent on them. His dependence on them signifies the total dependence of all human creatures on their Creator for their salvation.

In devising a common hierarchy of virtues and sins for the three regions of Dante's afterworld, I have considered how the different virtues and sins are ranked in the segmental hierarchy. In Hell Vergil explains that the sins of Lower Hell are more serious than the sins of Upper Hell – i.e., the gravity of the sins is the standard for ranking the different sins. If so, we have to face the next question: what determines the gravity of sins? For the determination of the gravity of sins, Seung cites the Platonic standard. He recognizes the three parts of the soul and ranks them in a hierarchy. Since the three parts are the basis of all virtues and sins, Seung uses the hierarchy of the three parts as the hierarchy of virtues and sins – according to the medieval philosophical standard: vegetative, sensitive and spiritual. The three parts of the soul are its three powers – according to the medieval standard: the concupiscible, the irascible and the intellectual. By virtue of these three powers, the human soul is, according to St Augustine, an *imago Dei*, an image of

God, or, more precisely, an image of the Trinity. This notion establishes the analogical correspondence between the three powers of the soul and the three persons of the Trinity.

By virtue of this analogical correspondence, Seung extends the hierarchy of virtues and sins to the Trinity. As long as the hierarchy is restricted to humanity, it is a single hierarchy. But when it is extended to divinity, it becomes a double hierarchy. The operation of the double hierarchy is hardly discernable in Hell, whose main object of discourse is the sins of human creatures. The notion of divine virtues appears only in allegorical inversions. For example, the story of Ugolino and his eating of his sons allegorically and inversely represents Christ or the Son feeding his flesh and blood to his children (*Inf.* XXXIII, 4–75). In Purgatory the manifestation of divine virtues is more easily noticeable because the divine virtues are the models for the penitents, for instance when the sin of pride is purged to the virtue of humility. In Paradise the operation of divine virtues is unmistakable; they are on full display. The divine virtues perform two functions. First, they are the exemplars for all Christians. For example, the first two heavens exemplify humility and mercy, the two great virtues of the Son. Dante scholars have argued that the first two heavens represent something awfully shabby and deficient. But to this we can reply that true humility and mercy do indeed look shabby and deficient. Second, by their divine virtues, the three persons of the Trinity inspire the human souls. This point is best illustrated by the Friars in the heaven of the Sun. Thomas Aquinas and Bonaventure tell the history of the Dominicans and the Franciscans. The centre of their stories is the power of the Holy Spirit, which inspired the dramatic inception and development of the two monastic orders.

In the discussion of the descriptive reading, I have argued that the state of the souls after death is not the central topic of Paradiso. In Seung's reading, the central topic is what the Trinity and God's chosen vessels have done in the mortal world. But the chosen vessels are like Dante the traveller; they cannot do anything important on their own. They can undertake great things only with the grace of God, as demonstrated by the careers of St Francis and St Dominic. Their virtues are not human; they are infused virtues – infused by God. This is the way the double hierarchy of virtues operates in Paradiso, according to Seung. Every heaven manifests one divine virtue and one infused virtue, which is modelled on the corresponding divine virtue. The infused virtue is inspired by the divine virtue. The operation of the double hierarchy of virtues is not restricted to Paradiso. Although its operation is not as manifest in Hell and Purgatory as it is in Paradise, Seung argues that it is noticeable everywhere in Dante's afterworld. In the operation of the double hierarchy, there is no single human being who manifests all the virtues. Hence there can be no human epic hero in Dante's epic. However, the Trinity sustains its action from the beginning to the end of his epic. This is why Seung argues that the Trinity is Dante's epic hero.

Ranking types of reading

Now that I examined the different ways of reading the *Comedy*, let me end by ranking them. I take the epic reading to be better than the descriptive reading, in part because the state of the souls after death cannot capture the thematic content of Paradise. Let me now extend this view to the other two parts of the poem. Although the first two parts talk at length about the mechanisms of punishment and purgation, they are also concerned with the sinful activities in this world; they are concerned with what the sinful souls have done in the mortal world. Even in Hell Dante expresses his concern for the living world by repeatedly referring to and describing the sinful character of Florence and other parts of his living world. For this reason, it makes more sense to read his poem not as a book of the dead, but as a book of the living. On this basis, I would rank the epic reading as better than the descriptive reading. In addition, among the particular epic readings, I would rank the reading that takes the Trinity to be the epic hero as better than the reading that takes Dante the traveller to be the epic hero because the latter is a poor candidate for the epic role, while the former is a better candidate.

There is one more reason for ranking Seung's Trinitarian reading as better than the other readings. The reason is the thematic hierarchy of virtues and sins which can function as the common thematic frame for the three parts of the poem. It is better than any other hierarchy of sins and virtues that has been proposed in Dante studies for three reasons in particular. One, Seung's hierarchy is simpler than any other in Dante studies. Two, it has the quality of completeness in that it covers all the circles of Hell, all the terraces of Purgatory and all the heavens of Paradise. Other proposals are usually incomplete. Third, Seung's hierarchy alone is a double hierarchy; it accommodates both human and divine virtues. Other proposals are normally limited to human virtues and sins. Seung's double hierarchy provides a richer thematic scope than the single hierarchies often encountered in Dante studies.

The difference between the single and the double hierarchy leads to the difference between the man-centred and the God-centred reading of the *Comedy*. Seung's double hierarchy need not dictate only the God-centred reading. In fact, it can provide two centres for reading Dante's epic: one for man, and one for God. But the two centres are not equal. In Seung's reading God is the primary centre, and man is only a secondary centre. Only with God at the centre of Dante's epic can we justify its popular name, the *Divine Comedy*. If the man-centred reading is taken to be the adequate way of reading, Dante's poem should be called the *Human Comedy*.

The problem of double reception.
On the dialectic of simple and complex apprehensio in the Divine comedy

Ülar Ploom

The aim of this paper is to study the problem of double reception or the dialectic of simple and complex *apprehensio* in Dante's *Comedy*. This problem is closely connected to the dialectic of the perceptive and intellective planes of Dante the character and Dante the author. A work of both cognitive and moral/didactic purport, one of the basic strategies of the *Divine Comedy* is to have Dante the character make wrong decisions about what he perceives to have them adjusted by Dante the author who, of course, in doing so, applies in his poetic two basic (in reality more) allegorical figures, Virgil and Beatrice. Virgil and Beatrice therefore assume the function of the two principal agent intellects, the intellective powers which inform the possible intellect of Dante the character. It is tempting to compare this basic scheme (which could be called a model of representation) with the cognitive model of St Thomas Aquinas. Yet it is even more tempting to see whether and to what extent this model really works out in the *Comedy* which, besides being a book of moral instruction, is a great work of art.

The first part of the present article discusses St Thomas views of the intellective processes, the second part deals with some of Dante's own considerations on the same theme and the third part discusses one concrete example in the *Divine Comedy*.

In his reasoning about the problematic of intellection, the relation between ontology and gnoseology, St Thomas of Aquinas states very clearly (*De Veritate* I, 2) that things in themselves have no meaning. They mean or, as St Thomas puts it, they may be known as true which signifies their being only with reference to the intellect, "[...] for being cannot be known without the true, for it cannot be known unless it agrees with or conforms to intellect"(*De Veritate* I, 1) (Answers to Difficulties). The intellect may be the human intellect, but there is of course also the Divine Intellect. Aquinas says that "[...] even if there were no human intellects, things could be said to be true because of their relation to the Divine Intellect. But if, by an impossible supposition, intellect did not exist and things continued to exist, then the essentials of truth would in no way remain (*De Veritate* I, 2) (Reply)."

Fortunately it is not so, for man possesses the capacities of perception and intellection. There is certainly a difference between man and God and the angels with regards to their intellectual capacities and their mode according to St Thomas. In God seeing is already the ultimate understanding, for God is one power, simple power which is his own existence which is also the Divine Intellect (*ST* I, 77, 2; 79, 2). God's vision is always *apprehensio absoluta*. God sees what things mean ("I see" in English in both meanings simultaneously). In man there are several powers (*ST* I, 77, 2), therefore in man *simplex apprehensio* is actually complex, i.e. the human intellect perceives things as they first appear to the senses which provide phantasmatic material for further operations. Things do not appear in the human perception as they are in their divine intention (the ontological structure, the "capacity in the form to signify its own structure", as Umberto Eco has wittily put it (Eco 1988, 190)), but in their concrete realized forms as matter, i.e. in man's perception and understanding of them as a structure (Cf. *ibid.*). Eco therefore distinguishes between the ontological truth and the formal truth with reference to St Thomas, whereby the ontological truth "means the very existence of things in their determinate structure" – or God's intention – and the formal truth means "the correspondence of a thing to the human intellect" (*Ibid.* 191–192). But let us turn to the problematic which interests me in connection with Dante's *Comedy*, the dialectic of the *ad hoc* perceptions and intellection in re-ordered judgements.

How does a thing in its whatness, *quidditas*, present itself to the human intellect in St Thomas' study of the process of cognition? Thomas speaks of two main stages in understanding things: 1) *simplex apprehensio* and 2) judgement. St Thomas: "For since the intellect passes from potentiality to act, it has a likeness to things which are generated, which do not attain to perfection all at once but acquire it by degrees. And likewise the human intellect does not acquire perfect knowledge by the first act of apprehension; but it first apprehends something about the thing, such as its *quiddity*, and this is its first and proper object; and then it understands the properties, accidents, and the various relations of the essence. Thus it necessarily compares one thing with another by composition or division [...]" (*ST* I, 85, 5 (I answer that)).

But let us consider *simplex apprehensio* very briefly. As I have already said, man's simple *apprehensio* is epistemologically rather complex, which shows man's imperfection in relation to God's vision or simple absolute apprehension.

Figure 1a
sensible objects → sense organs and sensitive powers// phantasmata ← agent intellect

Figure 1b
agent intellect ----- // intelligible species ----- possible intellect

First (figure 1a), some object is presented by the outer sense organs (the five senses) and perceived by inner sensitive powers (proper and common sense, fantasy or imagination, estimation and memory) as sense images or what are known as phantasmata. Sensible objects are concrete individual forms actualised as matter and not any kinds of separate forms, as was postulated by Plato (*ST* I, 84, 4 (I answer that)). The phantasm is the likeness of an individual corporeal thing, a sense image, which is then turned to by the incorporeal agent intelligent (*intellectus agens*).

Second (figure 1b), acting upon the phantasmata, the agent intellect abstracts from them the universal general intelligible species or concepts in the *intellectus possibilis*. It is the possible intellect which will finally apprehend, for "the species preserved in the possible intellect exist there habitually when it does not understand them actually" [...], (*ST* I, 84, 7) (Reply to Objection 1)[1] yet it needs the agent intellect to bring its potentiality to act.

---

1 It is clarified by St Thomas that the mind is not born possessed of likenesses, but must acquire them.

We could say that there are two inputs: that of the sense image and that of the mental image. If the phantasms are sense images, then the intelligible species are kinds of intellectual images, and they both provide likenesses. Aquinas speaks of the nature of these images or likenesses thus: "But phantasms, since they are likenesses of individuals and exist in corporeal organs, have not the same mode of existence as the human intellect [...] and therefore have not the power of themselves to make an impression on the possible intellect. This is done by the power of the agent intellect which by turning towards the phantasm produces in the possible intellect *a certain* likeness which represents the thing of which it is the phantasm only so far as regards the nature of the species (*ST* I, 85, 1) (Reply to Objection 3)."

What "a certain likeness" is, of course, remains unclear, but one thing is certain – these are no longer truly individual images of which nothing could be communicated in common speech but they represent some universal nature of the intelligible species "since by the power of the agent intellect we are able to take into consideration apart from individual conditions the nature of species [...] in accordance with whose likenesses the possible intellect is informed (*Ibid.*)."

St Thomas does not of course discard individual existence, for there are no separate intelligible species existing detached from matter in this world, yet we can perceive the individual in its individualizing principles which are common to it. Aquinas says that "[...] the nature itself to which it falls to be understood, or to be abstracted or to bear the intention of universality is only in individuals; but that it is understood, abstracted or bears the intention of universality is in the intellect (*ST* I, 85, 2) (Reply to Objection 2)."[2]

Of course St Thomas is very much concerned with the possibility and the problematic of communicating the intention of things which need not be what man apprehends. He says, although in another place (*Summa Contra Gentiles*), when discussing the difference in God's intention and man's apprehension, "[...] I mean by the "intention understood" what the intellect conceives in itself of the thing understood. To

---

2 The Benzinger Brothers' translation reads even more radically about the supremacy of the universal nature of the intelligible species: "[...] as by the power of the active intellect we are able to disregard the conditions of the individuality, and to take into consideration the specific nature, the image of which informs the passive intellect."

be sure, in us this is neither the thing which is understood nor is it the very substance of the intellect. But it is a *certain* likeness of the thing understood conceived in the intellect, and which the exterior words signify. So, the intention itself is named the "interior word" which is signified by the exterior word. Indeed, that the intention aforesaid is not within us the thing understood is clear from this: it is one thing to understand a thing, and another to understand the intention itself, yet the intellect does so when it reflects on its own work [...]" (*SCG* IV, 11, 6).

Figure 2
agent intellect → things conceptualised// likeness ← possible intellect // word in concepts

We may conclude then that the possible intellect, the function of which is receiving and knowing the concepts (intelligible species), which have been abstracted by the agent intellect, establishes a likeness of the concept received with the thing conceptualised. The possible intellect informed in this way forms a definition, or a division or a composition, expressed by a word (*ST* I, 85, 2) (Reply to Objection 3). (Perhaps we could compare it to cutting a form into the linguistic mass similar to cutting a form into the material mass, as presented by Saussure.)

According to St Thomas' system there is no primary intuition of form in the concrete sensible before the abstraction. This (intuition) is carried out by the possible intellect (logically and temporally) after the abstraction of the concept and returning to the phantasmata to understand a thing in its singularity. Aquinas says that "[...] the mind knows singulars through a certain kind of reflection, as when the mind, in knowing its object, which is some universal nature, returns to knowledge of its own act, then to the species which is the principle of act, and, finally, to the phantasm from which it has abstracted the species. In this way, it attains some knowledge about singulars." (*De Veritate* X, 5) (Reply). This may be illustrated as follows:

Figure 3
mind (*intellectus agens* acting in the possible intellect) →1. knowledge of the species as the principle of its act → 2. knowledge of its own act → 3. phantasmata from which the species have been abstracted

Here we are already transgressing the *ad hoc* character of simple apprehension, for St Thomas says that "as it [the intellect] turns to the phantasms, composition and division of the intellect involve time" (*ST* I, 85, 5) (Reply to Objection 2).

This raises the problem of whether several things can be understood at the same time. Here too Aquinas' answer is complex. It appears that whatever things the intellect understands under one species, it can understand them at the same time, but whatever things the intellect understands under different species, it understands at different times. Aquinas also postulates that parts of objects cannot be understood as existing in the whole simultaneously. They are understood through one form at a time, whereby the overall image is thus understood in a confused way (*ST* I, 85, 5).

What is the confusion caused by? St Thomas states that our intellect proceeds from a state of potency to a state of actuality, and every power thus proceeding from potentiality to actuality comes first to an incomplete act, which is the medium between potentiality and actuality, when the object is known indistinctly and confusedly. A thing thus imperfectly known is known partly by act and partly by potentiality (with reference to Aristotle's *Physics* I, 1). Only afterwards can we know it by distinguishing its principles and elements: "Now it is evident that to know an object that comprises many things, without proper knowledge of each thing contained in it, is to know that thing confusedly. In this way we can have knowledge not only of the universal whole, which contains parts potentially, but also of the integral whole. [...] as to 'animal' to know indistinctly is to know it as 'animal'; whereas to know 'animal' distinctly is to know it as 'rational' or 'irrational animal', that is, to know a man or a lion: therefore our intellect knows 'animal' before it knows man." (*ST* I, 85, 3) (I answer that).

There is, then, the second stage of intellection which enables one to see and understand a thing in its relatedness to other things, and it is only *sub specie integritatis*, for St Thomas believed in the unified and hierarchical order of things: "The human intellect must of necessity understand by composition and division. For since the intellect passes from potentiality to act, it has a likeness to things which are generated, which do not attain to perfection all at once but acquire it by degrees:

so likewise the human intellect does not acquire perfect knowledge by the first act of apprehension; but it first apprehends something about its object, such as its *quiddity, and this is the first and proper object*; and then it understands the properties, accidents, and the various relations of essence. Thus it necessarily compares one thing to another by composition or divison; and from one composition and division it proceeds to another, which is the process of reasoning." (*ST* I, 85, 5) (I answer that).

To conclude the first part of this paper, I would reiterate *that the quidditas, the primary whatness, must be related to general structures*. This relatedness occurs in the related process of reasoning operated by the intellect. Aquinas also points out that the relatedness of a thing to other things or of parts to a whole corresponds but is not the same to the composition and division of the intellect.

Figure 4
quidditas/whatness ------ mind ------ overall structures

We could of course proceed with Aquinas' theory of intellection, but I think that it is already possible to see whether and to what extent St Thomas' cognitive model might be detected in Dante's *Comedy*. As I have already mentioned in the opening passage of this article, I would prefer to call the models of Dante representational models, for Dante creates a fictional world, although at least partly in the mould of the natural one (as has been convincingly proven by Auerbach and many other scholars).

Dante as a thinker has not left us with a consistent corpus of cognitive and intellective standpoints. Even in the *Convivio* Dante appears first as a poet and then as a commentator of the truths hidden in the *canzoni* with which three out of the four books of treatises begin. Therefore his ideas about and understandings of the problematic of intellection, to my understanding, seem rather dispersed and mixed with other ideas on language, cosmology, political ideas, morals etc. Neither is it of course correct to say that he only imbibes from St Thomas, for the Philosopher *par excellence* is Aristotle: indeed, Dante also mentions Thomas' commentaries on Aristotle. In any case, there are various places in the *Convivio* which suggest that the Thomistic model could be taken as a basis for intellection in the *Divine Comedy*, yet there are also some things worth considering which require further analysis.

For example in *Convivio* III, II Dante refers to Aristotle's *De Anima* II, and speaks of the capacities of the soul: vital, sensitive and rational (*vivere, sentire, ragionare*) and stresses the unique capacity in man, that of reasoning which occurs thanks to participation in the divine nature "[...] a guisa di sempiterna intelligenzia; però che l'anima è tanto in quella sovrana potenza nobilitata e dinudata da materia, che la divina luce, come in angelo, raggia in quella" ("in the form of the everexisting intelligence, for the soul is so much in this sovereign capacity ennobled and liberated from matter, that the divine light, like in an angel, pours into it" – here and further on my translation, Ü.P.) (CV III, II).

Liberated from matter seems rather different from Aquinas, for Aquinas does not speak of liberation from matter in this life, which would mean Platonic separate forms. Dante possibly means that intellect itself is not material, but St Thomas of course stresses that human minds exist in bodies (for example, in a different way from the angels), thus the need for sense images. But no doubt, Thomas speaks about the divine light as the principle of all intellection: "For just as the light of the sun is the principle of all visible perception, so the divine light is the principle of intelligible knowledge; since the divine light is that in which intelligible illumination is found first and its highest degree." (*SCG* I, 10, 6).

Further on in the quoted chapter, referring to Aristotle's *Etica* VI, Dante speaks of the virtues/capacities which reside in the rational mind: "[...] there is one which is called scientific, and one which is called reasoning or rather the counselling: and with these there are certain virtues/capacities like [...] the inventive virtue/capacity and judgement." (CV III, II)

Here the inventive virtue/capacity (*virtù inventiva*) together with judgement (*giudicativa*) are of very special interest, for in the next but one chapter the virtue of our inventiveness or fantasy is said to be deficient: "[...]dico che nostro intelletto, per difetto de la virtù da la quale trae quello ch'el vede, che è virtù organica, cioè la *fantasia*, non puote a certe cose salire (però che la fantasia nol puote aiutare, ché non ha lo di che), sì come sono le sustanze partite da materia; de le quali se alcuna considerazione [sanza] di quella avere potemo, intendere non le potemo né comprendere perfettamente." (I say that our intellect, for the deficiency of our capacity from which it takes what it sees, which is the organic capacity, that is *fantasy*, cannot rise to certain things (for fantasy cannot help it, as it does not have the means), such as how substances are detached from matter, of which [substances] if we may have any consideration at all [without it], we cannot understand their intention nor comprehend them perfectly) (*Ibid*. III, IV).

And this quotation proves that Dante at this point is clearly following Aquinas' thought that the soul, because of its deficient fantasy, cannot know detached forms. This quotation is important from two more points. Aristotle in *De Anima* and *De Memoria et Reminiscentia* mentions imagination and supposition as important factors in the process of knowing.[3] And St Thomas in his commentaries on Aristotle also stresses the role of imagination, quoting for example Aristotle's "for the same thing happens in understanding as in geometrical diagrams, where we draw a triangle of a certain size, even though we don't use the particular size. [4] And he concludes that "human minds don't only need images as a source of ideas, but also as something in which they can be observed." (*Ibid*.). This leads to imagining not merely as seeing just like perceiving the phantasmata, but to figuring, whereby imagining is the medium through which the abstraction (or rather construction) of concepts becomes possible.

To be able to understand "this triangle" as "a triangle" or to understand that "this something" is "not a triangle", we have to figure, to construct "the triangle" first and then measure what we see against it. Imagining as figuring and constructing therefore provides the necessary third or the missing link between the two image inputs.

The other point of interest is that Dante says outright in a pure, medieval spirit that our fantasy is deficient in rising to seeing higher things, to understand substances, i.e. the divine intention of things. Therefore it is absolutely no wonder that in the *Comedy* (which represents not only human intellection but also divine intellection, for Dante the character is enraptured miraculously from his everyday perceptive and intellective activities to supernatural intellection, and Dante the

---

3 *De Anima* 427b–429a; *De Memoria et Reminiscentia* 449b – 450a.
4 e.g. *Commentary on Aristotle's De Memoria and Reminiscentia* 449 b30–450 a25.

author is enraptured to its poetic representation), Dante the author refers several times to the high fantasy.

Italo Calvino in his *Lezioni americane* begins the chapter dedicated to visibility with Dante's quotation: "Poi piovve dentro a l'alta fantasia" (*Purg.* XVII, 25).

("Then into my deep [high] fantasy there rained [one who was crucified].") (Calvino 1988, 81)[5]

The passage about the origin and nature of imagining in Purgatorio XVII, 13–18, quoted and interpreted by Calvino (Ibid. 82), is as follows:

> O imaginativa che ne rube
> talvolta sì di fuor, ch'om non s'accorge,
> perché dintorno suonin mille tube,
> chi move te, se 'l senso non ti porge?
> Moveti lume che nel ciel s'informa
> Per sé o per voler giù lo scorge.
>
> O fantasy, you that at times would snatch
> us so from outward things – we notice nothing
> although a thousand trumpets sound around us –
> who moves you when the senses do not spur you?
> A light that finds its form in Heaven moves you –
> directly or led downward by God's will.[6]

Calvino's interpretation:

> O imagination, which hath the power to accost our capacities and our will to take us into the inside world detaching us from the outside so that we do not notice anything, from where do you have the visual messages, if they are not formed by the

---

[5] The English quotations of the *Divine Comedy* are all by Allen Mandelbaum, except for the extract from Inferno V.
[6] The English quotations of the *Divine Comedy* are all by Allen Mandelbaum, except for the extract from Inferno V.

sensations which get imprinted into memory? You are either moved by the light which is informed in the skies on its own or by the virtue of some higher will
(Ibid.) (My translation)

And Calvino adds that according to Dante but also according to St Thomas Aquinas there is a kind of luminous fountain in the skies which transmits ideal images which are formed according to the intrinsic logic of the world of imagining (per sée) or according to the will of God ("o per voler che giù lo scorge") (Ibid.).

I do not know what Calvino means exactly by the intrinsic logic of imagining (perhaps what St Thomas has explained as "[…] the imagination forms for itself an image of an absent thing, or even of something never seen" (*ST* I, 85, 2) (Reply to Objection 3) but I understand that in the second sense it means the revelation of some ideal forms by some higher *intellectus agens*, which corrects the erroneous *simplex apprehensio* of the human intellect.

But here there is one more problem to tackle. Dante the character appears in the *Commedia* as a living being and has the divine light poured into him by high fantasy, but St Thomas says that it is not possible for man in this life to know either separate substances (that are detached from sense material) or God, who can be known rather through creatures according to the Apostle (Paul) (*ST* I, 88, 3).

However, Dante seems to solve this knot with a direct quotation from Thomas' *Summa contra Gentiles*, which states that man should not measure things with his intellect only: "Tommaso nel suo Contra li Gentili [dicendo]: "Sono molti tanto di suo ingegno presuntuosi, che credono col suo intelletto poter misurare tutte le cose, estimando tutto vero quello che a loro pare, falso quello che a loro non pare." ("Thomas in his *Summa contra Gentiles* [says]: "Many people are presumptuous about their ingenuity that they think to be able with their own intellect to measure all the things, considering to be true all that seems them to be so, false that which does not seem so."(*CV* IV, XV))

Possibly St Thomas means here faith and revelation, under special conditions, but this already seems to be the realm of faith.

And near the very end of the *Convivio* Dante calls his work in the spirit of Thomas "Contra- li erranti mia", which is also a line from the

Canzone with which the fourth book begins and which Dante says to have be taken as an example of the good brother Thomas, for it was him who gave to one of his books, in which he throws into confusion all those who tend to lead astray our Faith, the name "Contra gentiles". The exact quotation is the following: "Questo *Contra-li-erranti* è tutto una parte, e è nome d'esta canzone, tolto per essemplo del buono frate Tommaso d'Aquino, che a un suo libro, che fece a confusione di tutti quelli che disviano da nostra Fede, puose nome contra li Gentili" (Ibid. IV, XXX).

To conclude this very brief and insufficient presentation of what I could find of Thomas and Aristotle dispersed in Dante' s *Convivio*, it appears that even though the simple and the complex *apprehensio* might suffice while considering things of an ordinary nature, whereby sense organs first produce phantasmata from which the agent intellect abstracts intelligible species (simple apprehension) and then, second, mixed forms are constructed as a result of defining and dividing (complex apprehension), this *apprehensio* is clearly insufficient to understand things in their intention, to get man's vision to correspond to God's Vision, for which some higher fantasy and some higher *intellectus agens* are required.

Therefore in the *Commedia* which tasks itself with speaking (sometimes directly and sometimes allegorically) of some higher order of things, Dante necessarily has to turn to some higher *Intellecti* to take the place of the *intellectus agens* in the process of the complex *apprehensio* pouring into his possible intellect.[7]

The first one (in Inferno and in Purgatorio) is Virgil, who has been informed from the skies by Beatrice who has been informed by Lucia who has been informed by Mary etc (*Inf.* II); the second is Beatrice (in terrestrial Paradise), after Dante having been on his own for a brief period (when he sees Matelda, a very intriguing episode indeed in which Dante has to deal with his own fantasy, educated of course by Virgil)

---

7 Cf ST 1, 84, 4 (Reply to Objection 3):"Our possible intellect is reduced from potency to act by some being in act, that is, by the agent intellect, which is a power of the soul [...] and not by a separate intellect, as proximate cause, although possibly as a remote cause". Therefore Virgil and Beatrice and others are to be understood in this light as either allegorically Dante's own soul power or, which I think is to be preferred, as the remote cause.

and Paradise proper (where Beatrice will first recommend Dante to St Bernard and then to his own High Fantasy liberated by the prayer).

Therefore from a philosophical point of view the Agent Intellect proper in the *Commedia* does not seem to appertain to man.

And from a semiotic point of view the centre of cognition (either high fantasy or higher *Intellectus agens* that guarantees the true conceptualization) is always outside the cognitive system itself. The only exception seems to be the very end of *Commedia* in which Dante makes an attempt to interpret his vision of God as the Holy Trinity in three concentric circles. He sees

> La forma universal di questo nodo
> credo ch'i' vidi
> (*Par.* XXXIII, 92–93)

> I think I saw the universal shape
> which that knot takes

But of course he does not understand, for there is no higher Intellect or fantasy to pour into him, for this pouring is inside the Trinity Itself.

> O luce etterna che sola in te sidi,
> sola t'intendi, e da te intelletta
> e intendente te ami e arridi!
> (124–126)

> Eternal light, You only dwell within
> Yourself, and only You know You; Self-knowing,
> Self-known, You love and smile upon Yourself.

Dante is miraculously blended and blinded inside the concentric circles through the one in whom he sees his own effigy, Christ.

> [S]e non che la mia mente fu percossa
> da un fulgor in che sua voglia venne.
> (140–141)

> But then my mind was struck by light that flashed
> and, with this light, received what it had asked.

This is the mystical reunion between man and God, but does not suffice either philosophically or semiotically, for he should again have some *Intellectus Agens* to inform him from the outside and make him understand, but as far as the lightning which strikes is concerned, it is: : 1. either not possible to understand whence it came, for Dante does not say anything about it; or 2. it is the pure inside. The only outside (if we of course discard the idea that the pure inside is the outside) is Dante himself who refers to this receiving, but this is the vicious circle, unless we say that the high Dante has to inform the ordinary Dante. But this is something Dante cannot say, for in fact Dante states that

[a] l'alta fantasia qui mancò possa
(142)

here force failed my high fantasy

Dante cannot imagine, he cannot construct the Trinity. Mario Casella has said that where "knowledge becomes pure intellect, fantasy [...] which is mediation between the sensitive and the intellect [...] ceases altogether" (In Bosco and Reggio 2002, 598).

But of course the *Divine Comedy* is not a book of philosophy or theology but primarily a work of fiction and only then of philosophy and theology, therefore tension and conflict are as important as the attempt to resolve them. The primary *quidditas* is generally the construction of Dante the character (or sometimes by some other characters or perceived thus by the reader who might identify himself with Dante the character or some other character), whereas the judgement, especially the revised judgement, is the outcome of some higher *Intellectus Agens* in Dante the character, i.e. generally Virgil or Beatrice. But of relevance is that the artistic form is very often much more complicated than this kind of representative model. Of course if we take the level of representation, we have the dialectic of Dante the character (with whom the model reader, the medieval reader in the first place, should identify himself) and Dante

The problem of double reception

the author (who yields, so to speak, his intellect to the High Fantasy and Higher Judgement – God Himself). Dante the character is involved in action, Dante the author provides a higher intellectual meaning to and moral evaluation of the actions in which Dante the character is involved. Ideally Dante the author tasks himself with providing answers to the intellective problems which Dante the character and the model reader have to tackle. But I shall now observe one concrete example from the *Divine Comedy* to test the correspondence of these kinds of cognitive and representative models to the artistic plot.

In the second circle (first circle proper) of Hell, Dante and Virgil see Minos, the infernal judge. The fifth Canto opens by focusing on Dante the character who descends with Virgil into the first circle.

> Così discesi del cerchio primaio
> giù nel secondo, che men loco cinghia
> e tanto più dolor, che punge a guaio.

> From this first circle thus I came descending
> To the second, which, in narrower compass turning,
> Holds greater woe, with outcry loud and rending.[8]

The focus here is on Dante the character, but in the next *terzine* the focus already shifts to Dante the author, and the past simple tense is now generalized into the present simple:

> Stavvi Minòs orribilmente, e ringhia:
> essamina le colpe nell' intrata;
> giudica e manda secondo ch'avvinghia.
> Dico che quando l'anima mal nata
> li vien dinanzi, tutta si confessa;
> e quel conoscitor del le peccata
> vede qual loco d'inferno è da essa:

---

8 The English translation of this and the following extracts of Inferno V are all by Dorothy L. Sayers.

cignesi con la coda tante volte
quantunque gradi vuol che giù sia messa.
(*Inf.* 4–12)

> There in the threshold, horrible and girning,
> Grim Minos sits, holding his ghastly session,
> And, as he girds him, sentencing and spurning;
> For when the ill soul faces him, confession
> Pours out of it till nothing's left to tell;
> Whereon that connoisseur of all transgression
> Assigns it to its proper place in hell,
> As many grades as he will have it fall
> So oft he belts him round with his own tail.

Here we in fact already have, from the very beginning, a result of complex apprehension, the judgement which should only later grow out of the simple apprehension: we understand (if we are well informed or if we read the commentaries) that Dante the author has turned Minos, the dignified Virgilian character, into some kind of monstrous being, a strange mixture of human, animal and demon. A grotesque figure indeed. As the text reveals, first and foremost we have the judge destined to mete out divine punishment to sinners. And this is already the overall moral structure. Although Minos has a bizarre tail, it has become the instrument of weighing sins and signifying just sentence. It is now our task as critical readers to imagine what may actually have happened on a cognitive level. Dante the character might have seen a strange figure, he might have not known how to place its *quidditas*. He may have wondered: "Is it man or bull? Animal, according to St Thomas, sure, but is it sensitive or rational too?" Dante the character may have even thought of "a human bull", a strange man, or a strange bull, a Minotaur, just as the rhinoceros seen by Marco Polo was taken by him to be a strange unicorn (about which Eco writes in *Kant and the Platypus*). Dante the character might really have taken it for a Minotaur on the basis of his knowledge of Greek mythology, (especially after recently having met Charon), but surely not for Minos (whom he very well knew from Virgil's *Aeneid* and who is no monster there, just a simple human shadow). Yet we as readers know thanks to

The problem of double reception

Dante the author that this *is* Minos ("Stavvi Minòs ...") although we are also informed of its monstrous characteristics ("[...] orriblimente, e ringhia"). On the artistic level, therefore, this *ad hoc* perception and primary placement of the *quidditas* is at once counterbalanced, even preceded by the judgement. Therefore it presents at once the problem of double reception: we as readers have a mixture of Dante the character's ("Good God, who is it, a bull or the Minotaur?") simple apprehension and Virgil's – expressed by Dante the author – complex apprehension ("Well, well, this is Minos, the infernal judge, terrible, yet dignified in its function to mete out our Lord's will").

Dante the author surely does not maintain the chronological logic of simple apprehension and judgement, but supplies the judgement first and then enriches it with further details, thus gradually making Minos' figure complete. Dante's Minos is necessarily a complex apprehension (or judgement) which is thus presented and enriched with further details when we see, together with Dante the character, the appalled sinners (for Dante the character already knows that in this place there are only sinners) who stand before him and then apprehend how that *quidditas* girds his tail round them and launches them downwards into the Hell.

I wonder whether Virgil could have managed to explain anything to his disciple about the primary figuring of Minos, for the *quidditas* yells:

"O tu che vieni al doloroso ospizio",
disse Minòs a me quando mi vide
(16–17)

"Ho! Thou that comest to the house of pain,"
Cried Minos when he saw me [...]

And it is clear that the focus is again on Dante the author for there is no proof that Virgil may have whispered, "this is actually Minos that you know from my book, *Aeneid* VI, 432–433, but he is different."

"[G]uarda com'entre e di cui ti fide:
non t'inganni l'ampiezza de l' intrare!"
(19–20)

"How thou dost go, in whom is thy reliance;
Be not deceived by the wide open door!"

And only now do we see Virgil's first actual intervention:

"Perché pur gride?"
(21)

"Wherefore this loud defiance?"

which could be translated into a plain "why the hell are you shouting?"

It is of course very complicated if not impossible to analyse the whole episode of the Canto in this way, so I shall have to simplify.

Minos is horrible, he roars. The perceiver's senses register these characteristics and many more of that *quidditas* (which Dante the author calls Minos) and create phantasmata (in the mind of Dante – the character, other characters – sinners, and the reader, if he thinks backwards) which the agent intellect turns to and transforms into intelligible species – a primary concept – monster – in the possible intellect, whereby a likeness is established between the conceptual image and the primary *quidditas*. Thanks to the power of the agent intellect, the possible intellect receives and processes/knows the concept (intelligible species), whereby the mind, in knowing its object, which is of some universal nature, returns to the knowledge of its own act, and, finally, to the phantasm from which it has abstracted the species. Thus the knowledge of the singular in the specific is obtained by definition, division or composition, and is expressed verbally: Minos – the strange, grotesque, terrible, yet judge of God' s will. It is really very puzzling to operate this kind of cognitive model consciously, for I am liable to simplify. Minos is by no means a stable image, as we have already seen. It is transformed even later in the text. In Canto XXVII, 124–127, we find out that if the sin is especially tremendous (as is the case with Guido da Montefeltro, the ill advisor of Pope Bonifacius VIII) this "embodiment of Justice" will bite his tail ferociously. This could seem grotesque, even comic. Virgil's words might also be perceived as comic by the present-day reader who cannot see himself as a sinner before Minos. And Minos' authority which he enjoys in Virgil's *Aeneid*, but also the authority of Hell and of God, would be undermined if this was really perceived as grotesque or even comic.

And this is the very point of double reception which philosophically depends on whether we accept the primary impression in phantasmata as *quidditas* or as *haeccitas*.

Either "This is Minos" or "Minos is the judge". For the first one translates as "*Haeccitas* or thisness is Minos." The second translates as "*Quidditas* or whatness is the judge".

Haeccitas or thisness (the term coined by Duns Scotus) signifies the individuality in what is an individuality, on the one hand. And this is therefore not communicable. But another important aspect according to Scotus is that the unity of a composite object does not require a unity of *form*, only the subordination of the forms of the parts, none of which is annulled in its difference, to an ultimate form. And as Eco remarks in the *Aesthetic of Thomas Aquinas*, this is the opposite of St Thomas' views (Cf Eco 1988, 205–207). *Haeccitas* is an individual property. It does not perfect form, which cannot be anything but universal, but rather gives to the whole composite a concrete particularity, uniquely individual with respect to every other composite.

I am of the opinion that Dante the author means to apply the Thomistic model of the homogenous unity in its forms, whereby all the grotesque and distorted figures of the Inferno – from Charon to Minos to Pluto to Nimrod or strange events and misunderstandings, whether in the Inferno or Purgatorio (e.g. Lucifer standing on his head in Dante's primary opinion when passing with Virgil from the Northern hemisphere along Lucifer's body to the Southern hemisphere etc) or the secrets and mysteries of Paradiso (thanks to the intervention of Beatrice) –become resolved. In this light (the higher *lumen*), Minos girding his tail around a sinner will be seen as a sign of a verdict and biting his tail as closing the circle (*ourobros* – the snake biting its own tail, like the snakes closing around the thieves in the seventh subcircle of the Malebolge where Vanni Fucci and the Florentine thieves appear) etc.

The higher agent intelligent – Virgil – thus already prepared Dante to understand Inferno from outside itself; the reason for it is in Paradise, whence sinning angels fell, yet the centre of cognition is still outside, and everything is understood from that aspect, and a unity is aspired to. Inferno is meant to be understood in the Thomistic way on the macro-level.

Figure 5
Roaring and biting *quidditas*, ← Virgil/lumen naturalis/ → Minos/fierce judge
Minos displaced   Dante the author   of sinners in Hell,
                                                          Minosreplaced

But I am not convinced whether the unity works out on the micro-level, especially when considering the uniqueness of the incongruous forms of all the episodes, e.g.. Mohammed's foot in the air when walking with his body cloven in twain while speaking, and then continuing walking, the rhapsodies of the devils in Malebolge, etc. There are even episodes in which Virgil the higher *intellectus agens* is led astray and beaten (the devils, Kaifas etc), but of course he is informed again by the higher powers and the cognitive journey continues to the Trinity.

If we understand the *Divine Comedy* as a philosophical and/or theological work (and in this case we should only consider the fabula, not the artistic plot), in which the Holy Trinity and man's cognitive triumph are predicated from all its details, even the distorted ones, then of course the structure works out, though not semiotically as we have seen, for it cannot be explained for the final lack of the outside.

Yet if they were seen as subordinate to the artistic whole, and therefore often incongruous and heterogeneous, there is room for both the grotesque and the comic and non-understandable, and the Thomistic model of cognition – even though it might be regarded as the basis for Dante's general representative model – appears necessarily to be insufficient in describing Dante's poetic.

Galeotto fu il libro e chi lo scrisse.
Some remarks about intertextuality in Inferno V

Leonardo Cecchini

Of the many approaches to the revolution in the sensibility of love which took place in twelfth-century Western Europe and that we usually label 'courtly love', one of the most productive is, in my opinion, offered by C. Stephen Jaeger in his *Ennobling Love. In Search of a Lost Sensibility*.

According to Jaeger, courtly love evolved from another and earlier form of love which he terms *ennobling love*. This is an ethic of love and friendship that was prevalent in medieval monasteries and universities as well as at court. It was the result of the meeting between the Classical culture heritage (in which Cicero's *De Amicitia* played an especially important role) and the new Christian worldview.

The objective of this form of love and friendship (between both man and woman and man and man) was to attain *virtus*, moral elevation. Virtue arose from overcoming the sexual impulse and abstaining from the physical expression of sexuality. According to Jaeger, ennobling love was "love subjected to reason and discipline, love as a source of virtue, love as a learnable discipline that one can put into practice like any other ethic of behaviour," and it was "primarily a way of acting and behaving, and only secondary a feeling" (Jaeger 1999, 200), a kind of ritualised play in public life "inseparably connected with the social concerns [...] of court society: rank, standing, reputation, prestige" (Jaeger 1999, 154).

In Jaeger's view, the twelfth century completely revaluated and redefined *ennobling love* by attempting to reconcile it with physical love. He calls this new phenomenon *passionate love* and finds evidence of its social manifestation in the letters of Abelard and Heloise and in literary expression as for example Gottfried von Strasburg's *Tristan* and the Arthurian romances.

In this form of love, one attempts to conciliate two irreconcilable forces: love as moral virtue and love as a sexual act. This means that when love becomes "passion", i.e. suffering, pain and illness (according to the original meaning of the Latin word *passio*), carnal love can lead to moral elevation: "Those [...] who accept the difficult philosophy of love-suffering, love-passion, align themselves with nobility of mind and soul" (Jaeger 1999, 193).

The most radical change brought about by the union of what had until then been incompatible forces was the migration of love from the public to the private sphere. Passionate love is at odds with public reputation and social institutions, but its esoteric nature nevertheless aided the aristocracy in setting itself apart from the rest of society and in the Middle Ages it became an important element in the self-understanding and behaviour of the European nobility. As literary characters such as Tristan or Lancelot illustrate emblematically, "love with high potential for disgrace and for the destabilizing of states is declared the source of all worth and reputation." (Jaeger 1999, 194)

A kind of paradox is established here, one which Jaeger expresses in this way: "How can it [i.e. passionate love] claim virtue, while admitting virtue's old enemy, the sexual act, as the natural end of love and full partner in the exalting process?" (Jaeger 1999, 159)

According to Jaeger the medieval sensibility (and the Romantic after that) struggles in vain between these two poles and cannot resolve the dichotomy: the union of *virtus* and passion cannot be justified rationally. While *ennobling love* leads to the betterment and increased social status of the individuals involved, *passionate love*, polluted by sexuality, is highly prejudicial for the social order and is not socially acceptable. The result can be only tragedy and self-sacrifice, love and death.

And such a story of love and death is precisely what Dante tells us about in Inferno V: the story of Francesca da Rimini and Paolo Malatesta, one of the most famous and best known episodes in the *Divine Comedy*. Unlike other famous couples representing *passionate love* such as Tristan and Iseult or Lancelot and Guinevere, all the players in Dante's drama are historical characters. Francesca, from the Da Polenta family, rulers of Ravenna, married in about 1275 Gianciotto

(Giovanni "the Lame", died 1304) of the Malatesta family, rulers of Rimini, possibly to seal a political alliance between the two families; between 1283 and 1284 she and her brother-in-law, Paolo Malatesta, with whom she had committed adultery, were killed by her husband.

The whole episode occurs in the canto without any kind of introduction of the characters or the event and is thus presented by Dante as universally known, as a famous "social scandal of the century" in Northern Italy, as Ole Meyer, the Danish translator of the *Divine Comedy*, writes in his comments. We do not know if it did take place just as Dante tells us – his account is the oldest known source of the episode and other sources from the period are too sparse to completely confirm or refute wholly his version. In all likelihood, however, the adultery and the subsequent double killing did take place.[1]

There is no doubt however that Dante has thought of the story of Paolo and Francesca as presented in V canto of Inferno as a contribution to the debate about moral issues and the ethical and religious consequences of what Jaeger calls *passionate love* and as a contribution to the literature dealing with it; at that point a debate had been going on for a couple of centuries in medieval society. This can be seen in the famous intertextual reference to Lancelot and Guinevere, which Dante puts into Francesca's mouth.

In the canto it is Francesca herself who tells her tragic story. She is the first of the many souls that Dante meets and talks to on his journey in the hereafter and she is the only one in the *Divine Comedy* who is directly encouraged to remember the circumstances of her sin. With her lover Paolo, who utters not one word in the whole episode, she is in the second circle of the Inferno, where "*i peccator carnali, che la ragion sottomettono al talento*" (the carnal malefactors, who reason subjugate to appetite, v. 38–39) are punished by being thrown about by a violent storm symbolising the inescapable strength of lust. Similar to a long line of other characters from Antiquity and more recent characters (among whom Tristan is mentioned), Francesca and Paolo belong to the sub-group whose common denominator is their all having suffered violent deaths because of passion.

---

1 Recently Tedolinda Barolini has once more conducted a study of the historical sources of Francesca and Paolo's story in her "Dante and Francesca da Rimini: Realpolitik, Romance, Gender." *Speculum*, 75 (2000): 1-28.

At the end of the episode Dante asks how they could commit adultery, how they could transgress the boundary between *i dolci sospiri*, the sweet sighs, i.e. to paraphrase Jaeger, the ritualised, continent "courtly" game of love and *i dubbiosi desiri*, the dubious desires, the dangerous and socially unforgivable *passionate love*. The answer which Dante puts into Francesca's mouth makes her and Paolo's story "one of the earliest and more powerful manifestations of the modernistic topos of life imitating literature" (Valesio, 68).

The couple, brother- and sister-in-law – Francesca says – were betrayed by literature, so to speak: one day they were together reading the story of Lancelot the knight's love of Queen Guinevere. When they came to the episode in which Lancelot – with Prince Gallehaut as a go-between – meets Queen Guinevere and gets to kiss her for the first time, Paolo too kissed Francesca:

Noi leggiavamo un giorno per diletto di Lancialotto come amor lo strinse; soli eravamo e sanza alcun sospetto.	One day we read, for our delight, Of Lancelot, how Love did enthral him. Alone we were and without any fear.
Per più fïate li occhi ci sospinse quella lettura, e scolorocci il viso; ma solo un punto fu quel che ci vinse.	More than once our eyes together drew That reading, and drove the colour from our faces; But one point only was it that overcame us.
Quando leggemmo il disïato riso esser basciato da cotanto amante, questi, che mai da me non fia diviso,	When we read how the longed-for smile Being by such a noble lover kissed, This one, who never from me shall be divided,
la bocca mi basciò tutto tremante. Galeotto fu 'l libro e chi lo scrisse: quel giorno più non vi leggemmo avante. (Inferno V, 127–138)	Kissed me on my mouth all trembling. Galehaut was the book and he who wrote it. That day we read in it no more."

Here Dante is referring to a central episode in one of the most famous medieval chivalric romances, *Le livre de Lancelot du Lac*, an anonymous prose romance from the so-called *vulgata* version of the Arthurian romances (written around 1220–1235). Together with the story of Tristan and Iseult, these prose romances were among the best known and most read all over Europe in the Middle Ages. In Italy, too, they were very popular, especially at the Northern Italian courts but also among prosperous merchants in towns like Florence and Venice (Del Corno Branca 1998, 143–150).

The intertextual reference to the Arthurian romances has drawn the attention of many scholars. At the beginning of the 1900s eminent Danteists (Crescini, Paris, Rajna, Toynbee, Torraca) dwelled on this paragraph and a vivid discussion arose.[2] At the centre of attention was the question of the discrepancy between what Francesca affirms to had read, namely that it is Lancelot who kisses Guinevere (*il disïato riso esser basciato da cotanto amante*; the longed-for smile being by such a noble lover kissed), and what the romance actually says, that it is the Queen who took the initiative to kiss Lancelot.[3]

Hypotheses that Dante had read a different version of the romance from the one that has reached us, or that Dante had not remembered it correctly were formulated (this latter hypothesis is contradicted by the precision with which Dante quotes the same paragraph in Paradiso XVI – see below – and the Lancelot cycle elsewhere[4]), or that he might deliberately have changed it (see below).

Recent research conducted by Daniela Del Corno Branca has confirmed that the phrase *sot quil la besoit* (she [the Lady of Malehaut] realised that he kissed her), which Rajna had already found in a Lancelot manuscript at the Biblioteca Laurenziana in Florence, is also present in a certain number of other manuscripts, some of them Italian (Del Corno Branca 1998, 146). It is thus possible that Dante had read the

---

2   A useful critical account of the question in A. Hatcher & M. Musa "The Kiss: Inferno V and the Old French Prose Lancelot." *Comparative Literature* 20 (1968): 97–109.
3   Et la reine voit que li chevaliers n'an ose plus faire, si lo prant ele par lo menton, si lo baise devant Gelehot assez longuement, si que la dame de Malohaut sot que ele lo baisoit. *Lancelot do Lac: the non-cyclic Old French Prose Romance*, ed. F. Kennedy, Oxford, Clarendon Press, 1980, vol. 1. 348, 28–30.
4   Dante quotes the last romance of the cycle, *Mort Artu*, in *Convivio*, IV, XXVIII, 8 and in Inferno XXXII, 61–62.

Lancelot romance in a version in which Lancelot kisses Guinevere which, probably, was popular mostly in Italy.

By virtue of the new methodologies of textual readings such as narratology and structuralism gaining ground from the fifties onwards, Dante's relationship to *Le livre de Lancelot du Lac* has again begun to interest the Danteists as these methodologies have permitted subtler interpretations of the intertextual reference to the Lancelot present in Francesca's discourse.

Based on the important narratological dividing line between Dante-the poet (and architect of the whole *Comedy*) and Dante-the pilgrim (i.e. the person or actant who travels through the work itself), modern Dante research has also introduced a similar contradiction on an ethical and hermeneutic level and ascribes to the fictive pilgrim the compassion and dismay which Dante clearly feels for Francesca and Paolo throughout the episode in Inferno V, while Dante as *theologus-poeta* condemns and can only condemn Francesca and her brother-in-law.

As a contrast to the traditional romantic interpretation of the canto anchored in Francesca's *pathos* and tragic passion and of her as an icon of romantic love (a interpretative tradition which goes back to Ugo Foscolo and Francesco De Sanctis), the (self-)deceiving and manipulative character of the beautiful words of this *intellettuale di provincia* (small-town intellectual, Contini, 42) or "Madame Bovary of the 1200s" (Sanguineti, 28) has been pointed out, and the episode has been interpreted as Dante warning against the dangerous power of fascination of the chivalrous love rituals and secular courtly literature and culture. In this context some scholars have ascribed to Dante the intention of wanting to present Francesca in the act of an unintentional misreading, or an outright manipulation of the French text (Hatcher & Musa, Noakes), thus resuming one of the hypotheses that was already present in the discussion at the beginning of the 1900s.

Nevertheless, it seems to me that Romantic research with its emphasis on Francesca's *pathos* and *romance* did point out an aspect actually present in the text[5] and not only an anachronistic projection of Romanticism's own sensibility. It seems to me that from a narratological point of view, the now traditional dichotomy between the

---

5 See also Barolini's article p. 9–12.

role of the pilgrim and that of the poet is employed in this case too mechanically, and it is not subtle enough to facilitate determining the poetic value of the text; it does not take into consideration the complex nature of Dante's text.

The intertextual strings played on by Dante in canto V of Inferno are very complex. He does not present the love story of Francesca and Paolo in phrases that allude to an older text hidden in the background (with what Gerald Genette and others may call an allusion); on the contrary, he quotes directly from the romance of chivalry. In this way Dante implicitly reveals the "literary" origin of a "true" story (Valesio, 69; Noakes, 223). Thus, the Lancelot story is underlined a number of times as the source of Francesca and Paolo's existential drama. For example, it can be seen how Dante, in the course of a few verses, insists on words such as *leggevamo* (reading) (v. 127), *lettura* (reading) (v. 131), *leggemmo* (we read) (v. 133 and v. 138) and on the attraction the book about Lancelot and Guinevere has on Francesca and Paolo.

But not only that, Dante also refers to *Le livre de Lancelot du Lac* elsewhere in the *Divine Comedy* in the episode in *Paradiso* XVI, 13–16 in which Dante, accompanied by Beatrice, meets his ancestor Cacciaguida (died before 1198) and as a sign of respect addresses him using the formal *Voi* ('you' in the plural), whereas in the previous canto – when he did not know with whom he was speaking – he addressed him using the informal *tu* ('you' in the singular). Beatrice, who has noticed a certain inappropriate proudness and human vanity in Dante's *Voi*, smiles and thus (a comparison which Dante makes) assumes the same role as Guinevere's maid of honour, the Lady of Malehaut, who, in the romance of chivalry, coughs to let Lancelot know that she knows his identity and his secret:

Onde Beatrice, ch'era un poco scevra,	Whence Beatrice, who stood somewhat apart,
ridendo, parve quella che tossio al primo fallo scritto di Ginevra.	Smiling, appeared like the Lady who coughed
(*Par.* XVI, 13–16)	At the first fault inscribed of Guinevere.

Thanks to the same intertextual "go-between", the episode from the Lancelot romance, the episode in Paradiso XVI is interesting because it establishes a textual "link" between "the woman" in Inferno and "the woman" in Paradise, i.e. between Francesca and Beatrice, who are traditionally seen as antipoles in the *Divine Comedy*. The language in this episode is also strikingly similar to that in Inferno V (Valesio, 75): a courtly, secular, self-conscious language with remarkable similarities to Dante's stilnovistic writing in the work from his youth, *Vita Nuova*.

In the same way as some of the elements Dante used in his composition of Beatrice in the stilnovististic works of his youth later came to colour the character of Francesca in Inferno (see especially the famous first part of her speech, v. 88–107), elements from the character of Francesca are again reflected in the picture of Beatrice in Paradiso. The question deserves more thorough treatment than I can provide in a few lines here, but I think that there is some evidence that we should at least problematise and introduce light and shade to the traditional, idealised way of seeing Beatrice *tout court* as a Christological figure (as we are used to doing since Singleton) and Francesca as an anti-Beatrice.

Thereby Dante-the narrator intervenes twice in his own source: indirectly through Francesca's discourse and directly by structuring the whole episode in his own way as a literary discourse (his transferral of elements from the French romance to Paradiso XVI included).

I would like now to look further at the famous verse 137 (*Galeotto fu il libro e chi lo scrisse*; Galeotto was the book and he who wrote it) which has a fundamental function in the episode linking together literature and life. What does Dante mean by this verse? Rhetorically –as many scholars have pointed out – the verse contains a metonymic meaning, i.e. it replaces the word "romance" with one of the main characters in the romance (Gallehaut = Lancelot romance) and it can be paraphrased as follows: the book in which one of the main characters is Gallehaut – in Francesca and Paolo's real world – assumes the same role as the one Gallehaut establishes in the fictive world of the book. As we have already seen, Dante here juxtaposes and thereby links two levels: the real world and the fictional world. But the structure of the verse makes it difficult for the reader to apprehend the metonymic meaning because in this case the metonymy does not (as it usually does) consist of two elements, but three: Gallehaut = Lancelot romance = the author of the romance. In itself this further reference to the French author of the book is not necessary semantically because the reader should already be able to understand the meaning after the first "part" of the metonymy. It could thus be seen as a conscious textual clue on Dante's part – a clue which should indirectly draw the attention of the reader back to Dante himself and his role as the writer (he also "writes" books, this book: the *Divine Comedy*). Narratologically, with the anonymous author of the Lancelot romance as a pretext, the shadow of Dante-the writer materialises next to Dante-the pilgrim, who compassionately attends to Francesca's drama (Valesio, 70). It can thus be claimed that the reference to the author of the romance in verse 137 is a textual clue to Dante's metaliterary intentions.

I believe that Peter Dronke is right when in his article *Francesca and Héloïse* (p. 117) he asks himself rhetorically: "Did it ever occur to Dante, I wonder, that for some later readers Francesca's words might become as inflammatory as the tale of Lancelot and Guinevere had been for her and Paolo?" It is possible that Dante wants to draw the reader's attention to the fascination and power of literature, not only on the reading actants in the work, Francesca and Paolo, but also on the actual readers of the *Divine Comedy*.

Dante's narration will have the same influence on us as Lancelot's story had on Francesca and her brother-in-law: the poetical power and pathos emanating from Francesca's discourse will, throughout the centuries, act as "Gallehaut" on subsequent generations of readers. The fascination that literature exerts over Francesca and Paolo will, thanks to Dante's poetic power, live on in the reader and work against the ethical and theological frame of the episode, as the canto's reception over the centuries demonstrates.

This is not an attempt to reject the "palinode" dimension of the canto which by now is generally accepted by all critiques of Dante, i.e. the attitude of "moral" denial of this kind of courtly literature and also a self-critical retrospection of Dante's own past, thus distancing himself from and overcoming his own previous stilnovistic production.

However, it is not possible to rid oneself of the impression that in the canto there is a certain ambiguity in Dante's approach: a text (Inferno V) which refers to another text (the Lancelot romance) and distances itself from it by calling it "Gallehaut", but which at the same time functions in the exact same way. *Passionate love* literature is accused of being socially, ethically and theologically dangerous while at the same time passion (and literature's) forceful power of empathy is recognised.

A generation later, Dante's first great creative interpreter, Giovanni Boccaccio, showed that he had understood perfectly Dante's play in Inferno V when on the title page of the *Decameron* – i.e. at the beginning of a literary work dedicated to the women who love – he writes with a clear allusion to Inferno V: *Comincia il libro chiamato Decameron, cognominato prencipe Galeotto* (Del Corno Branca 1998, 150).[6]

On a more cultural and historical level the story of the two lovers from Rimini – as Dante tells it to us – exemplifies the paradoxical nature of one of the most prevailing phenomena stemming from medieval sensibility: *passionate love* (the way Jaeger has reconstructed it). Passion and the physical love between two lovers is basically hell (and in Francesca and Paolo's case it literally takes them straight to Hell), but at the same time they have something redeeming in them.

---

6 The *same* Boccaccio who plays a decisive role in establishing a "romantic" interpretative tradition of Inferno V with his own version of the love story between Francesca and Paolo in his *Esposizioni sopra la Commedia di Dante*; see Teodolinda Barolini's article (especially pp. 13–16). Also one of the most famous stories of the *Decameron* (IV, 1 which narrates the sad love story between Ghismunda and Guiscardo) has clear intertextual references to Inferno V.

Dante and the Bible.
A reading of central passages in
the Vita nuova and the Commedia[1]

Asbjørn Bjornes

Dante uses the Bible in part to give his own poetry authority and depth and his use of Scripture is an enormous and complex field of research. In this article I shall provide a short account of how the Bible is situated in medieval culture, after which I shall exemplify Dante's use of religious language and some of his quotations from the Bible in the *Vita nuova* and the *Divina Commedia*. Using selected examples, I shall seek to underline the variety of biblical texts we find in central passages by Dante, and shall illustrate how he adapts the texts to fit into his descriptions, arguments and explanations.

The Bible in the Middle Ages[2]

In the fifth canto of the Paradiso Beatrice speaks to Dante the wanderer. In it, she says something essential about the unique role and position the Bible had in the Middle Ages – and for Dante himself: "Avete il novo e 'l vecchio Testamento, / e 'l pastor de la Chiesa che vi guida; /

---

1 This article is mainly based on my thesis; see Bjornes 2002. The thesis and the lecture given at the Nordic Dante Network Conference in 2006 resulted in an article (written in Norwegian) in the literary magazine *Prosopopeia* (No. 2, 2007, University of Bergen). Some of the revisions and adjustments from *Prosopopeia* are in this article. I am greatly indebted to Robert Marsalis for his assistance with the English translation as well as for his useful comments on the text.
2 Under the headline "The Bible in the Middle Ages" I have consulted Hawkins 1993, pp. 120–22, Smalley 1964, p. xiv, Dante 1995 (*Convivio*), p. 105, and Dante 1990 (The Banquet), p. 67.

questo vi basti a vostro salvamento"[3] (*Par.* V, 76–78). No other book has had a greater influence on Dante's literary production than the Bible. Among several other important books in the Middle Ages, the Scriptures hold a unique position as *God's own Word*: "All Scripture is God-breathed and is useful for teaching, rebuking, correcting and training in righteousness" (2 Tim 3:16).

The Holy Writ is the basic textbook for the age and culture in which Dante grew up. Understood to be God's holy and inerrant Word, the Bible had an authority that exceeded all other writings during the Middle Ages and was the most studied book throughout this long period. It was used in the teaching of the *artes liberales* (the seven liberal arts), and it was the most important book in the churches and monasteries.

Dante's use of the Bible – first of all the Vulgate (*exemplar Parisiensis*) – is primarily based upon his experience of the Bible in the way its language, symbols and ideas influenced medieval culture. Unusual for a layman, Dante seems to have studied the Bible in line with the prevailing exegetical traditions of his time. In the *Convivio*, Dante probably refers to the convent schools established by the Dominicans at Santa Maria Novella and by the Franciscans at Santa Croce: "le scuole de li religiosi e a le disputazioni de li filosofanti" (*Conv.* II, xii, 7).[4] In these spiritual environments he would have been exposed to the *lectio divina* as well as lectures about the Scriptures.

The academic practices of the two convents were similar, but the exegetical atmosphere of each was quite distinct. From the Dominicans Dante would have received the Thomistic methodology of the *Summa*, whereby the words of Scripture (along with citations of Aristotle and the Church Fathers) serve to substantiate or dispute theological points. This technique is amply demonstrated throughout the Paradiso, and particularly in Paradiso 13, where Dante the wanderer meets with St. Thomas and listens to his explanations. (Hawkins 1993, 122)

---

3 *Par.* V, 76–78: "You have the New Testament and the Old, and the Shepherd of the Church, to guide you: let this suffice for your salvation." The translations from the *Comedy* are by Singleton, in Dante 1970, 1973 and 1975.
4 *Conv.* II.xii,7: "[...] to the schools of the religious orders and to the disputations held by the philosophers" (Lansing's translation; p. 67 in Dante 1990).

The Bible in the works of Dante

Dante's poetry is swarming with quotations from and references to the Bible. His works contain no less than 575 biblical citations, compared to 395 from Aristotle and 192 from Virgil (Manetti 1984, 120; Hawkins 1993, 134). The Scriptures Dante most often uses come from the very books that are privileged by the worship of the Church: the Gospels, the Psalms, and the Epistles of Paul. (Genesis, Proverbs, and Isaiah are also important sources, but in the prose treatises and epistles rather than for the *Commedia*.) (Hawkins 1993, 123).

Most interesting here, however, is to take a closer look at how Dante *uses* the Bible and its world, how he absorbs and adapts biblical material and how citations from the Bible support his love for Beatrice in the *Vita nuova* and his journey to God in the *Comedy*. It is also very useful to take a closer look at Dante's forms of argumentation and how meaning in the *Vita nuova* and the *Comedy* is brought forth and fortified by the greater referential context of the Bible (Kleinhenz 1986, 225).[5]

Religious language and Bible citations in the *Vita nuova*

Dante probably composed the *Vita nuova* (or *Vita Nova*) between 1293 and 1295. The work consists of 42 short chapters and is a combination of prose and poetry. The main theme is the "new life" the protagonist finds in his love for Beatrice. In Dante's time it was common to glorify a woman through poetry, whether she was a real person or mere fiction. Perhaps Dante is writing about Beatrice on the basis of real meetings with her, or perhaps she is a poetic construction. In the *Comedy* she symbolizes theology, the virtuous life in faith, the Christian faith, etc. (Reynolds 2006, 6; Ulleland 2000, 37). The *Vita nuova* hints at the same.[6]

The poetry of praise has a very long and rich tradition in Western literature and the *Vita nuova* is rooted in it. As Fineman (1986) points out, "the poetry of praise is regularly taken to be, from Plato and

---

5 Kleinhenz treats the *Comedy* here, but his account is also relevant to the *Vita nuova*.
6 Particularly in chapters 19–21; 24; 26; 27; 29; 33:8, and 40–42.

Aristotle through the Renaissance, the master model of poetry per se; furthermore, [...] this is a central fact for the Renaissance sonnet, which, from Dante onward, characteristically presents itself as something panegyric" (p. 1). But praise in the *Vita nuova* is not just anchored in a Classical literary tradition. The work is also influenced by a Christian tradition of praise that stretches back to the Bible, not least to the Book of Psalms.[7]

The biblical verses and allusions in the *Vita nuova* intensify the theological meaning of Beatrice and of the protagonist (i.e. the fictitious Dante's) inward focus and the work at times directly reflects biblical themes.

Dante's language is in many ways a mediator between heavenly and earthly things. Dante himself uses – through the protagonist's poetical and spiritual understanding – a physical language to describe Beatrice's divinity, and he uses a religious or theologically charged language to describe her physical beauty. This shows how the *Vita nuova* can be understood both theologically and poetically. The protagonist's development towards divine love becomes an expression for both a poetic and spiritual "conversion", a "new life" ("vita nova"; ch. 1).

Beatrice's beauty and divinity is the starting point for his love and idealization. Beatrice appears as a heavenly being in many ways: through her physical and spiritual beauty, her virtues, social rank, humility, death and ascension, and in her role as Dante's guide to God.

Dante's vision of Beatrice, whose name means "beatifier", constitutes the very seed of Dante's knowledge of divine love. Because of her beauty, she is compared to an angel (2:8; 26:2). Beatrice "non parea figliuola d'uomo mortale, ma di deo" (2:8).[8] When she greets the protagonist, Dante's choice of words and expressions signalizes that she is divine: "mi salutoe molto virtuosamente, tanto che me parve allora vedere tutti li termini de la beatitudine" (3:1).[9] Dante's knowledge of

---

[7] In my account of Dante and the biblical tradition I have consulted Collins 1989, p. 38; Hawkins 1999, p. 40, and Mazzaro 1981, p. 39.

[8] *Vita nuova* 2:8: "She [Beatrice] seemed no child of mortal man, but of god." The translations from the *Vita nuova* are by Cervigni and Vasta, in Dante 1995. Italian words and expressions are from the edition by Michele Barbi 1932, in Dante 1995 (*Vita nuova*).

[9] *Vita nuova* 3:1: "she greeted me with exceeding virtue, such that I then seemed to see all the terms of beatitude."

Beatrice is not only associated with a greeting ("mi salutoe": "she greeted me"). In Italian the expression also alludes to salvation (Harrison 1988, 22). Instead of the customary *felicità* ("happiness"), Dante uses the theologically charged word *beatitudo/beatitudine* ("beatitude") to describe the protagonist's joy (ch. 3). In Dante's time, the term *beatitudine* was normally reserved for the eternal happiness attained in the direct vision of God in heaven. Such an ecstatic joy, the state of being *beato*, is really only for angels and saints (Ryan 1993, 137; Shaw 1965, 99, note 4). The protagonist is completely beside himself with joy and by using such a word he is signalling that the happiness he knows through Beatrice ultimately comes from God (Ryan 1993, 137). She is his "gentilissima", his most gentle lady. The expression helps to describe Beatrice's perfect conduct and appearance, but it also carries a deeper religious meaning. Through her greeting in chapter 3, Dante alludes to Beatrice's role as his spiritual guide to God: through her physical beauty and piety she will lead his mind up to heaven. Joan M. Ferrante (1985) writes:

> [Dante] is able to affirm secular love as the first stage of divine love: if a woman's beauty reflects heavenly beauty, if her powers to refine man come from God, then it is by seeking the source of her beauty, not by rejecting her, that man should reach God. Dante accepts the attraction he feels to physical beauty and ascribes it to the reflection of a higher beauty, so that he is able to preserve his love for a woman without letting it come into conflict with his love for God.
> (Ferrante 1985, 129)

Beatrice's greeting may be said to be a starting point for the analogy of Christ which, according to many, Beatrice represents in the *Vita nuova*, particularly from chapter 23 onwards.

The *Vita nuova* contains only four direct quotations from the Bible. The first biblical verse occurs in chapter 7. To underline his grief over a beautiful lady who was obliged to leave the city and journey to a faraway place (7:1), the protagonist quotes the words of the prophet Jeremiah who says: "O vos omnes qui transitis per viam, attendite et videte si est dolor sicut dolor meus" ("O all you who pass by, attend and see if there be a sorrow like my sorrow"; Lamentations 1:12). The protagonist turns to a solemn biblical verse in Latin to emphasize his pain at losing this lady. He calls upon the words from Lamentations as his authority. In a way the poetry borrows its authority from theology (here too).

We find an example of an allusion to the Bible in the twelfth chapter of the *Vita nuova*. The protagonist falls asleep, and in a dream he sees Love (Amore) in the figure of a young man: "Avvenne quasi nel mezzo de lo mio dormire che me parve vedere ne la mia camera lungo me sedere uno giovane vestito di bianchissime vestimenta" (12:3).[10] The incident is reminiscent of the young man dressed in white sitting in Christ's sepulchre after the Resurrection: "As they entered the tomb, they saw a young man dressed in a white robe sitting on the right side, and they were alarmed" (Mark 16:5) (Musa 1973, 112–113; Shaw 1965, 84). A reasonable interpretation here is that the young man in the *Vita nuova* represents a higher, spiritual aspect of the protagonist's love for the divine Beatrice (Musa 1973, 112; Shaw 1965, 84). I will not go into a longer interpretation of the text here, but wish only to emphasize that Dante, through his allusion to Mark 16:5, wants to accentuate the seriousness of the protagonist's exalted love for Beatrice, symbolized by the young man in white apparel. This love has its source in God.[11]

The deification of Beatrice increases from chapter 19 onwards. The protagonist erupts in a glorification of Beatrice that secured Dante a central position in world literature. This is most explicit in the 'chapters of praise' (19–21; 24; 26; 27; 29).

The praise or glorification in the *Vita nuova* really commences with the groundbreaking canzone "Donne ch'avete intelletto d'amore" ("Ladies who have understanding of love"; ch. 19:4–14). This poem marks the change from Dante's youthful, purely Florentine style to a

---

10   *Vita nuova* 12:3: "It happened that almost in the middle of my sleep I seemed to see sitting alongside me in my room a young man dressed in whitest garments."
11   I give a more detailed reading of *Vita nuova* 12 in Bjornes 2002, pp. 45–52.

new style, the style of praise ("lo stilo de la loda").[12] Dante and other *stilnovisti* intensify or reinforce the poetic glorification or divinization of the Woman. In the *Vita nuova* we may find many descriptions of Beatrice's outer and inner grace and virtuousness. Dante uses analogies, hyperboles and metaphors of light (metaphors in terms of light) to express Beatrice's divinity. She reflects the vision(s) of physical and spiritual beauty.

A number of descriptions may remind us of the hymns in the Book of Psalms (cf. the poems in *Vita nuova*, ch. 19–21 and 26).[13] Klara Myhre (1985) writes that "[...] many psalms have *description* as their form. God's being and works is described in a poetic style" (p. 15). She also points out that "in the main part of the hymn the Lord's works and "qualities" are described with strong and varying words. Active verbs and characterizing adjectives are used as a way of expression" (p. 41). And: "Many psalms are [...] in a direct way testimonies about God. [...] The psalms are born out of a relation of faith, where the whole foundation rests in God" (p. 15).[14] But just as *God* is the Psalmist's source of inspiration, Beatrice – fundamentally an *earthly* woman – is the protagonist's inspiration in the *Vita nuova* and the *Commedia*.

Dante's use of analogies, hyperboles and imagery of light gives a dazzling introduction to divine and ennobling love – personified in Beatrice. Her soul shines with a force that even reaches heaven, which is imperfect without her (19:7). Dante uses metaphors[15] which express Beatrice's divine goodness and her virtue(s) ("virtu"; 19:9) in terms of light (Boyde 1971, 133). This light she has from God Himself, who is light.[16] Beatrice is a reflection and a mediator of God's true light, "that gives light to every man" (John 1:9), and which is a condition for a deeper knowledge of God's being. The light that radiates from Beatrice

---

12 Cervigni and Vasta, in Dante 1995 (*Vita nuova*), p. 15. Harrison (1988) writes: "When the protagonist of the *Divine Comedy* encounters Bonagiunta Orbicciani [...] in Purgatorio XXIV, that rhymester from Lucca recognizes the lyric poet of the *Vita Nuova*. This frequently cited passage [cf. vv. 49–63] stands as Dante's posthumous comment on the poetics that underlies his ideal lyric" (pp. 31–32).
13 See for instance Psalm 8; 19:1–7; 29; 33; 47; 65; 100; 104; 105; 111; 113; 117; 135; 136; 145–50. Cf. Myhre 1985, p. 40.
14 The translation from Myhre 1985 is mine.
15 Metaphors of light, see *Vita nuova* 19:7; 31:10; 33:8; 41:11.
16 God is light: John 1:9; 1 Tim 6:16; James 1:17; 1 John 1:5 etc.

is reflected by the angel who invokes the Lord or entreats within the divine mind ("divino intelletto"; 19:7)(Cf. Ginsberg 1999, 59). In this way Beatrice is, through the divine light she reflects, a representative of God Himself.

Beatrice reflects ideals of the Spiritual Franciscans, such as humility: "Ella coronata e vestita d'umilitade" (26:2); miraculousness: "par che sia una cosa venuta / da cielo in terra a miracol mostrare" (26:6); and poverty: "E sua bieltate è di tanta vertute, / che nulla invidia a l'altre ne procede, / anzi le face andar seco vestute / di gentilezza, d'amore e di fede" (26:11).[17]

It becomes clear that her divinity is of a *universal* character: people who see her are struck by her beauty and divine power. They run to see this shining angel on earth (26:1). Every sweetness and every humble thought is born in the hearts of those who hear her speak (21:3). They who go with her are bound to render thanks to God (26:10). Through her beauty she clothes them in gentleness, love, and affection (26). The one Beatrice finds worthy, experiences her power: "ché li avvien, ciò che li dona, in salute, / e sì l'umilia, ch'ogni offesa oblia. / Ancor l'ha Dio per maggior grazia dato / che non pò mal finir chi l'ha parlato" (19:10).[18]

The other quotation from the Bible is in chapter 23 in the vision of Beatrice's death and ascension. The protagonist hears angels sing in Latin: "Osanna in excelsis" ("Glory in the highest"; 23:7; see also 23:25). I quote from chapter 23:5 and verse 7:

> [...] pareami vedere lo sole oscurare, sì che le stelle si mostravano di colore ch'elle mi faceano giudicare che piangessero; e pareami che li uccelli volando per l'aria cadessero morti, e che fossero grandissimi tremuoti. [...] Io imaginava di guardare verso lo cielo, e pareami vedere moltitudine d'angeli li quali

---

17 *Vita nuova* 26:2: "She, crowned and clothed with humility." *Vn* 26:6: "[Beatrice] seems a thing come down / from heaven to earth to reveal miraculousness." *Vn* 26:11: "And her beauty is of such power / that no envy flows to the others from it; / rather it makes them go with her clothed / in gentleness, love, and devotion." Cf. Mazzaro 1981, pp. 43–44.
18 *Vita nuova* 19:10: "[...] for what she gives him turns into salvation, / and so humbles him that he forgets every offense. / God has given her an even greater grace: / that one cannot end in evil who has spoken to her."

tornassero in suso, ed aveano dinanzi da loro una nebuletta bianchissima. A me parea che questi angeli cantassero gloriosamente, e le parole del loro canto mi parea udire fossero queste: *Osanna in excelsis*; e altro non mi parea udire.[19]

"Osanna in excelsis" is a direct quotation of the crowd's shouts during the triumphal entry of Jesus into Jerusalem (Matt 21:9; Mark 11:10). "Hosianna" is a Hebrew expression meaning "Save!" which became an exclamation of praise (*The Holy Bible* 1984, 754). In the *Commedia* the angels or the souls in glory sing "Hosianna".[20]

The apocalyptic descriptions in *Vita nuova* 23 have clear associations with the death of Christ on the cross – cf. Matthew 27:45 and v. 51: "From the sixth hour until the ninth hour darkness came over all the land. [...] The earth shook and the rocks split" (see also Mark 15:33; Luke 23:44–45). Beatrice's ascension is reminiscent of the ascension of Christ: "[...] he was taken up before their very eyes, and a cloud hid him from their sight. They were looking intently up into the sky as he was going [...]" (Acts 1:9–10). The allusion to the death and ascension of Christ strengthens Beatrice's divine status.

Dante's daring use of the Bible to praise Beatrice is also confirmed in chapter 24 where we may find the third biblical quotation in the *Vita nuova*. In a vision, the protagonist sees a gentle lady coming towards him. Her name is Giovanna, and she was given the name *Primavera* (Springtime) because of her beauty. Behind her he sees the divine Beatrice approaching, and Love seems to speak in the lover's heart:

Quella prima è nominata Primavera solo per questa venuta
d'oggi; ché io mossi lo imponitore del nome a chiamarla così
Primavera, cioè prima verrà lo die che Beatrice si mosterrà dopo
la imaginazione del suo fedele. E se anche vogli considerare lo

---

19 *Vita nuova* 23:5 and v. 7: "[...] and I seemed to see the sun darken, so that the stars appeared of a color that made me think that they wept; and it seemed to me that birds flying through the air fell dead, and that there were tremendous earthquakes. [...] I imagined myself looking toward heaven, and I seemed to see multitudes of angels who were returning upward, and they had before them a small cloud of purest white. It seemed to me that these angels sang gloriously, and the words I seemed to hear of their song were these: *Osanna in excelsis* [Glory in the highest]; and nothing else I seemed to hear."
20 "Hosianna": *Purg.* 11, 11; 29, 51; *Par.* 7, 1; 8, 29; 28, 118; 32, 135.

primo nome suo, tanto è quanto dire 'prima verrà', però che lo suo nome Giovanna è da quello Giovanni lo quale precedette la verace luce, dicendo: 'Ego vox clamantis in deserto: parate viam Domini.'
(24, 4)[21]

The quotation is from the paragraph in the New Testament in which John the Baptist denies being the Christ.[22] The wordplay and the parallel between Giovanna and Giovanni (John) are obvious. Likewise, by virtue of the quotation from the Vulgate, Beatrice is associated with the coming of Christ and His salvation: "Ego vox clamantis in deserto: *parate viam Domini*" – "I am the voice of one calling in the desert, 'Make straight the way for the Lord'" (John 1:23). Just as John the Baptist was a forerunner of Christ and predicted His coming, Giovanna becomes a forerunner of the divine Beatrice. Giovanna is *Primavera*, because she will "come first" (it. "prima verrà"), just as John (Giovanni) came before Christ, "la verace luce" – "The true light" (John 1:9).

The analogies to Christ also reflect – in addition to the true nature of Beatrice – the protagonist's deeper understanding of her true nature. Through her death and ascension she directs the protagonist's mind towards heaven.

In the vision of chapter 23 we received a premonition of Beatrice's death and ascension. In chapter 28 we read about what seems to be a description of Beatrice's actual death. The chapter opens with a quotation from Lamentations 1:1: *Quomodo sedet sola civitas plena populo! facta est quasi vidua domina gentium* ("How deserted lies the city, once so full of people! How like a widow is she, who once was great among the nations!"). The biblical verse – the fourth and last in the *Vita nuova* – seems to reflect a universal grief at Beatrice's demise (Singleton 1983, 23). The whole city, which we can assume is Florence, seemingly bemoans

---

21 *Vita nuova* 24:4: "She who comes first is called *Primavera* uniquely for this, today's coming; for I inspired the bestower of her name to call her *Primavera*, because she will come first [*prima verrà*] on the day that Beatrice will show herself following the imagining of her faithful one. And if you also wish to consider her first name, it is tantamount to saying, 'She will come first,' in that her name Giovanna derives from that John who preceded the true light, saying: 'Ego vox clamantis in deserto: *parate viam Domini*'" ['I am the voice crying in the wilderness: prepare the way of the Lord']".
22 John the Baptist: see Matthew 3:1–15; Mark 1:1–9; Luke 3:1–18; John 1:19–28.

her death. Beatrice has gone to high heaven, to the realm where the angels have peace (31:10). God called her to glory under the sign of the blessed queen, the virgin Mary (28:1; cf. 26:6). For her great worth God placed her in the heaven of the humble, where Mary dwells (34:7). There Beatrice sees Christ's beautiful countenance in eternal glory (40:1; cf. 42:3).

Dante's symbolic use of the number nine is also an important factor to underline her divinity. In chapter 28 and 29 the protagonist makes a spiritual connection between Beatrice and the sacred number. In chapter 29 Dante connects the number nine with the moment Beatrice died. At her conception all nine moving heavens were in the most perfect relationship to one another (29:2). Beatrice is a miracle, just like the number nine. Yes, she is a nine *herself* – analogically and metaphorically. Here Dante relates Beatrice to the wondrous Trinity, the Father, the Son, and the Holy Spirit (29:3).

It is also useful to take a closer look at the last chapter of the *Vita nuova*. After the sonnet in chapter 41 a wonderful vision appears to the protagonist. This vision makes him resolve – for some unknown reason – to write no more of Beatrice until he can treat her more worthily. To achieve this, he applies himself as much as he can, as she truly knows. If it be pleasing to God, he hopes to say of her what was never said of any other woman (42:1–2). He has this wish:

> E poi piaccia a colui che è sire de la cortesia, che la mia anima
> se ne possa gire a vedere la gloria de la sua donna, cioè di
> quella benedetta Beatrice, la quale gloriosamente mira ne la
> faccia di colui *qui est per omnia saecula benedictus*.
> (42:3)[23]

Dante's formulation in Latin (qui est [...]) alludes to the description of God in Romans 1:25, here in English: "the Creator – who is forever praised".[24]

---

23 *Vita nuova* 42:3: "And then may it please Him who is the Lord of courtesy that my soul may go to see the glory of his lady: namely, that blessed Beatrice, who in glory gazes upon the face of Him *qui est per omnia s[a]ecula benedictus* [who is for all ages blessed]."
24 See also Romans 9:5: "[...] who is God over all, forever praised!" And 2 Corinthians 11:31: "The God and Father of the Lord Jesus, who is to be praised forever, [...]"

In terms of a medieval theological context, Dante goes far not only in praising God through an earthly woman, but also in praising this earthly woman herself. Dante's use of the Bible and his religious language in the *Vita nuova* (and the *Comedy*) is a very daring undertaking, but the central aspect – in a theological sense – is that this praise is to a high degree part of a Christological context (see in particular chapters 23 and 24), and therefore it basically points towards Christ the Lord, and not only towards Beatrice herself.[25] This is a possible way of reading Beatrice's role as a figure of Christ in the *Vita nuova* (and the *Comedy*), a way of reading that can be combined with modern methods of interpreting literary texts, where the emphasis is not upon the *Vita nuova* as Dante's religious manifesto of literary conversion, but for instance mostly on Dante's experimentation with the conventions from Provençal troubadour poetry and the *stilnovisti*, his preoccupation with poetics, with metaliterary concerns, with the ontological status of analogy and metaphor, and with the search for a literary idiom adequate for Beatrice (Menocal 1991, 13; Harrison 1988, 10). There is no absolute divide between "theological" and "literary" approaches to the *Vita nuova*. In fact, these approaches point to the need for each other (Ginsberg 1999, 21; Harrison 1988, 4).

Dante's use of the bible in the Divine comedy

Dante's use of the Bible is clearest in the *Divina Commedia*, which first was given the addition 'Divina' (Divine) in a Venetian edition from 1555 (Grønlie 2006, 6). With its didactical aim,[26] the *Comedy* underlines that obedience to God and His Word is the fundamental condition for salvation, something that Purgatorio particularly emphasizes. The Holy Scriptures are also the basis for the theological meaning of Beatrice and her spiritual education of Dante the wanderer.

Dante integrates the biblical text into his own text so that the reader can catch the biblical resonance. Sometimes Dante quotes directly from the Bible or a song from the rich tradition of the Church, but

---

25 I wish to thank Dr.art. Henrik Syse for useful comments on Beatrice in a Christological context.
26 See for instance *Purg.* IX, 70–71; X, 106–11; XV, 130–32; XVII, 103–05, and vv. 127–39; *Par.* V, 76–78.

most often one hears Dante's own voice clearer than the Bible text itself. Often the allusion to the Bible is there, but it is not always easy for modern readers (or students of literature) to catch it or even understand what Dante means by using it. Our knowledge of the Bible and our familiarity of Dante's ways of using it are insufficient. Dante expected that the listeners of his own time would know what he was talking about when he referred to the Bible (Kleinhenz 1997, 75).

Nel mezzo ...

The tradition of biblical hermeneutics contains a very rich typology, allegory and Providential history about God's intervention in this world. This tradition forms the intellectual, literary and theological basis of *the Divine Comedy* (Kleinhenz 1986, 225).[27]

In composing his major work to conform to that special kind of allegory – "the allegory of theologians" – Dante has chosen, in Charles S. Singleton's words, "to imitate God's way of writing." (Singleton 1954, 15; Kleinhenz 1986, 225). Let us for instance take a look at the opening line of the *Comedy*. Dante opens his work by establishing the timeframe for the story: "Nel mezzo del cammin di nostra vita" – "Midway in the journey of our life". Commentators remind the reader that Dante the wanderer sets out on his journey through the afterlife during Holy Week of 1300, when he was thirty-five years old. But as Peter S. Hawkins (1993) remarks, "none of this additional information is necessary for one who remembers that the span of "our life" is already a known quantity" (Hawkins 1993, 121). This is stated in Psalm 89 [90]:10: "dies annorum nostrorum in ipsis septuaginta anni" ("The length of our days is seventy years").[28]

The very first line of the *Commedia*, "Midway in the journey of our life," can also be said to be an echo from King Hezekiah's writing in

---

27 On the same page, Kleinhenz writes: "The rich and complex relationship between Dante and the Bible has been studied by numerous critics over the last century, and even the earliest commentators on the poem were sensitive to those passages which displayed Scriptural origin or influence." Among the earliest commentators are for example Guido da Pisa, Pietro di Dante, and Giovanni Boccaccio. Kleinhenz ibid., p. 235, note 3.
28 See also *Purg.* XIII, 114, where Sapia says "già discendendo l'arco d'i miei anni" ("when I was already descending the arc of my years").

Isaiah 38. After the king's illness and recovery, he says: "In the prime of my life must I go through the gates of death and be robbed of the rest of my years?" I said, "I will not again see the LORD, the LORD, in the land of the living; no longer will I look on mankind, or be with those who now dwell in this world" (Isaiah 38:10–11). This biblical verse is far more than an ordinary allusion to being at the midpoint in one's life (cf. "In the prime of my life"). Rather, this is a scriptural subtext for Dante's larger effort in the *Comedy*. He appropriates the parallel experience of King Hezekiah (as Isaiah describes it) in his own story about his salvation from hell, about his own way to – and through – the *Inferno*. In a way he shares King Hezekiah's own experience because God was with him and saved him: "In your love you kept me from the pit of destruction" (Isaiah 38:17b). Just like Dante, he looks back and writes about his salvation.

Here (and in other places in the *Comedy*) Dante adapts an ancient exegetical tradition in his own text, a tradition concerning what it means to face Hell: "Nel mezzo del cammin di nostra vita."

The opening line of the *Inferno* can be said to be a sign of Dante's use of the Bible in the *Comedy* as a whole: Dante gives us glimpses of the Bible and the vast theological tradition. Most often we will not find direct quotations from the Bible but rather words and expressions, allusions and paraphrases which are coloured by biblical language. These references are included in a metaphorical and/or allegorical context, and they say something important about the direction Dante's journey takes.

The use of certain words and metaphors is influenced by biblical or theological language. For example Virgil's admonition to Dante in Inferno I, 112–17 can give associations to several verses in the Bible: Ond' io per lo tuo me' penso e discerno / che tu mi segui, e io sarò tua guida, / e trarrotti di qui per loco etterno; / ove udirai le disperate strida, / vedrai li antichi spiriti dolenti, / ch'a la seconda morte ciascun grida.[29]

---

29 *Inf.* I, 112–17: "Therefore I think and deem it best that you should follow me, and I will be your guide and lead you hence through an eternal place, where you shall hear the despairing shrieks and see the ancient tormented spirits who all bewail the second death."

The Bible has several verses about the spirit or souls in torment,[30] and "la seconda morte" alludes to the death of the soul on Judgement Day. According to Revelations 21:8, the place of the damned will forever "be in the fiery lake of burning sulfur. This is the second death".

From the Purgatorio I, 1: "miglior acque" ("better waters") indicate Dante's journey towards Mount Purgatory and the hope which is connected to that mountain. Purgatorio I, 24: "la prima gente" ("the first people"), i.e. Adam and Eve.

In Paradiso I, for example, we find two expressions for *heaven*: "del regno santo" ("the holy kingdom;" v. 10), and "in segno lieto" ("a joyful target;" v. 126).

We will find most quotations from the Bible in the middle space of the Purgatorio. There are no less than thirty direct citations and roughly forty allusions. The souls of the Purgatorio have hopes of coming to Paradise, the goal of their journey, but they have not yet reached their eternal destination. They are still under the conditions of time and change. Therefore they need the Word of God for guidance and instruction – just like Dante and others who are living on earth. Therefore the Word of God – which can both save and restore – has such a central position in this realm, and therefore the souls (most of them) hurry up the mountain. Dante and Virgil are no exception (Hawkins 1993, 125).[31]

The souls receive instruction through the Word of God – in Latin or in Italian. Here are both translations and paraphrases from the Bible. The souls sing psalms or prayers[32] of the Church, and they receive instruction through visual pictures, as they see the figures on the bas reliefs and the terrace in Purgatorio X and XII. Important here are also the souls in prayer and the souls who are interceding for people

---

30 See for instance Matthew 8:29: "Have you come here to torture us before the appointed time?" Matthew 25:46: "Then they will go away to eternal punishment." Mark 5:7: "Swear to God that you won't torture me!" Luke 16:23: "In hell, where he was in torment." Revelations 14:11: "And the smoke of their torment rises for ever and ever."
31 Compare *Purg.* II, 46 ("In exitu") with v. 63, and vv. 118–33.
32 References to psalms and liturgy in Latin, see *Purg.* XIII, 10–21 ("Te lucis ante"); 9, 139–41 ("Te Deum laudamus"); 13, 49–51; 25, 121 ("Summae Deus clementiae").

living on earth,[33] allusions to the Christian (hermeneutical) tradition, Classical mythology and literature and church politics.[34] As for politics, some of the characters in the *Comedy* remind us of prophets of the Old Testament in the way they rebuke religious life in Dante's own time. In Paradiso XXVII, for example, St. Peter rebukes his successors and the corruption of the Church, and in the same canto Beatrice laments the greed of mankind, the corruption of man's will, which is not governed on earth. As a conclusion she announces that mankind will change its course (cf. *Par.* XXVII, 148).

In exitu Israël de Aegypto ...

In Purgatorio 2 God's angel brings the souls of the redeemed to the foot of the mountain of Purgatory (II, 28–54). All the souls are singing, and in line 46 we find the poem's first exact quotation from the Vulgate: "*In exitu Israël de Aegypto* / cantavan tutti insieme ad una voce / con quanto di quel salmo è poscia scripto" (II, 46–48).[35] We, the readers, only "hear" one line from Psalm 113 in the Vulgate (Psalm 114 in modern translations of the Bible) but it is as if Dante – once again – expects the reader or listener to know where the reference is in the Bible and how the rest of the psalm goes.

Dante quotes the opening line (incipit) of Psalm 113: "In exitu Israhel de Aegypto" – "When Israel came out of Egypt." The souls are singing a central psalm of redemption; Dante refers to Israel's celebration of the Exodus of Israel from Egypt (cf. Exodus). Psalm 113:1–2: "In exitu Israhel de Aegypto domus Iacob de populo barbaro facta est Iudaea sanctificatio eius Israhel potestas eius." ("When Israel came out of Egypt, the house of Jacob from a people of foreign tongue, Judah became God's sanctuary, Israel his dominion".) From the time of the early fathers, the Exodus of Israel had served Christian exegetes as the

---

33 Intercession and prayer: See Romans 8: 25–27 and v. 34; Philemon 1:22; Hebrews 7:25; Matthew 7:7–8. Examples of prayer and intercession in *Purgatorio*: VI, 26–51; XIII, 124–29, and vv. 142–47; XVI, 49–51; XXII, 142–44; XXIII, 85–90; XXVI, 127–32, and vv. 142–48.
34 See *Purg.* XVIII, 130–38; XX, 73–75, and vv. 87–91.
35 *Purg.* II, 46–48: ""*In exitu Israel de Aegypto*" all of them were singing together with one voice, with the rest of that psalm as it is written."

textbook example of the four interpretive senses of Scripture (Hawkins 1993, 126).

In his allegedly authentic letter to Can Grande della Scala, Dante (1996) comments on these verses. He makes use of Psalm 113 to illustrate the Bible's polysemous or "multiple meanings" approach – the literal, allegorical, moral and anagogical meanings:

> If we look at it from the letter alone it means to us the exit of the Children of Israel from Egypt at the time of Moses; if from allegory, it means for us our redemption done by Christ; if from the moral sense, it means to us the conversion of the soul from the struggle and misery of sin to the status of grace; if from the anagogical, it means the leave taking of the blessed soul from the slavery of this corruption to the freedom of eternal glory.[36]

Psalm 113 best presents the notion of liberation and thus provides the most succinct statement of the movement of the poem as a whole (Kleinhenz 1997, 82). By placing this particular text in the foreground of the Purgatorio, Dante claims the Exodus as a prefigurement of his own journey of conversion and self-discovery, and joins his literary enterprise with the exegetical traditions of the Church (Hawkins 1993, 126). Nothing less.

The beatitudes in the Purgatorio

The purgation in the Purgatorio is fundamental with a view to Dante's use of the Scriptures in the *Comedy*. Here Dante weaves the Beatitudes of the Sermon on the Mount (Matthew 5:3–11) into the process of purgation. He changes the order of seven of the nine Beatitudes so they fit into the structure of the Purgatorio. An angel proclaims the words of Christ at the exit to each terrace, which means that one of the seven deadly sins has been purged away and a corresponding virtue attained. Except for Dante's paraphrase of the fourth Beatitude into Italian in canto XXIV, 151–154, every Beatitude is indicated by one

---

36 Dante 1996. *Epistle to Can Grande*. Translated by James Marchand. http://www.english.udel.edu/dean/cangrand.html.

or more words in Latin. For example, Dante tells about the angel who sings in canto XXVII, 7–9: "Fuor de la fiamma stava in su la riva, / e cantava "*Beati mundo corde*!" / in voce assai più che la nostra viva."[37] The Vulgate says: "beato mundo corde quoniam ipsi Deum videbunt" – "Blessed are the pure in heart, for they will see God" (Matthew 5:8). The sixth Beatitude is especially appropriate for the souls here, who have purged themselves of all lustful inclinations. Soon they are to enjoy heavenly beatitude in the vision of God in Paradise.[38]

In my work on the way Dante uses biblical texts as an integral part of his own text, I have found Christopher Kleinhenz's (1986) research very valuable. Kleinhenz identifies six basic types of biblical "citation" or reference in the *Commedia*. They are: 1) exact citation of the Latin text; 2) slightly modified citation of the Latin text; 3) incomplete citation of the Latin text. The fourth, fifth, and sixth categories are the same as these except that they comprise those citations in an Italian translation or paraphrase.

One of many examples of direct citation of the Latin text is the verse from Matthew – "Venite benedicti Patris mei" ("Come, you who are blessed by my Father;" Matthew 25:34). Here Christ speaks of the just souls on Judgement Day. Dante incorporates these exact words in Purgatorio XXVII, 58–60: "*Venite, benedicti Patris mei,*" / sonò dentro a un lume che lì era, / tal che mi vinse e guardar nol potei."[39] By these words the angel leads Dante, Virgil and Statius after they are out of the fire that purges the lustful. Soon they ascend to the earthly paradise at the top of the mountain, where they can see the triumphal procession of the Church (*Purg*. XXIX).

In canto 30, 19 we find an example of a slightly modified citation of the Latin text. Those who are part of the triumphal procession declare the advent of Beatrice with the words "Benedictus qui venit" – "Blessed

---

37 *Purg*. XXVII, 7–9: "He stood outside the flames on the bank and sang "*Beati mundo corde*" in a voice far more living than ours."
38 Singleton, in Dante 1973, Vol. 2 (*Purgatorio*), p. 650.
39 *Purg*. XXVII, 58–60: "*Venite, benedicti Patris mei;*" sounded from within a light that was there, such that it overcame me and I could not look on it." See also *Purg*. IX, 81, where Dante is dazzled by the sight of the guardian angel who sits on the threshold of the gate of Purgatory: "[...] tal ne la faccia ch'io non lo soffersi" ("[...] in his face he was such that I endured it not"). Cf. the Son of Man in Revelations 1:16: "His face was like the sun shining in all its brilliance."

is he who comes". Here Dante makes a connection between the advent of Beatrice and that of Christ, i.e. the triumphal entry of Christ into Jerusalem.[40] By writing *venis* for *venit*, Dante makes the phrase more direct and personal. Even more important is that he stresses the central analogy between Christ and Beatrice by retaining the masculine inflection of *benedictus*. In this way he places Beatrice in a Christological context. The analogy between Christ and Beatrice is, according to the beliefs of many scholars, central in this part of the Purgatorio, and the analogy lies at the heart of Dante's concept of Beatrice throughout the entire *Comedy* (Kleinhenz 1986, 226).

In the *Comedy* there are far more quotations from the Bible in Italian than in Latin. As previously mentioned, Kleinhenz's fourth, fifth, and sixth categories are either an Italian translation or paraphrase.[41]

The triumphal procession of the church

In Purgatorio XXIX we meet the mystical procession of allegorical figures. The procession takes place prior to the advent of Beatrice in Purgatorio XXX.

Dante sees a file of "ventiquattro seniori, a due a due" – "four and twenty elders, two by two" (XXIX, 83). Most commentators claim that the elders stand for the books of the Hebrew Scriptures (Ulleland, in Dante 2000, 404; Hawkins 1993, 129). The verse is a clear allusion to Revelations 4:4: "Surrounding the throne were twenty-four other thrones, and seated on them were twenty-four elders. They were dressed in white and had crowns of gold on their heads." In his prologue to the Vulgate, St. Jerome compares the twenty-four elders with the twenty-four books of the Old Testament.[42]

---

40 Matthew 21:9. See also Mark 11:9; Luke 19:38, and John 12:13.
41 For Kleinhenz's fourth category, compare *Purg.* XV, 89–92 with Luke 2:48. For the fifth category, compare *Purg.* XI, 1–24 with Matthew 6:9–13. For the sixth and last category, compare *Purg.* XXII, 142–154 with John 2:1–5; Daniel 1:1–21, and Matthew 3:1–6; 11:11.
42 In reality there are thirty-nine books in the Old Testament, but according to the enumeration of St. Jerome in his prologue to the Vulgate, the exact number is twenty-four. For this and the next paragraph, see Singleton, in Dante 1973 (Vol. 2: *Purgatorio*), p. 711. See also Ulleland, in Dante 2000, p. 404.

In canto XXIX, 85–87 the men sing: "*Benedicta* tue / ne le figlie d'Adamo, e benedette / sieno in etterno le bellezze tue!"[43] This greeting is reminiscent of the angel Gabriel's greeting to Mary in Luke 1:28: "Greetings, you who are highly favored! The Lord is with you." The Vulgate: "Et ingressus angelus ad eam dixit: Ave, gratia plena, Dominus tecum, benedicta tu in mulieribus." ("The angel went to her and said, "Greetings, you who are highly favored! The Lord is with you."") See also Elizabeth's greeting to Mary in Luke 1:42: "Benedicta tu inter mulieres." ("Blessed are you among women".) Dante has, not inappropriately, changed "in mulieribus" ("among women") to "ne le figlie d'Adamo" ("among the daughters of Adam"). This is now the Garden of Eden, where Adam was first placed.[44] There is some disagreement among scholars whether the men greet Beatrice or Mary, but most likely they salute Mary here.

Behind the elders come four living creatures (v. 92) which probably symbolize the four Gospels. In this connection Dante (in vv. 100 and 105) refers directly to Ezekiel 10:4–14 and Revelations 4:6–8.[45]

In the fourteenth and fifteenth centuries, the four animals were identified as the great doctors of the Church: Augustine, Jerome, Ambrose and Gregory the Great (Hawkins 1993, 129).

A griffin pulls a triumphal chariot on two wheels (XXIX, 107). The griffin is a fabulous animal, half-eagle and half-lion. The most usual interpretation is that the griffin symbolizes Christ, that the triumphal chariot symbolizes the Church, and that the two wheels stand for the two classes of clergy: cloistered monks and secular priests (Ulleland, in Dante 2000, 405).

Three ladies come dancing in a round at the right wheel (vv. 121–129). With their colours – white, green and red – the women symbolize the three theological virtues of faith, hope and love (1 Cor. 13:13).

---

43 *Purg.* XXIX, 85–87: "Blessed art thou among the daughters of Adam, and blessed forever be thy beauties."
44 Singleton, in Dante 1973 (Vol. 2: *Purgatorio*), p. 713.
45 Ezekiel 1:10: "Their faces looked like this: Each of the four had the face of a man, and on the right side each had the face of a lion, and on the left the face of an ox; each also had the face of an eagle." Revelations 4:7: "The first living creature was like a lion, the second was like an ox, the third had a face like a man, the fourth was like a flying eagle."

Beside the left wheel we read about four other women (vv. 130–132). These are dressed in purple and represent the four moral or cardinal virtues: Prudence, Temperance, Justice and Fortitude.

Behind the whole group Dante sees two old men. They are differently dressed, but similar in bearing, venerable and grave (vv. 133–135). The first one is probably Luke, for he is wearing the robes of a physician (cf. Col. 4:14, where Luke is described as "the doctor"). Here Luke represents Acts, of which he is the author. The other man frightens Dante with his sharp and shining sword (v. 140; cf. Isa. 49:2; Heb. 4:12; Eph. 6:17). This is probably St. Paul, who represents his various Epistles.

Then Dante sees four men of lowly appearance. Many commentators claim that they stand for the minor canonical Epistles of James, Peter, John and Jude.

Behind them all we see an old man coming alone, "dormendo, con la faccia arguta" – "asleep, with keen visage" (v. 144). This is the visionary John, who symbolizes The Book of Revelations, the last book of the Bible. In the fourteenth and fifteenth centuries commentators believed that this man could be interpreted either as Moses or Bernard of Clairvaux (Hawkins 1993, 129).

It seems that the exalted creatures are aflame above their eyebrows (vv. 149–150), and they stop short straight opposite Dante (v. 154).

The hundred ministers and messengers of life eternal who rise upon the divine chariot (XXX, 17) must be angels (XXX, 82), but they are compared with the blessed who will rise ready at the last trumpet, each from his tomb, to gather at the right hand of Christ.

Exalted as she is, Beatrice speaks to the frightened Dante in *pluralis maiestatis*: "Guardaci ben! Ben son, ben son Beatrice. / Come degnasti d'accedere al monte? / non sapei tu che qui è l'uom felice?" (*Purg.* XXX, 73–75).[46] The angels are praying to God for Dante (see also vv. 94–95), but they are also, indirectly, praying for Beatrice's mercy when they now sing the first part of the thirtieth psalm (Ps. 30:2–9 [31:1–8]).

---

46 *Purg.* XXX, 73–75: "Look at me well: indeed I am, indeed I am Beatrice! How did you deign to climb the mountain? Did you not know that here man is happy?"

Purgatorio XXX, 82–84: "Ella si tacque; e li angeli cantaro / di sùbito "*In te, Domine, speravi*"; / ma oltre "*pedes meos*" non passaro."[47]

Later Beatrice upbraids Dante (XXX, 76–31, 63). He finally confesses his guilt and is refreshed in the holy water of the River Eunoë. Beatrice leads him on the rest of the way in Purgatory and through Paradise (to canto 31).

The procession in Purgatorio XXIX is the most striking example of Dante's allegorization of the Scriptures in the *Comedy*. Here he does more than remind us just of the importance of the Scriptures and the biblical tradition. He conjures up a *vision* of the Bible itself – from Genesis to the end of the Apocalypse. Like Dante, we too become spectators of a theological masque, the procession of the holy texts (Hawkins 1999, 58–59). Like him, we must follow Mathelda's exhortation (XXIX, 61–63) to look towards the Scriptures and what they represent.

Paradise

Inferno is the part of the *Comedy* which contains fewest quotations from the Bible. This is hardly a surprise. As for the Paradiso, this part of the *Comedy* contains far more allusions to the Bible than quotations. Since the souls here have reached their heavenly goal, they do not need God's Word as admonition, education and guidance anymore, unlike the souls in Purgatory and people living on earth. The blessed have become so completely one with God's Word that they assimilate it in their own speech. They have passed beyond the mediation of the Scriptures and into the reality they signify. Now they are so near God that they are "ingodded" in heaven's glory (Hawkins 1993, 125).[48]

Here are some examples of how Dante uses the Scriptures in Paradiso. In Paradiso III, 121–22 Dante writes: "[…] "*Ave, / Maria*" cantando, e cantando vanio."[49] "Ave Maria" is Latin and means "Greetings,

---

47 *Purg.* XXX, 82–84: "She was silent; and the angels all of a sudden sang: "*In te, Domine, speravi*," ["In you, O LORD, I have taken refuge"] but beyond "*pedes meos*" ["my feet"] they did not pass." Cf. Singleton, in Dante 1973 (Vol. 2: *Purgatorio*), p. 746.
48 Hawkins writes: "The blessed [are] … "ingodded" (to recall the neologism "indiarsi" which Dante invents in Paradiso IV, 28 to describe the state of beatitude)" (p. 125).
49 *Par*. III, 121–22: "*Ave Maria*, and, singing, vanished."

Mary" and The Angel Gabriel uses these words to open his speech to the Virgin Mary in Luke 1:28 (cf. the Vulgate).

In Paradiso XXIV Peter examines Dante about faith. On the question of what faith is, a part of Dante's answer is "fede è sustanza di cose sperate / e argomento de le non parventi" (XXIV, 64–65).[50] Here Dante is translating Hebrews 11:1: "Now faith is being sure of what we hope for and certain of what we do not see." Dante answers by quoting God's Word:

[...] E io: "La larga ploia
de lo Spirito Santo, ch'è diffusa
in su le vecchie e 'n su le nuove cuoia,
è silogismo che la m'ha conchiusa
acutamente sì, che 'nverso d'ella
ogne dimostrazion mi pare ottusa."
(XXIV, 91–96)[51]

The old and the new "parchments" ("cuoia") are respectively the Old and the New Testament.

In Paradiso XXVI, 67–69, in a paragraph in which John asks Dante what the final goal of his love is, we find an allusion to two verses in the Bible: "Sì com' io tacqui, un dolcissimo canto / risonò per lo cielo, e la mia donna / dicea con li altri: "Santo, santo, santo!""[52] In Isaiah 6:3 we read about the seraphim who call to one another: "Holy, holy, holy is the LORD Almighty; the whole earth is full of his glory." In Revelations, the four living creatures never stop saying: "Holy, holy, holy is the Lord God Almighty, who was, and is, and is to come" (Rev. 4:8). In this way Dante connects the Old and New Testament.

As mentioned above, the souls in Paradise have reached their heavenly goal, and they have become so completely one with God's Word

---

50 *Par.* XXIV, 64–65: "Faith is the substance of things hoped for and the evidence of things not seen."
51 *Par.* XXIV, 91–96: "The plenteous rain of the Holy Spirit which is poured over the old and over the new parchments is a syllogism that has proved it to me so acutely that, in comparison with this, every demonstration seems obtuse to me."
52 *Par.* XXVI, 67–69: "As soon as I was silent a most sweet song resounded through the heaven, and my lady sang with the rest, "Holy, Holy, Holy!""

as to assimilate it in their own speech. In this context Dante most often provides short references to persons or events in the Bible. Here are some examples: In Paradiso XXV, 91–93 Dante refers to the prophet Isaiah: "Dice Isaia che ciascuna vestita / ne la sua terra fia di doppia vesta: / e la sua terra è questa dolce vita; …"[53] In Isaiah 61:7 we read about the Year of the Lord's Favour: "they [God's people] will rejoice in their inheritance; and so they will inherit a double portion in their land, and everlasting joy will be theirs." Other allusions are for example the reference to the six wings of the seraphim in Isaiah 6:2; cf. Paradiso IX, 77–78. In Paradiso IX, 116 Dante mentions Rahab, a prostitute who helped Joshua's spies (Joshua 2:1–24 and 6:17–25); Paradiso X, 107–108 alludes to the poor widow's offering (Mark 12:41–44; Luke 21:1–4). Another example is the reference to David and the Ark in Paradiso XX, 38–39 (cf. 2 Sam. 6:1–17); Paradiso XXIV, 1–3 alludes to the great wedding supper of the blessed Lamb (Rev. 19:9); Paradiso XXVIII, 136–139 echoes Paul's great revelations in 2 Cor. 12:1–4), and Paradiso XXXII, 68–69 refers to the story of Esau and Jacob in Gen. 25:22f.

Closing remarks

As we have seen, Dante builds references to the Bible into the *Comedy* and the *Vita nuova* in several ways. Through Dante's quotation technique, the poetic-theological language in (all of) his works is a bearer of both biblical truths and profane *fictio*. Theologically, there is a great challenge in his use of the Bible and biblically coloured language, especially when seen in light of medieval terminology and thinking. Yet at the same time his works have had and continue to have a mind-opening and didactic function in that they reflect the sacred texts of the Bible. As we have seen, this is particularly noticeable in the *Commedia*, "'l poema sacro / al quale ha posto mano e cielo e terra" (*Par.* XXV, 1–2).[54]

---

53 *Par.* XXV, 91–93: "Isaiah says that each one shall be clothed in his own land with a double garment, and his own land is this sweet life; […]"
54 *Par.* XXV, 1–2: "[…] the sacred poem to which heaven and earth have so set hand."

The domestication of vernacular poetry. Measuring authority in the De vulgari eloquentia

Espen Grønlie

Scholars have tended to treat the *De vulgari eloquentia* either as a work concerned with supposedly transcendent issues such as poetic form and ideal language, or as one primarily related to the historical situation in which it was written, to Dante's historical project or his exile.[1] How are these theoretical and socio-political aspects to be linked? Some recent investigations have tried to read the unfinished treatise in light of the medieval notions of authorship and authority, as theorized for example by Erich Auerbach and A J Minnis. In Auerbach's study of the literary institution and the changing relations between author and public throughout history, Dante is said to have introduced a social aspect into a literary practice which until then had been considered a solitary activity. More recently, Minnis has placed Dante at the midpoint between the "impersonal" author function of the Middle

---

1   Drawing a slightly different distinction, Joseph Luzzi refers to Francesco D'Ovidio and Pio Rajna as philologically orientated scholars concerned with poetics, and to Bruno Nardi and Antonio Pagliaro as scholars who reject seeing Dante's ideal language, the "vulgare illustre," simply as a poetic language, instead claiming that it reflects historical and socio-political aspects of language (Luzzi, "Literary History and Individuality in the De vulgari eloquentia," *Dante Studies* 1998, pp. 161–88). Like Luzzi, I would refer to Albert Russell Ascoli's extensive bibliography in his "'Neminem ante nos': Historicity and Authority in the De vulgari eloquentia," in *Annali d'Italianistica* VIII (1990), pp. 186–231, and to Pier Vincenzo Mengaldo's *Linguistica e retorica di Dante* (Pisa: Nistri–Lischi, 1978). When Luzzi subsequently speaks of a mediating, "dialogical approach," he links it to Ascoli and Mengaldo, as well as to Gustavo Vinay.

Ages and the modern one invested with "personality."² What these approaches have in common is their interpretation of the *De vulgari eloquentia* as an important work in Dante's career, representing an investment in his future poetic authority. Notable among the recent authority-centred interpreters of the *De vulgari eloquentia* is Albert Russell Ascoli.³ Ascoli centres his attention on the last four chapters

---

2 Erich Auerbach: *Literary Language & its Public in Late Latin Antiquity and in the Middle Ages*, tr. Ralph Manheim (Princeton: Princeton University Press, 1993). A. J. Minnis: *Medieval Theory of Authorship. Scholastic Literary Attitudes in the Later Middle Ages* (London: Scolar Press, 1984). Cf. also *The Cambridge History of Literary Criticism. Volume 2: The Middle Ages*, ed. A. J. Minnis and Ian Johnson (Cambridge: Cambridge University Press, 2005). Both Luzzi and Ascoli cite Auerbach and Minnis as important to their own work.

3 The bulk of this article was written before the publication of Ascoli's *Dante and the Making of a Modern Author* (2008), and originally referred to the individual articles published by Ascoli, of which revised versions are now included in this thorough and very convincing study. Since Ascoli has made quite a lot of stylistic revisions of his phrasing, I have chosen to refer to the book rather than the articles when actually quoting him. Generally, there is reason to indicate that if some of the individual articles published by Ascoli may have seemed "rhetorical" in a somewhat formalistic manner, his book as a whole is far more historically orientated, and it will no doubt count as the standard work on the role of *auctoritas* in Dante for a long time. Moreover, the introduction sees Ascoli expanding in important ways on the very concept of authority, partly by referring to a broadly conceived notion of "cultural capital," partly by drawing on the theories of Hannah Arendt, Roland Barthes and Michel Foucault. According to Ascoli, Dante gained his cultural capital by consciously negotiating between Latin and vernacular language, and by making seemingly different sorts of investments in the notion of authority at different stages of his work, for example in the obvious instance of his referring to two different etymologies of *auctoritas* (from *autentin*, "worthy of faith and obedience," as well as from *avieo*, "bind [tie] words together"). In his book, Ascoli claims that Dante transforms the medieval notion of authorship by placing the existing words designating authorship under the umbrella of the single Italian word *autore*, thereby giving birth to "Barthes' dead, modern, author" (Ascoli 2008, 226). These observations made by Ascoli represent an important perspective on *auctoritas* in Dante, and they provide a relevant framework for the claims I make in this article. As will become clear, however, my investigation is somewhat less concerned with the notion of the individual author than Ascoli's; what I hope to do is supplement his study by showing that the *De vulgari eloquentia* relates not only to the *auctoritas* so central to medieval thought, but that the work is fundamentally – if to some degree implicitly – governed by the hierarchical structures of Scholasticism, and more specifically to the relation between form and matter, as well as to the politically loaded notions of measuring and weighing, which tie the philosophical system to the world of Florentine politics. It is worth noting that, in Ascoli's view, Dante deploys an "elaborate metaphorics of coinage [...] throughout [the *Divina Commedia*]" (*Op.cit.*, p. 10), even if Ascoli does not elaborate on how such a metaphorics may have affected Dante's views on poetry.

of Book I, thereby continuing the investigation suggested by Gustavo Vinay who saw those chapters as important to be able to realize the way in which Dante inscribed his linguistic-poetic ideals into the realm of contemporary Italian politics.[4] The following investigation will focus on the same passages and draw on Ascoli's analyses, but will read them as having a greater significance than Ascoli seems to have acknowledged, both when it comes to understanding Dante's treatise as a deeply formal theory, and to stressing the historical importance of Dante's concept of domesticating vernacular poetry by stating that it needs to governed by "rules", or *regula*.

I shall attempt to show that the *De vulgari eloquentia* is a deeply scholastic work. Such a reading questions the legitimacy of a simple authority-centred approach, and represents what I would claim to be a more coherent view of the work. I shall suggest that the agenda of the work is not only to situate the poets of Dante's generation in an authoritative position, but to do so in a way heavily influenced by philosophical conceptualization: the poets of Dante's generation become representatives of a new and *rational* way of composing poetry in the vernacular. I shall indicate that Dante makes a conscious attempt to develop the tradition of vernacular lyric poetry by showing how authority is to be *measured* rationally, thereby "housing" vernacular poetry in its proper political home. In my view, this idea of finding a way to measure authority is an integrated part of the conceptual framework of the *De vulgari eloquentia*, and central to understanding the link the work tries to establish between political power and linguistic form. This would suggest that the recent authorship/authority-centred interpretations of the *De vulgari eloquentia* may need revising – perhaps even a revision advocated by the work itself.

From poetics to poetological theory

Dante's entire body of work is somehow concerned with poetics. Chapter xxv of the *Vita nuova* discusses the notion of allegory and

---

[4] Pier Vincenzo Mengaldo gives credit to Gustavo Vinay for having demonstrated the importance of these four chapters, and for having shown that the "vulgare illustre" cannot be based solely on literary criteria, but on criteria that are "fondementalmente sociali e politici" (Mengaldo 1978, 84–85).

sketches out a literary history in which Dante obviously wishes to situate the poets of his generation. In this work, Dante's focus seems to be both one of stressing the amount of thought that has been put into each individual poem, and assigning a role for himself and his contemporaries in the poetic tradition at large. It is clearly important to him that vernacular poets need not only be referred to as "trovatori" (*Vita nuova* iii, 9), but should actually be compared to the Roman poets (xxv, 4). In the *De vulgari eloquentia* this point is stressed once again (II, iv, 2), but now the claims on behalf of vernacular poetry are both broader and at certain points rather different. Whereas the *Vita nuova* is fairly general in its references to the poetic craft, the *De vulgari eloquentia* is immensely technical – and this is probably the main reason why scholars have had such problems establishing any link whatsoever between the "transcendent" and the socio-historical aspects of the work.

One way of approaching this "formalist problem" posed by the *De vulgari eloquentia* is to read it in connection with the *Convivio*, written at approximately the same time. This, however, confronts us with a much-debated paradox: the *De vulgari eloquentia* is, in Steven Botterill's words, "The Declaration of Independence of the Modern Languages,"[5] yet written in Latin; the *Convivio* states the superior, eternal stability of Latin, even though it is itself written in Italian. Albert Russell Ascoli recognizes this chiasmic structure, then goes on to explain that it is precisely the differing elements of the two works which suggest that they are a part of Dante's rhetorical-strategic moves to gain authority as a poet.[6] Centring one's interpretation on Dante's build-up of poetic authority may to some extent weaken the strict barriers between his seemingly different statements in the two works, thereby providing a response to those who have seen a massive contradiction between the views on language expressed in them. Nevertheless, one might wonder whether such a newly found rhetorical flexibility would not simply maintain an essentially *thematic* interpretation of Dante's prose texts and thus disregard the option that a historical perspective on genre might explain the differences between them.

---

5 See Botterill's introduction to his edition of the *De vulgari eloquentia* (1996), p. viii.
6 See Albert Russel Ascoli, "The unfinished author – Dante's rhetoric of authority in *Convivio* and *De Vulgari Eloquentia*," (1993), pp. 45–66.

The domestication of vernacular poetry

The two works are rather different thematically: while the *De vulgari eloquentia* is concerned with poetic form, the *Convivio* offers a more general philosophical background for the moral content of Dante's mature *canzoni* – something that may seem liberating to the interpreter who expects Dante to explain in didactic prose what he actually thinks he is doing in verse. The question remains, however, whether we are right to compare the *De vulgari eloquentia* to the *Convivio* in the first place – whether we by doing so might not be too drastically limiting ourselves to a thematic reading that risks ignoring that the Latin text would have been met historically with very specific expectations, simply because of its status as a scholastic treatise written in "the eternal language." In short, it is striking that authority-centred interpreters such as Ascoli do not dwell more on the need to pose what one might call Skinnerian questions to the text they are reading, ones such as: what genre does this text belong to? what kind of discourse does it inscribe itself into? and: what questions can we reasonably assume that it was meant to answer?

There is reason to stress that Dante, insofar as he is concerned with political issues, is clearly entering into a discussion with other theoreticians at the time (whether of a "rhetorical" or "Scholastic" leaning, in Skinner's terms), among others Brunetto Latini and Remigio de' Girolami. The existence of such an "intellectual context" is perhaps more obvious when it comes to the *De monarchia* than the *De vulgari eloquentia*. But if – as I assume – the *De vulgari eloquentia* contains the first sketches of the very ideas Dante was later to develop at greater length in the *De monarchia*, this ought to make the question of intellectual context relevant even when it comes to the *De vulgari eloquentia*. This means that we ought to be careful when asking what characterizes Dante's view of "the State," for example, since this is obviously a point on which he deviates only marginally from his contemporaries – and perhaps we instead should ask in what way his *de facto* role as a poet could be relevant to his perspective. One could, for instance, imagine that being a practising poet influenced Dante's way of approaching the whole idea of *theory*.

The fact that the *De vulgari eloquentia* is composed in the manner of a scholastic treatise has seldom been given any substantial weight in the interpretations of the work, probably because it is taken for granted that scholastic Latin would be the "normal style" of Latin texts at this historical stage. But if we stop for a moment to ask ourselves what such a scholastic disposition is normally taken to mean when we read medieval texts, it would be hard to claim that we think of it as being simply a *stylistic device*. Rather we would say that it is linked to some very important philosophical concepts and distinctions. I would suggest that the so-called Aristotelian distinction between form and matter, which is all-important to medieval philosophy, also in fact contains the key to Dante's views on the role of poetry as they are expressed in the *De vulgari eloquentia*.[7]

Dante's use of the word *forma* in *De vulgari eloquentia* is limited (II, vi, 2–5; I, xii, 4; II, v, 7), but what is implied when talking about the form/matter distinction in a medieval context can obviously not be reduced to the use of those actual words. One is in fact talking about a worldview modelled on the medieval understanding of Aristotle's *Physics* and *Metaphysics*. If there is such a thing as "the medieval world picture," that picture would imply that *everything* can – and ought to – be understood via those two concepts.

In writing about the different types of metric verse the vernacular poet may choose to use, Dante states:

> [L]ines with an even number of syllables are only rarely used today because of their lack of sophistication; for they retain the

---

7 One could of course question whether the *De vulgari eloquentia* really is that scholastic compared to the other prose texts Dante wrote. I would nevertheless claim that it, as well as the *De monarchia* and the *Questio de aqua et terra*, stands out as scholastic in its entire disposition (although one could get the feeling that Dante "masters" such a disposition somewhat better in those other two texts, written at a later stage than the *De vulgari eloquentia*). Stressing the scholastic nature of these texts does not mean that there is no clear influence of scholastic thought in for example the *Convivio* – scholastic thought was the very road to truth, and a "trattato" like the *Convivio* is of course also dependent on this sort of reasoning. This does not undermine the uncontroversial assertion that for Dante, as well as for others at the time, Latin was *the* theoretical language. When it comes to Dante's letters, they are of course also influenced by the author's knowledge of scholastic Latin, more or less like any other medieval text in Latin – yet they are obviously not treatises. Even more obvious is the case of the *Vita nuova*, which of course could be read as developing arguments in a way which is influenced by scholasticism, and may be said to have a structure somewhat analogous to a scholastic treatise – but that in no way portrays itself as actually *being* such a treatise.

nature of the numbers that govern them, which are inferior to odd numbers as material is to form.

Parisillabis vero propter sui ruditatem non utimur nisi raro: retinent enim naturam suorum numerorum, qui numeris imparibus quemadmodum materia forme subsistunt.
(II, v, 7)[8]

Dante's way of speaking of form as inferior to matter is a commonplace in medieval scholasticism. These fundamental metaphysical categories are made into a laden dichotomy, in which it would probably be illuminating to speak of only one *principle*, "the ordained," that which introduces order into the disorderly, and on the other hand of this disorderly *something*, being the flux of the world, the fundamentally worldly matter that one would not be able to know in any systematic way unless it had a form.

As a function of this quasi-implicit logic, a *formal* focus becomes the *sine qua non* of any theoretical discipline, and since the *De vulgari eloquentia* is obviously a scholastic treatise, it should be read as belonging to a theoretical discipline. The *De vulgari eloquentia* is indeed a *poetological treatise*, a "theory of poetry" – perhaps more so than simply a *poetics*. Dante is, I believe, trying to explain what poetry *is*, and what role it assumes in relation to reason, justice, power and language in general. It would in fact be hard to understand the role of the second – and unfinished – book if one did not postulate such an issue (the role of poetry in general) for the first book.[9] The question of how

---

[8] I quote Dante's Latin text from the edition of Pier Vincenzo Mengaldo in *Opere minori*, vol. II (Milano–Napoli: Riccardo Ricciardi 1979), and the English translation by Steven Botterill, *De vulgari eloquentia* (Cambridge: Cambridge University Press, 1996).

[9] Ascoli responds to this dilemma by arguing against the need to find a logical continuity from the first book to the second, and in a polemical flash he blames such conflicts on the idea that there is any unity to Dante's thought. Ascoli claims that, until recently, only Pier Vincenzo Mengaldo had argued that the *De vulgari eloquentia* is "shot through with 'contraddizioni teoriche' [...] which are not susceptible to logical conciliation" (Ascoli 2008, 139). One can of course question the ambition of finding any reading that "fuses" different parts into a whole. But such "fusing" should not be condemned *a priori*. A *zooming out* which tries to find a more general perspective may at certain times be useful in order to take a fresh look at a text that is constantly infused

Dante could possibly have conceived of the *De vulgari eloquentia* as having *any unifying subject whatsoever,* cannot be satisfactory solved unless one has established a *framework* for all his – more or less dry – formal observations in Book II.[10] I believe that all the "theorizing" taking place in the *De vulgari eloquentia* is in fact a way of inscribing poetry into a specific historical situation. What happens if we try to see Dante's understanding of this situation as determined by his specific views of the nature of poetry?

Domesticating vernacular poetry

What is poetry, according to Dante? In the instance where he most clearly seeks to define it, it is "a verbal invention composed according to the rules of rhetoric and music" (*fictio rhetorica musicaque poita*; II, iv, 2). This definition is often mentioned and commented upon, and it is rightly considered important to understand the *De vulgari*

---

with new meanings as new winds blow into the ever-open windows of semiotics, rhetoric and literary theory. This clearly does not refute the value of studying minute parts and isolated aspects of such works. On the contrary: all the different interpretations of the different parts make the task of general interpretation all the more demanding, and thus more interesting.

10 Although what we may wish to term "dry formality" is of course a complex set of criteria, many of which have interesting normative tendencies, such as Dante's preference for the eleven-syllable line (the most extensive one that exists, he tells us), his preference for the canzone form (once again the most extensive of all the available vernacular lyric forms he is familiar with), and his analysis of himself as a poet who in his poetry – in contrast to poets writing about "prowess in arms" and "ardour in love" – primarily elaborates on the subject matter he refers to as "control of one's will" (*directio voluntatis*; II.ii.7). A meticulous study of the most formal and technical aspects of the *canzone* craft and the sources of Dante's ideas within it is Mario Pazzaglia's *Il verso e l'arte della canzone nel* De vulgari eloquentia (Firenze: Pubblicazioni della Facolta di magistero dell Universita degli studi di Bologna, 1967). In Marianne Shapiro's *Dante's Book of Exile: The* De vulgari eloquentia (Lincoln: University of Nebraska Press, 1990), the observations are in many instances taken from Pazzaglia's study, and represent praiseworthy attempts at untangling the complex specificities of Dante's normative poetics. The *De vulgari eloquentia* was written at approximately the time of Dante's last great moral canzoni, such as "Amor, che muovi tua virtù dal cielo" and "Doglia mi reca ne lo core ardire", placing the treatise in a very interesting relation to Dante's post-exilic phase. But I shall have to leave all this to one side and just hint at the stylistic poetic position Dante is trying to stake out for himself in his formal ideals in the *De vulgari eloquentia*.

The domestication of vernacular poetry

eloquentia as a whole. It implies that the very formal nature of poetics as a theoretical discipline rests on two pillars: *rhetorica* and *musica* – once again linking Dante's treatise to the general world of scholastic reasoning. As Giuseppe Mazzotta has made clear, Dante's definition of poetry is not best seen as a claim that poetry should be considered a sub-discipline of rhetoric in any restricted sense, but rather that it is an art that is capable of *uniting* the rhetorical-linguistic arts of *trivium* and the numerical-musical arts of *quadrivium* (Mazzotta 1993a, 19–22). This fusion of the mathematical discipline of music with the rhetorical disciplines represents in my view one of the clear instances that fuses the linguistics and the poetics of the treatise: Book I indicates a general view of language, and Book II lays out rules for formalizing language.

The description of the disorderly state of vernacular language occupies much of Book I of the *De vulgari eloquentia*. Chapters iii to xv trace the disordering of spoken language from the building of The Tower of Babel to Dante's contemporary Italy, where language is divided into different dialects – 19 in total, according to Dante. The spoken language experiences an ever-continuing disordering. A way of resisting this process at a given stage in history is the *invention* of *gramatica* – Dante in fact refers to the origin of this orderly language in such a manner, i.e. as if it were a craft, or in the same way that one in Antiquity spoke of "the invention of rhetoric."

The primary characteristic of *gramatica* as Dante conceives of it is that it *does not change* (I, ix, 11) – the grammatical perhaps "simply denoting any systematic body of rules," as Marianne Shapiro puts it (Shapiro 1990, 145).[11] *Gramatica* in the *De vulgari eloquentia* ought to be seen as *language in its purest form*, i.e. language matter made

---

11 Shapiro makes some interesting observations in her study, particularly concerning the relation between Books I and II, and she argues in a way rather similar to the one suggested here. For example, her study clearly shows how Dante's work rests on the central canon of the scholastic tradition: "The laws of proportion and analogy Dante outlines in Book 2 repose solidly on a principle of universal harmony, derived proximately from the *De institutione musicae* of Boethius as well as from Augustine's *De musica*" (Shapiro 1990, 36–37). Nevertheless, Shapiro tends to discuss possible parallels between the *De vulgari eloquentia* and other texts to such an extent that she neglects the systematic theorizing that takes place in Dante's text itself.

orderly by being given *one* identifiable and lasting form.¹² If *gramatica* is a language of order, the vernacular is correspondingly a language of disorder. If we suppose that all this relates to the inherent hierarchy of the form–matter dichotomy, we could think that *gramatica* is best understood as a superior language, at least superior in the sense that it is the language most closely in contact with reason. But as is well known, Dante does *not* think of *gramatica* as inherently superior to the vernacular (I, I, 4). This is an important indication: it tells us that in Dante's view it is in fact possible to *formalize* the vernacular "matter." The notion of the "vulgare illustre," Dante's ideal language – whether it was meant solely for use in poetry, or on a general basis – should be understood broadly as this: as a rhetorical formalizing of the vernacular language matter.¹³

---

12 What Dante implies by *gramatica* in the *De vulgari eloquentia* is, of course, an age-old discussion. Ascoli dismisses the much-debated claims proposed by Maria Corti in *Dante a un nuovo crocevia* (1982) in which Dante's view of *gramatica* is said to be influenced by the so-called speculative grammarians, or *modistae*, who established *gramatica* as a technical concept denoting a universal way of systemizing language. Asoli's criticism of Corti seems to me accurate: She postulates some sort of continuity from Adam to the post-Babelic vernaculars, something that Dante himself condemns as being both "logically impossible" and "a clear instance of idolatrous pride" (Ascoli 2008, 147).Umberto Eco seems to be doing much the same as Corti in his inclusion of Dante's "vulgare illustre" among the representatives of adamittic longing, in his *The Search for the Perfect Language* (1995). Eco's chapter on Dante is somewhat too willing to postulate an identity between pre-Babel language and Dante's "vulgare illustre." There is clearly an analogy between the two, but it is more of a structural analogy than anything else. Even if Dante conceived of linguistic change as historically inaugurated by the building of the Tower of Babel, this does not imply that a project that leads towards a greater degree of linguistic oneness will ever be able to restore the damage made by this building. Dante's linguistic project seems to lie closer to a modern idea of a national standard for language rather than a mystic-religious quest for a lost epoch of semiotic oneness. Even though there are some fundamental problems with Corti's claims, she has nevertheless contributed to raising a fully legitimate and relevant interest in how Dante's conception of *gramatica* might have been influenced by an understanding of language *as a system*. As suggested by many scholars, the link between Dante and the *modistae* may certainly be there, but probably in a more indirect way than was implied by Corti: What the *modistae* did for grammar was to make it into a theoretical science in the Aristotelian sense, and one could easily suggest that such a general ambition is also present in the *De vulgari eloquentia* – but that what is theorized here, i.e. made "scientific," is poetry rather than language in general.

13 Steven Botterill makes the observation that *gramatica* in the *De vulgari eloquentia* could be understood in the sense of "Latin as it is used by the best [Classical] poets" (1996, 90). This seems hard to reconcile with the fact that *gramatica* in Dante's view

The domestication of vernacular poetry

The second book of the *De vulgari eloquentia* deals specifically with *harmonizing* the otherwise chaotic world of vernacular poetry by way of numerical techniques – "musical" in the medieval sense of the word. In doing this, Dante introduces a set of limitations to maintain a *rational* grip on the otherwise wild-running vernacular poetry, *measuring* it in a way that may indeed seem very formal – but this does not mean that it is *formalist* in the sense of "supposedly context-free." On the contrary, the tendency to postulate that rational poetry brings formal unity to the vernacular matter becomes for Dante a clue to determine the proper context for poetical language, the place it ought to occupy when no longer wild but *domesticated*: this point of rational unity is where the political and the poetical meet.

To show how history and poetic form are interconnected, Dante introduces three epithets for his ideal language in addition to *illustris*, namely *cardinalis*, *aulicus* and *curialis*. Dante's explanations of the meaning of these epithets are, as Steven Botterill puts it, "notable for the frequency with which they draw on the rhetoric of politics." (Botterill 1996, 23). Numa Pompilius and Seneca are mentioned to explain what is meant by *illustris*: they represent power (*potestas*) and knowledge (*magisterium*) respectively (I, xvii, 2). The word *cardinalis* is perhaps best understood as something governing all the individual parts, indicating the ambition of a united language for all Italians. The idea of the "vulgare illustre" being *cardinalis*, i.e. having the function of a *cardo* – the "hinge" of a door, if you like – also suggests the fundamental *domestic* metaphorics that is at work here. *Aulicus* and *curialis* both mean something like 'pertaining to the court', denoting something similar to political power in the case of *aulicus*, and juridical reason in the case of *curialis*. To explain what he means by the word

---

is an unchanging language, invented as such once and for all – this should not suggest any implicit hierarchy in the uses of this language that should affect how we think of Dante's definition of it. I do think, however, that Botterill in his phrasing here indicates a good understanding of the "vulgare illustre": *This* is precisely language *as it is used by the best (vernacular) poets*. In order to defend Botterill's attribution of such a characteristic to *gramatica* and not only to the "vulgare illustre," one could of course stress the obvious similarities between the two formalized languages. Here, I would simply suggest seeing a difference in flexibility, one in which *gramatica* is already formed and the "vulgare illustre" is still being formed.

aulicus, Dante indicates once again the connection between language and politics:

> The reason for calling this vernacular 'aulic' [...] is that if we Italians had a royal court, it would make its home in the court's palace. For if the court is the shared home of the entire kingdom, and the honoured governor of every part of it, it is fitting that everything that is common to all and yet owned by none should frequent the court and live there; and indeed no other dwelling-place would be worthy of such a resident. And this certainly seems to be true of the vernacular of which I speak. So this is why those who frequent any royal court always speak an illustrious vernacular; it is also why our illustrious vernacular wanders around like a homeless stranger, finding hospitality in more humble homes – because we have no court.
>
> Quia [...] aulicum nominamus illud causa est quod, si aulam nos Ytali haberemus, palatinum foret. Nam si aula totius regni comunis est domus et omnium regni partium gubernatrix augusta, quicquid tale est ut omnibus sit comune nec proprium ulli, conveniens est ut in ea conversetur et habitet, nec aliquod aliud habitaculum tanto dignum est habitante: hoc nempe videtur esse id de quo loquimur vulgare. Et hinc est quod in regiis omnibus conversantes semper illustri vulgari locuntur; hinc etiam est quod nostrum illustre velut acola peregrinatur et in humilibus hospitatur asilis, cum aula vacemus.
> (I, XVIII, 2–3)

This "shared home" of Italians, the *domus* where the "vulgare illustre" is supposed to reside, is indeed such a "form" as we speak of here, "common to all and yet owned by none," a scholastic universal that will always exist in some way, even if not materialized as such (as a house) – there is no need for this to be a "literal" *domus*, no more than the stanza is a literal room. Dante is simply suggesting that there has to be some sort of institution, which he conceives of as a *domus*, more precisely as a "House of Reason" that is capable of actually *replacing* the lacking court, which now however goes under the name of *curia* rather than *aula*:

> [J]ust as the elements of the German tribunal are united under a single monarch, so those of the Italians have been brought together by the gracious light of reason. So it would not be true to say that the Italians lack a tribunal altogether, even though we lack a monarch, because we do have one, but its physical components are scattered.

> [U]t curia regis Alamannie, in Ytalia non sit, membra tamen eius non desunt; et sicut membra illius uno Principe uniuntur, sic membra huius gratioso lumine rationis unita sunt. Quare falsum esset dicere curia carere Ytalos, quanquam Principe careamus, quoniam curiam habemus, licet corporaliter sit dispersa.
> (I, XVIII, 5)

The "vulgare illustre" is in exile because there is no common governing *aula*, and the only thing that indicates that it exists is the faculty of reason possessed by the most competent users of language: the poets, who represent the scattered *curia*. Thus Dante here states: (1) that poetry is necessarily part of a governing house; (2) that such a house, though not materialized as such, still exists as far as reason exist, and in precisely the form of reason; and (3) that reason at this point in time is found among the scattered *membra* of the poets who are capable of attaining the "vulgare illustre," the rational language of government.

One could claim that this is mere sophistry: Dante is obviously trying to gain authority for the vernacular poets by calling their language *curialis* – but when he then goes on to explain what *curialis* implies when no literal *curia* exists, it appears that the poets are its only guarantee, and thereby the only guarantee for their own authority, making the argument circular. In a similar vein, Ascoli argues that there is no factual connection between the effective political power of the *Princeps* and disempowered reason as represented by the poets, and that this marks the failure of Dante's project in the *De vulgari eloquentia* (Ascoli, 1991, 195). My claim would be that Ascoli does not fully understand the nature of the link Dante's treatise tries to establish.

Measuring poetic authority

When Dante tries to link the political situation of the Italian City-States of his day with a theoretical understanding of poetry, what characterizes this theorizing? What does a rational "ordering" of poetry amount to? To answer such questions, we need to see that when Dante wants vernacular poetry to be rational and orderly this means that it ought to "follow rules," or more correctly, he wants it to be in accordance with *regula*. Botterill translates Dante's *regula* with "rule," and this is indeed a reasonable way of interpreting the general meaning of the word (especially if one implies a modern, say, Wittgensteinian interpretation of the concept of rules), but this translation cannot fully capture what is certainly not an irrelevant history of the concept of *regulation*. For when Dante speaks of a *regula*, he obviously conceives of it as a defining element in the long tradition of *imitatio*: the idea that poetic skills are acquired by imitating ancient, established models. In fact, the Latin word *regula* is a translation of the Greek word *kanon*, which was simply the name of a tool with which to measure something (more like a ruler than a rule), and which taken in a less literal sense names the features that are *worth imitating*, as such defining the fundamental principle for *canonical* works. To Dante, *gramatica* makes imitation possible because the language is orderly and unchanging. When we consider the way in which Dante envisages vernacular poetry, however, such an unchanging character seems to be lacking, and as a consequence no criterion has so far been defined with which to determine the mechanisms of vernacular *imitatio*.

It seems that part of the agenda in the *De vulgari eloquentia* is to find a technique to determine how vernacular poets or poems could be worth imitating. In chapter iv of Book II, this impression is enforced by Dante's reference to the Classical poets as a canon not only for poets who compose in Latin, but also for vernacular poets. The reference to Horace's *Ars Poetica* even suggests that this work is one that Dante relates to his own, because he in his own theory of poetry has to look to the Classics and "emulate their learned works of poetic doctrine" (*doctrinatas eorum poetrias emulari*; II, iv, 3). Dante then investigates which formal guidelines one ought to follow in the different parts of the poetic craft. When referring to the stanza, he explains in an interestingly nuanced manner how each stanza *mimes* the poem as a whole, mirroring itself to create the formal framework (II, ix, 2–3). This indicates how the entire argument of the *De vulgari eloquentia* is related to an understanding of the relations of the parts to the whole. The poem as a formal entity is composed of stanzas, i.e. the stanzas are the parts of the poem. Verses are of course parts of the stanzas again, and syllables parts of verses. This should lead us, via the simplest understanding of the scholastic notions of *genus* and *species*, to see that the whole that governs the individual poem is quite simply poetry itself. And indeed, Book II of the *De vulgari eloquentia* opens by discussing poetry in general, before it proceeds to the poem and its parts. But why then does Dante not tell the reader what, so to speak, *poetry itself is a part of*? I think he does: this is exactly what the first book of the treatise is all about.

What is poetry part of? And why is this something we ought to consider? My answer to the second of these questions is simply that it would be inexplicably "unscholastic" to enumerate all the parts of the poem, minutely clarifying what is their hierarchical relation to their respective whole, and then *not* explain what universal these relate to, i.e. what principle governs these individual entities. Poetry could not itself be such a governing entity: only God, or a principle of authority emanating from God, could have that status. What principle governs poetry, in Dante's view? I would suggest that it is quite simply reason (*ratio*).

Book II explains the nature of a poem by looking at its parts, such as the stanza, which is the central element in drawing up the room-structure of the poem – the vernacular word "stanza" is Latinized into *stantia*, and Dante states that "this word was coined solely for the purpose of discussing poetic technique" (*hoc vocabulum per solius artis respectum inventum est*; II, ix, 2). The stanza is said to be "a capacious storehouse or receptacle for the art in its entirety" (*mansio capax sive receptaculum totius artis*; II, ix, 2). Since Book II explains the formal "building blocks" of the poem, Book I should be assumed to say something about the "housing" of poetry itself, and as we have seen it does. Poetry is characterized by inhabiting the "House of Reason" – reason being simply *form-giving* as such, thereby preventing the part/whole-structure from leading to a *reductio ad absurdum*. This suggests that Dante's main concern in Book I of the *De vulgari eloquentia* is to demonstrate that even poetry partakes of reason. There is *only one* language worthy of inhabiting a common Italian court, Dante says – and the very *formality* of the *domus* that poetry inhabits is established by its nature of being the One from which the many derive. This suggests that poetry, the mastering of linguistic form, is to be included among the rational theoretical disciplines of scholasticism.

Let us for a moment return to chapter xvi of Book I, the first chapter after Dante has made his exilic journey through the Italian dialects, where all the four epithets are introduced. Here Dante states that to understand something, it is not enough to look at all the specific instances of a phenomenon – "we should carry out a more closely reasoned investigation" (*rationabilius investigemus*; I, xvi, 1). I would stress the way the expression *rationabilius* divides Dante's text into two parts: the obviously *less* closely reasoned investigations that have been attempted so far and the one introduced here, which – for some reason or other – Dante considers to be "more closely reasoned". How is this division to be interpreted? What is this "more closely reasoned investigation" all about? The scholastic logic in the passages that follow is clearly not to be understood as only a convenient tool and even less as a stylistic device, but rather something which is of prime importance to understand the meaning of Dante's entire enterprise:

> [I]n arithmetic, all numbers are measured by comparison with the number one,[14] and are deemed larger and smaller according to their relative distance from or closeness to that number. Likewise with colours, all are measured against white, and held to be brighter or darker as they approach or recede from that

---

14 It is worth noting that Indian-Arabic numerals are introduced to Europe at approximately this point in time, in Florence around the year 1300 – and are met with fierce resistance, for at least one central theoretical reason (in addition to all the possible practical reasons): The fact that the Indian-Arabic numerical system has a sign for zero. This very idea of zero – nothing – having some sort of sign to point to it, seems to have put vacuum pressure on the medieval worldview, creating an intensified *horror vacui*. The zero with its to us rather harmless oval shape gives form to something that according to scholastic physics or metaphysics *cannot have any form*: it gives form to a void, and not to essence or matter, thereby destabilizing the oneness of the universe. This reaction towards the new numerals is mentioned here simply to stress the obvious importance given to the idea of the necessary oneness of form, and the closely related idea that form is more rational than matter and void.

colour. And I hold that what can be said of things that have quantity and quality is also true of any predicate whatever, and even of substances: in short, that everything can be measured, in so far as it belongs to a genus, by comparison with the simplest individual found in that genus.

> [S]icut in numero cuncta mensurantur uno, et plura vel pauciora dicuntur secundum quod distant ab uno vel ei propinquant, et sicut in coloribus omnes albo mensurantur – nam visibiles magis et minus dicuntur secundum quod accedunt vel recedunt ab albo. Et quemadmodum de hiis dicimus que quantitatem et qualitatem ostendunt, de predicamentorum quolibet, etiam de substantia, posse dici putamus: scilicet ut unumquodque mensurabile sit, secundum quod in genere est, illo quod simplicissimum est in ipso genere.
> (I, xvi, 2)

This way of thinking is, of course, scholastic in an exemplary way and illustrates the figure often called *reductio ad unum*, which implies that the function of reason is to create – so to speak – the oneness appropriate for each set of things. Consequently, any *theory* will necessarily be closely linked to the idea of finding or determining the *proper unit*. The "vulgare illustre" is indeed such a unit: it is the standard by which all instances of language should be measured. There can be no doubt that this is what Dante is trying to indicate, for example with his phrasing in this passage:

> [W]e can define the illustrious, cardinal, aulic, and curial vernacular in Italy as that which belongs to every Italian city yet seems to belong to none, and against which the vernaculars of all the cities of the Italians can be *measured, weighed, and compared* [my italics].

> [D]icimus illustre, cardinale, aulicum et curiale vulgare in Latio quod omnis latie civitatis est et nullius esse videtur, et quo municipalia vulgaria omnia Latinorum mensurantur et ponderantur et comparantur.
> (I, xvi, 6)

The notions of *measuring* and *weighing* are in my view central to the whole structure of Dante's thought in the *De vulgari eloquentia*. Dante is in fact writing his text about 50 years after the City of Florence first introduced the monetary unit known as the *fiorino d'oro*, the Golden Florin, thereby establishing a standard to which all the other Italian City-States soon became eager to conform: determining the unit, the "one," by making it dependent on the amount of metal used for its production: one pound (*libra*).

There is some reason to stress that the parallel between money and language may have been more obvious to men at the time of Dante than it is to us today: that is if we see ourselves as having a "demystified" view of what money is, that money constitutes a strictly numerical system based simply on everybody's relative faith in the value of each unit. This contrasts with the thinking around 1300, when there was a strong sense of a necessary link between the value of the coin and the value of what the coin consisted of. The fact that the Golden Florin was made dependent on a common weight unit was precisely what made the invention such a success.

It was part of medieval metaphysics to see weight as somehow more essential than the ghostly, abstract idea of money, as is evident when a pupil of Thomas Aquinas, Ptolemy of Lucca (d. *c.* 1328), in his *De regimine principum*, says that "it seems that weights and measures take their origin from nature more than coinage does, and therefore they are even more necessary [than coinage] in a republic or kingdom." (Quoted in Wood 2000). This quote, at the very least, makes it easier for us to see why Dante is so concerned with discussing poetry in terms of weight and measures. In this perspective, it is not at all unlikely that what was at stake for him was finding a way to *measure the value* of any given poem – a "value" which might come close to denoting "authority" even in a rather modern sense of the word.

As we have seen, the "vulgare illustre" is to be considered to be a measuring unit in the domain of language. There is every reason to stress how closely related the words Dante uses are to the language used in documents about political life in the City-States at the time, even in the general cases of *ars* (as in "art of poetry") and *membra* (the word Dante used to describe the scattered elements of reason in Italy),

The domestication of vernacular poetry

both being Latin words used to denote a guild.[15] One might very well argue that what Dante does is to portray the poets as a guild in their own right – a guild that is not geographically limited or part of any direct struggle for power, but that represents a craft which is able to find a tool to dictate the appropriate standards of language used even in politics. Since poets simply by exercising their craft tend towards the "vulgare illustre", the very existence of poetry indicates that an idea of rational measuring and weighing is in fact *already operative* in Italian civic life:

> It is right to call this vernacular "curial", because the essence of being curial is no more than providing a balanced assessment of whatever has to be dealt with; and because the scales on which this assessment is carried out are usually found only in the most authoritative of tribunals,[16] whatever is well balanced in our actions is called "curial". Therefore, since this vernacular has been assessed before the most excellent tribunal in Italy, it deserves to be called "curial".
>
> Est etiam merito curiale dicendum, quia curialitas nil aliud est quam librata regula eorum que peragenda sunt: et quia statera huiusmodi librationis tantum in excellentissimis curiis esse solet, hinc est quod quicquid in actibus nostris bene libratum est, curiale dicatur. Unde cum istud in excellentissima Ytalorum curia sit libratum, dici curiale meretur.
> (I, xviii, 4)

The *curia* is a house of reason, and this house is nothing but the universal to which poetry belongs. Botterill tells us that *curialis* implies "law-court." (Botterill 1996, 96). In such a court the necessary fusion of poetics and politics can take place, the "court" being simply the very idea that Justice can in some way or other be expressed in language, completely in accordance with the way Dante in the *Convivio*

---

15 See for example John M. Najemy, *Corporatism and Consensus in Florentine Electoral Politics, 1280–1400* (1982, 3–78).
16 The most authoritative of tribunals (*excellentissimis curiis*) is – by internal definition – no more and no less than reason itself.

establishes the poetic art as an art trying to build a bridge from *belezza* to *bontà* (II, xi). The very idea of "the scales" (*statera*) for measuring actions, suggests some sort of – more or less conscious – reference to the goddess of Justice. Justice, as Dante explains in the *De Monarchia*, is itself "a kind of rectitude or rule" (*quedam rectitudo sive regula*; I, xi, 3).[17] In the perspective of the *De vulgari eloquentia* what *adds weight* to an argument, as we say, what gives the speaker authority, is envisioned as something that can be measured by rational means. This suggests that Dante was concerned with finding a rational way of measuring authority.

Trading poetry for politics

If Dante wanted to find a way to measure the authority of the vernacular poets, what were the motives behind such a project? The *De vulgari eloquentia* indicates that the historical background may well be relevant to find an answer to this question. When describing the splitting-up of languages from Babel to the Italian dialects with which he is familiar, Dante sneaks in a compressed history of vernacular poetry.[18] He describes the three major Romance languages (Occitan, Old French and Italian), and he does so by listing – this sort of thinking was rather common at the time – their individual relation to different genres: French is supposedly better suited to epic verse, Occitan to poetry, and Italian to those who according to Dante "have written vernacular poetry more sweetly and subtly" (*dulcius subtiliusque poetati vulgariter sunt*; I, x, 2). It seems, in fact, that this idea of refinement and subtleness – which Dante refers to on more than one occasion in the *De vulgari eloquentia* – forms an important link between his idea of rationally measuring poetic authority and the idea of a conscious development of an essentially unbroken tradition.

---

17 I quote from Prue Shaw's translation of the *De Monarchia* (*Monarchy* 1996).
18 As Barolini notes with reference to Mengaldo's 1968 introduction (*De vulgari eloquentia*, ed. Mengaldo [Padova: Editrice Antenore]), Dante's treatise is marked by a "revolutionary historicity": As a rule, the work structures its narrative in accordance with the sequence Provençal–Old French–Italian, moving chronologically from school to school (the Sicilians in chapter xii of Book I; the Tuscans in chapter xiii; the Bolognese in chapter xv), and its first-line quotes can be said to represent "miniature histories of the lyric" (Barolini 1984, 92).

The domestication of vernacular poetry

Dante certainly knew the Provençal *razos*, the short commentaries that provide introductions to troubadour poems in the manuscripts. Regarding the *De vulgari eloquentia* as belonging to the *razos* tradition does not, however, seem to fit. The *razos* are often "retellings" of the story of the poem, remaining much closer to the "content" of them than Dante does. Nevertheless, as Marianne Shapiro has pointed out, there are certain striking similarities between the *De vulgari eloquentia* and a text like Raimon Vidal's *Razos de trobar*: (Shapiro 1990, 112) This text, at least, shares Dante's focus on minute linguistic and grammatical detail.

It is hard to argue against Mengaldo's contention that the *De vulgari eloquentia* exemplifies what is already a tendency in medieval stylistic theory: the rhetorical discipline of *inventio*, i.e. the "the art of finding topics", becomes almost a pretext for entering into the technical specifics of *elocutio* or *ornatus*. (Mengaldo 1978, 53) But if we accept Giorgio Agamben's comments on *inventio*, and see the *ratio* (or *ars*) *inveniendi* as translated into the Provençal *razo de trobar* (Agamben 1999, 79), this would suggest that Dante is in fact relating his text to the discipline of *inventio*. What is interesting about this idea is that it can show how the move away from the central idea of "love" as the sole subject of poetry (stated by Dante himself in the *Vita nuova*) can be seen as fundamental to the *De vulgari eloquentia*: When Dante speaks of "control of one's will" (*directio voluntatis*; II, ii, 7) as the subject matter he himself pursues – once again showing how he at this stage identifies his project primarily with his moral *canzoni* – he might in fact be making a statement about the importance of "political poetry" that ought to affect the way we read his treatise and how we think about his views on the poetic tradition at large.

In our as well as in Dante's historical perspective, the tradition of vernacular poetry develops from Provençal troubadour poetry to the Italian poetry of Dante's contemporaries. Even though the notion of *courtly love* over time may have become somewhat contested, not least because of its very vagueness, and because love was obviously only one of the themes of troubadour poetry, the heterogeneity of which has become increasingly evident through studies conducted in recent decades, there is little doubt that the troubadours' poetry is *courtly* in some sense of the word in that it was performed at the courts by poet-performers who had some more or less established and lasting relationship to the court; and that this essentially *courtly* character of poetry was maintained by the poets that preceded Dante in what one may legitimately term "the first group of Italian vernacular lyric poets." (Barolini 1993, 14)

Aristide Marigo suggests that Dante might have got his notion of a *dictamen curiale* from Giovanni Garlandia's *Poetria*.[19] As so often in his commentaries on Marigo, Pier Vicenzo Mengaldo is sceptical, and claims that Dante simply uses the word in a stylistic sense quite common in medieval texts (Mengaldo 1978, 212–213). One might ask, however, how "stylistic" Dante's notion of *curialis* really is. Dante makes an ironic comment about Guittone d'Arezzo, Bonaguinta da Lucca, Galletto, Bartolomeo Macati and Brunetto Latini, who pretend to have reached the "vulgare illustre", but whose poetry, in his view, "we would find to be fitted not for a court but at best for a city council" (*non curialia sed municipalia tantum invenientur*"; I, xiii, 1). Should not this lead us to suspect that Dante's notion of poetical language as *curialis* indicates that his concerns are essentially political? It is striking that Dante uses the word *curialis* to denote even "whatever is well balanced in our actions" (*quod quicquid in actibus nostris bene libratum est*; I, xviii, 4). This makes it hard to state that Dante has an idea of the "courtly" that is purely – or even primarily – stylistic. It is obviously important for Dante to stress the relationship of the "vulgare illustre" to a *curia*, and to indicate that the appropriate example of such a *curia* would be the court of Frederick II in Sicily. In her study of the literary environment at Frederick's court, Karla Mallette stresses the geographical dissemination of Frederick's government: it would be very misleading to think of this "court" as a building where all those who worked for the Emperor met. On the contrary, the court was a *decentred* centre, Mallette says – not an institution located at one specific geographical point, but rather an "apparatus of court functionaries and dignitaries" (Mallette 2005, 71).

There is no doubt that numerous poets were affiliated to – but not, then, "residing at" – the court of Frederick II, at what, using a

---

19 Aristide Marigo in one of his notes to Dante, *De vulgari eloquentia*, ed. Marigo (1957, 155).

term borrowed from Dante, is usually called the "Sicilian School". This school is usually said to have flourished from about 1230 until Fredrick's death in 1250, and its poets were consciously modelling their poetry on the poetry of the troubadours: the Provençal (or Occitan) *canso* turning into the Italian *canzone*, and the *midons* (the revered lady) turning into the *madonna* – clearing the way for the important fusion of theology and love poetry as portrayed in what is termed the *donna angelicata*. What happens thematically to the vernacular poetic tradition in its "move" from the Provençal troubadours to Sicily is that the satirical and political genres of the troubadours practically cease to exist at the expense of an almost total focus on love poems – in Dante's words "no Italian poet so far has written about the theme of war" (*Arma vero nullum latium adhuc invenio poetasse*; II, ii, 8). This change coincides with the invention of the sonnet, an invention attributed to Giacomo da Lentini, the so-called Notary (a name given to him by Dante both in the *De vulgari eloquentia* and in the famous passage in canto 24 of Purgatory). From this point on, vernacular lyric poetry is primarily expressed in the strictly measured formal scheme of the sonnet: it is domesticated both formally and thematically. Nonetheless, accompanying the move *away* from a variety of subject matters in lyric poetry is a *de facto* institutionalisation of poetry as a craft associated with *governing*, and with the poet playing a significant role at the court *understood as a government*. When Dante refers to someone like Guido delle Colonne, who is one of the most famous Sicilian poets, as "judge of Messina" (*Iudex de Messana*; quoted in II, v, 4 and II, vi, 6), there seems to be no conflict involved in seeing the poet as determined by his official title, a title that places him in the political administration rather than in a geographical centre. The poets of the Sicilian school are in fact people working in Frederick's government, and Giacomo da Lentini – also known as the "head of the Sicilian school" – is called "the Notary" for the simple reason that that was his function at the court. It is worth noting that "Giudici e Notai" is the name of one of the guilds in Florence at the time.

This idea of the poets having an official position at the court has interesting implications, precisely because it stakes out a possible political function of poetry, even though this may not be explicit in the poems themselves. Dante might have thought of his project as an attempt to grant the poets the authority that Frederick's court once possessed, in what is for Dante a long lost time of peace.[20] It may be speculative to ask how Dante thought of Frederick's court, but it is at least not unlikely that he saw it precisely as a government characterized by having poets and scholars in central positions at different locations in the area Frederick controlled. I would stress once again that from Dante's perspective a common, unified court, such as existed at the time of Frederick, is not necessarily a physical building: although poetry and law-court are linked, there seems be no reason to think that this would have to mean that they imply any direct "cohabitation" with the Emperor.

It is, in short, *not* reasonable to think that the *curia* (reason) has to be institutionalised in a fixed relation to the governing power of the *aula* (effective political power). The very lack of "aulic" authority is instead rather to be seen as a consequence of this lack of unity of the "two courts" of power and reason. When Dante says that "writers of prose most often learn the vernacular from poets, and [...] what is set out in poetry serves as a model for those who write prose, and not the other way about" (*prosaycantes ab avientibus magis accipiunt et [...] quod avietum est prosaycantibus permanere videtur exemplar, et non e converso*; II, I, 1), this indicates that the vernacular poets are establishing the standard of imitation to which others must conform, much like the ones making the Florentine coin. What poets do in the "curial" house of justice and reason is create a unified language. This involves what we may term a structure of *double imitation*: first, the poets imitate the Classics and the modern masters of vernacular poetry, thereby establishing a tool to determine the proper use of language; this language can then be used by those in power for them to have legitimate authority – they in their turn have to "imitate," learn from, the language of the poets. In the perspective of the *De vulgari eloquentia*, the notion of the "vulgare illustre" cannot be reduced to something

---

20 Even though Frederick is to be found in canto 10 of the *Inferno* for his "Epicureanism," "atheism," "sensualism" or "materialism," he is nonetheless a heroic figure, especially in the *De vulgari eloquentia*. As Ascoli observes, Frederick clearly played a decisive role in Dante's historical imagination, at least in the first years of Dante's exile, above all indicating "the place where power, knowledge, and imagination might meet and collaborate" (Ascoli 2008, 288).

The domestication of vernacular poetry

that merely measures empirical uses of language in an isolated, "aesthetic" way; in fact, it indicates that language is a way of measuring authority: "[I]n so far as we are human beings who are Italians, there are certain very simple features, of manners and appearance and *speech, by which the actions of the people of Italy can be weighed and measured* [my italics]" (*in quantum ut homines latini agimus, quedam habemus simplicissima signa et morum et habituum et locutionis, quibus latine actiones ponderantur et mensurantur*; I, xvi, 3).

I believe that Dante saw the poetry of his day as partly traditional and partly different from both Classical and earlier vernacular poetry, and that he sought to provide a philosophical basis for the idea of a poetry concerned with moral issues analogous to the monetary innovation of the Italian City-States, thus launching a supposedly neutral method with which to measure the uses of language: this function is in fact what ensures language's relation to morality, to the court and to the law-court, where measuring is performed by weighing up words to make a balanced judgment. The ideas of the common home of the Italians, and of being worthy of such a home, are what make the ideal language not only a possibility, but a necessity: it must exist *as an ideal*, something to be found "everywhere and nowhere." Dante attempts to solve the political problems of the Italians by placing enormous weight on the exemplary judgement of the poets. The space occupied by the Italian-speaking population is in fact both linguistically and politically divided, although in essence politics and language are united, and the realization of this essential linguistic and political unity is primarily a linguistic project. In other words: the politics of language delimits and determines politics itself.

Legitimate authority is only possible if there is some sort of measuring tool that dictates imitation. To Dante, Classical poetry is characterized by already having such a tool. If we acknowledge that both the *aula* and the *curia* are divided in terms of form and matter, the very idea of *regulation* becomes the only possible way of rationally *formalising* the elements that provide vernacular poetry with its theoretical basis, lending it an authority that has not yet been recognized. In this way, Dante tries to establish a tradition of vernacular lyric poetry with its own mechanisms of progressive amelioration. By virtue of being the most competent users of language, the poets establish a formal framework for measuring authority, indicating that the form of legitimate power has to rest on a united and rational language.

Dante, of course, is in exile, and the *De vulgari eloquentia* is one of the first texts he writes after being banished. This exile is of fundamental importance to his idea of politics. In the *De vulgari eloquentia*, the Tower of Babel – the third offence committed by humanity against God – is portrayed as the decisive moment which seals the fate of human language, splitting the one into multiple languages and dialects. In his *Letter to the Florentines*, Dante alludes to the building of the Tower of Babel to illustrate the conflicts between the Florentines (vi, 8), perhaps referring to the twenty-one guilds that for the past fifty years or so were the means through which citizens could acquire political power in Florence. Dante obviously conceives of his own political exile as a part of a "history of exiles". But the *De vulgari eloquentia* is not only an allegory of Dante's exile. It is in fact a work that tries to solve the homelessness of Italian government by domesticating vernacular poetry, making it into a tool to measure and weigh up the legitimacy of different sorts of language. The poets' ability to locate the "vulgare illustre" makes them worthy residents of the common Italian home, and the linguistic ideal itself becomes nothing less than "the true head of the family" (*vere paterfamilias*; I, xviii, 1).[21] Dante even mentions the *paterfamilias* in the *De monarchia* in a passage in which he argues that the same priority of the intellectual faculty (*vis intellectualis*) is necessary for each man, for each family (*domus*), and for larger political units. It is up to the *paterfamilias*, Dante explains, to "guide everyone and impose rules on others" (*regulare omnes et leges imponere aliis*; I, v, 5). It should be noted here that Dante actually uses the word *leges*,

---

21 Gary P. Cestaro demonstrates the degree to which the *De vulgari eloquentia* is based on a metaphorical system involving the categories of masculine and feminine (*Dante and the Grammar of the Nursing Body* 2003). Cestaro's work draws up interesting perspectives on sex and society, which deserve to be studied more closely – for now, I shall simply mention that the categories of "male" and "female" are certainly not irrelevant when it comes to Dante's "rational housing" of poetry. One could, for instance, claim that the way the form/matter dichotomy is sexualized by Dante is highly relevant to the *De vulgari eloquentia* if one reads the work as a manual, i.e. a book written to teach poets how to compose poetry. This might give the idea of the *domus*, of the housing and the domestication I am referring to, a wider sense, involving both nurturing, "growing up" and preparing to be the head of one's family, i.e. it could enable us to see the entire work as part of more general – even practical – notion of education.

i.e. "laws", in this context – and that, later in the *De monarchia*, he will quote Seneca to the effect that "law is the bond of human society" (*"legem vinculum" dicat "humane societatis"*; II, v, 3). This is absolutely central to Dante's project in the *De monarchia*, in which every concord depends on unity of the will at all levels of society (I, xv, 8). Should we not expect that a similar concern is at the heart of the *De vulgari eloquentia*?

To grasp Dante's ideas about poetry, we have to realize to what extent they are dependent on the scholastic thinking of his time: it helps us understand the importance he ascribes to making poetry "rational". This might suggest some sort of institutionalisation of a modern notion of poetry as a form of art, or even literature as such, making it conform to certain standards, *housing it* in the home of political authority while removing the *unac-countable* elements: a line is drawn between more or less uncontrolled poetry (possibly a conscious move away from sung or even improvised poetry) and what is said to be a subtler and more rational poetry. The domestication of vernacular poetry, its move from disintegration and chaos to order and reason, is to Dante what makes it able to acquire the authority needed to take on political and moral subject matter – at this time, of course, any morality would also be said to be rational. In this way Dante is drawing up a "theory of poetry" in what he would consider to be *purely logical and formal terms*, where poetry's role is to provide a language to be used for political purposes. If we accept the idea that Dante seeks to find a way to *rationally* measure poetic authority, how are we to envision this "rationality" in the *De vulgari eloquentia*?

A defence of reason

How does one *measure* a vernacular poet's authority? The *De vulgari eloquentia*, I think, tries to come up with an answer to this question. To Dante, reason always works to find *a one*, a unit. The need for a measuring tool for language is the primary reason why Dante wants to establish such a rational unit for poetry, thus making the *regula* a device with which to determine which formal structures are to be seen as canonical, i.e. worthy of being imitated by vernacular poets. This is, in my view, the primary concern of the *De vulgari eloquentia*.

The distinction between form and matter is, to Dante, a difference between the disorderly and the orderly; in short, a difference between chaos and reason. And vernacular language is chaotic. But what, precisely, makes vernacular language chaotic, in Dante's view? Its very disintegration, one might say. But this disintegration is perhaps more precisely defined as a *lack of oneness*. To put it in very simple terms, when the chaotic language matter of the mother tongue is treated by a poet able to master the "vulgare illustre," the chaos of the vernacular suddenly becomes in accordance with what Dante calls *regula* – this means that *even vernacular poetry can be subject to the laws of imitation*. The "vulgare illustre" is the chaotic vernaculars *regulated* in precisely this sense, in terms of a unified tool. It is *formed* or *formalised* – and in this way it is made into something *worthy of imitation*, not only by other poets but by everyone who uses language to treat moral and political subject matter.

In Ascoli's interpretation, Dante in the *De vulgari eloquentia* assumes the role of a "self-confident voice of reason." (Ascoli 2008, 136) The "voice of reason" is quite clearly very important in the *De vulgari eloquentia*, but not necessarily for the reasons suggested by Ascoli: reading the category of "reason" as a figure representing Dante himself is a mere reduction of Dante's theoretical outlook. More than as a strategic choice of a "personal" style in the *Convivio* and a strategic focus on reason as a voice in itself in the *De vulgari eloquentia*,[22] these two works differ in genre, and belong to different discourses: speaking in the name of reason is quite simply the way one presents a theory in the world of scholastic theory.

Ascoli argues that Dante is not able to control the free-floating notion of the "vulgare illustre", it "slides from theological transcendence, to the immanence of human knowledge and power, to the formal marginality of the poetic style" (Ascoli 2008, 167). But this argument would only be relevant if one did not accept the central point Dante is trying to make: that poetry partakes of reason. Ascoli might, of course, say that his point is valid also for the "formal marginality" *even of reason* – as he seems to indicate when he says that "historical circumstances

---

22 Implicitly, of course, Dante involves himself at many stages in the text, by citing his own poems, as Cino's friend (*amicus eius*), and on one occasion even by speaking in the first person singular about one of his poems.

that deprived Italy of its regal *aula* have also forced the scattered *curia* in exile back onto the disempowered resources of reason alone" (Ascoli 2008, 166). But nothing suggests that Dante would see this as a failure – on the contrary, this very *forcing of the curia back to reason alone* is the main purpose of his treatise.In her book-length study of the *De vulgari eloquentia*, Marianne Shapiro claims that Dante constructs the logic of the work by making his exile a metaphor for the "exilic" nature of language. This is hard to argue against: Dante describes the Italian language as a homeless man seeking shelter in humble homes – and the very "hunt" for the perfect vernacular in chapters X–XV of Book I represents an erring journey by someone who has trouble finding his true resting-place. In Ascoli's view, the *De vulgari eloquentia* is an attempt by Dante to ground his authority in a dispassionate rationality made possible by his exile, which gave him knowledge of the variety of Italian dialects, and consequently the ability to choose the best elements from among them. This leads Ascoli to claim that Dante is portraying himself not only as a privileged user of the "vulgare illustre", but that he in fact *is* the very "vulgare illustre" (Ascoli 2008, 156). In this instance, Ascoli is obviously right: Dante models the descriptions of the "vulgare illustre" on his own journeys throughout the Italian peninsula while he is exilic and homeless. There is no point trying to deny the validity of this "biographical" or "existential" reading. In fact, one might ask if this is not the most simple and literal reading possible – there seems to be no hidden agenda in these descriptions, they are as straightforward as anything: Dante claims that he has come to know that there is no ideal dialect being spoken anywhere, that a common language consequently has to be made up of different dialectal elements, and that he has tried to do so in his post-exilic poetry. Claiming that Dante indicates that he "is" the "vulgare illustre" amounts to little more than stating that he knows what he is talking about. Claiming that the *De vulgari eloquentia* is a theory of poetry is itself a more daring reading: it means that the description of the "vulgare illustre" is not relevant only to Dante, but to other poets as well.

There is a danger that a reading focusing entirely on authorial rhetorical strategy ends up simply disregarding the socio-historical aspects of a specific work: if one sees every textual move as relative to every other move, one risks making the "will to authority" a kind of intrinsic constant governing every text. One may of course want to read Dante in a nominalist manner, in which all sets of ideas are nothing but fictions – this is, in my view, what Ascoli does.[23] And there is, of course, no point in discarding such readings *per se*. But simply claiming that Dante's theories are nothing but rhetorical strategies, with or without him being aware of this, what problems would such an approach solve? Ascoli's response is a mere repetition of a question to which the *De vulgari eloquentia* must reasonably be considered to be Dante's answer. Ascoli himself makes philosophical claims, stating that Dante has an "impossible desire to reconcile historicity with ideality" (Ascoli 2008, 139). But this seems like simply making the same claim that Dante set out to refute: the claim that there is no way of linking ideals with history. To Dante, using reason *is* precisely this: linking ideals with history; linking the One, the proper unit, with the chaotic matter of vernacular language.

If one, for some reason, should find such a portrayal of an "idealistically formalist" Dante inconvenient, one should simply think of the forms as theoretical tools, models in which a great deal of poetic license is given – on more than one occasion Dante points out the importance and the possibility of individual poetic choices. One could of course claim that if the forms are simply frameworks, they do not as such reflect Dante's concern with more important matters. My counter-argument is that the *De vulgari eloquentia* shows us that frameworks were all-important to Dante – at least when he expressed himself in the scholastic idiom. They were the only *rational* matrices, and the only ones that could save poetry from anarchy analogous to the way Dante in the *De monarchia* explains that the *monarcha* can guarantee the peace of the state.

I do not wish to discredit any of the interesting studies of the different styles Dante approached in his poetry – stylistic changes that no doubt were important to him, and that he obviously reflected upon precisely as changes, turns from one kind of poetic expression to another,

---

23 One quote to illustrate this point: "What Dante seems to know – and his career-long propensity for self-contradiction in matters philosophical bears this out – is that the terminology of rational philosophy is itself historical and contingent, subject to the will of the individual speaker and the specific circumstances of time and place, like all language after the Fall from Eden and the confusion of Babel" (Ascoli 2008, 171).

integrating new and often more complex subject matter. My point is of course not to dispose of any of the distinctions that one can make in order to better understand Dante's poetry and poetics: such distinctions are tools for explaining why we love Dante: his development and his reflections on it, his dialogue between poetry and prose – these elements constitute the complexity that makes Dante's work so rich, that made him the most heterogenous writer in history at the time of his death. Nonetheless, this question strikes me as legitimate enough: could it be that the *De vulgari eloquentia*, by itself, represents a more "old-school" scholastic understanding of the poetic craft than is implied by more modern stylistic distinctions?

One can of course stick to the idea, which I believe to be true, that Dante stopped working on the *De vulgari eloquentia* simply because he preferred to address his ideas about poetry in verse – and because he at the time had acquired a better idea of how this was to be done. Nonetheless, the scholastic nature of the *De vulgari eloquentia* is certainly able to tell us something about the development of vernacular poetry at large. Reading the *De vulgari eloquentia* as an allegory of exile, as a search for a unified or adamittic language, or speculating about Dante's strategic motives for writing the *De vulgari eloquentia*, should not prevent us from seeing that what led Dante to establish a theory of poetry may in fact have been the reason that he himself indicates: the need to defend reason itself.

Dante's avant-gardism reinvented.
Past and present vernaculars in the 1920s

P.M. Mehtonen

> I like an old work for its novelty. Only contrast links us to the past.
> (Tristan Tzara, Dada manifesto, 1918)[1]

Discovering means of demonstrating what an old work has to communicate to us is an ongoing process, generation by generation. According to Stephen G. Nichols, recent medieval scholarship is also often motivated by the question of "how [the historical artefact] can interrogate or confirm the insights opened by new intellectual paradigms" (Nichols 2005, 424). One exemplary paradigm to Nichols is the twelfth-century 'linguistic turn' as a scene that inspired writers such as Marie de France, "the James Joyce of the twelfth century". She participated in the invention of the vernacular literary language – the vernacular as something that could be seen as real language and also as an object of analysis and cultivation.

The invention of the vernacular – either real or synthetic – has reoccurred both as a linguistic fact and as a poetic stimulus in the later European literary avant-gardisms. This paper will briefly explore two linguistic turns: the reception of Dante, the James Joyce of the fourteenth century, by the early twentieth-century avant-gardists. In English literature one landmark of the radical contemporaneity of the medieval sage consists of the young Samuel Beckett's comments on *De vulgari eloquentia* (1303–1305) in the manifesto "Dante...Bruno.

---

1 Trans. Mary Ann Caws, in Caws 2001, 303.

Vico..Joyce" (1929). The word 'manifesto' in the previous sentence is emphatic. While Beckett's text is often (e.g. Boldrini 2001, 14; Caselli 2005, 10–22) referred to as an 'essay' on James Joyce's *Work in Progress* – the future *Finnegans Wake* – the text would be in better company (in terms of its style and declaration) with the modern manifesto, a genre which was very much the product of the 1910s and 1920s.[2] Beckett, too, employs the stylistic devices of this genre, such as direct address – "if you don't understand it, Ladies and Gentlemen" – and shameless exclamation: "Basta!"

In this article the notion of the manifesto liberates us from the conventional reading of Beckett's text as a more or less adequate "commentary" on Dante and Joyce.[3] Beckett did not use Dante as a source for an essay but as an inspiration in an avant-garde declaration or – to reuse Nichols' terms – as a confirmation of the insights opened by a new intellectual paradigm. This paradigm in the 1910s and 1920s sought a means towards abstract, non-representative art. Thus in the context of the contemporary avant-garde it is possible to discern how Dante's quest for the noble vernacular was transformed by Beckett into a tenet of different "synthetic" invention.

The "genuine complexity" of medieval literature

Beckett's reading of Dante is deeply rooted in the Anglo-French poetic movements and the modernist attempts to revolutionise language. Both the avant-gardist figures in the literary circles of Beckett's youth (Jolas, Joyce) and the mainstream modernists (Yeats, Eliot, Pound) turned their gaze towards the Middle Ages in a quest for models of linguistic experimentation.[4] Beckett himself was inspired both by Dante and the poetry that inspired Dante: the complex forms of medieval vernacular troubadour lyric.[5] Whereas Dante's great influence on Beckett's later

---

2   See Mary Ann Caws (as referred to in Ivanov 2001 and Moréas 2001).
3   See Boldrini 15ff.; Caselli 10ff. Jean-Michel Rabaté has – correctly – observed "the snide and disparaging comments that are regularly lavished upon these essays [of the *Our Exagmination...*]" (Rabaté 1999, 249).
4   See for example Boldrini on Joyce's interest in Dante and the older layers of medievalisms before him: Blake's illustrations of the *Commedia*, the medievalism of the Romantics, the Pre-Raphaelites, and so forth (Boldrini 2–3 et passim).
5   On Beckett's "Alba," "Enueg I–II," "Dortmunder," and so forth, see Cohn 24–26, 33–34.

fiction has been admirably shown by Beckett scholarship (Cohn 2001; Caselli 2005), the direct influence of the avant-garde poetics of the 1920s has been studied less and therefore deserves a closer look here.

The poetic manifestos of the period reveal one eminent enemy that nurtured the broader interest in medieval poetics, namely the realism and naturalism of the earlier generations of writers. As an antidote to the clarity of realistic representation and "the impression of a chloroformed world" (Beckett, *Dream* 119), experimental writers welcomed the ambiguity and obscurity not only of their fellow modernists but also of the Classics that had successfully avoided the influence of realism simply by having been historically anterior to it.

The "Symbolist Manifesto" (1886) of Jean Moreás proclaims early on in defence of symbolism:

> So this art will never show details of nature, actions of humans, concrete phenomena: for they are only the appearances destined to represent to the senses their esoteric affinities with primordial Ideas.
>
> Readers will accuse this aesthetics of obscurity: we aren't surprised. What can you do? Weren't Pindar's *Odes*, Shakespeare's *Hamlet*, Dante's *Vita Nuova* [...] said to be ambiguous?
> (Moréas 2001, 50)

This re-born obscure aesthetics necessitates "an archetypal complex style" and "the good old language set on a sure footing and modernized" (Moréas 2001, 50, 51). In the later symbolism of the 1910s Dante continued to be celebrated as one of the archetypal modernisers of language. As if Dante were a true symbolist on a quest for the inner word, his vernacular poetry was seen to represent "a synthetic judgment" in which subjective symbols (such as love[6]) go through the poet's "mytho-creating intuition":

---

6 Ivanov refers here to the "concluding verse of Dante's Paradiso [*L'Amór / che muove il Sóle / e l'altre Stélle*]" where "images are composed into myth and music teaches its wisdom" (Ivanov 2001, 65).

> For the myth is the synthetic judgment where the predicate verb is joined to the symbol-subject. The sacred word, *ieros logos*, is transformed into the word as *mythos*.
> (Ivanov 2001, 66)

The later avant-garde in the 1910s and 1920s (Russian and Italian futurisms, dada) loved to hate the high-flown idealism and rhetoric of the symbolists, as evident in the citations above. Nevertheless, in their language-centred poetics these movements also cherished the ideas of anti-realism, the "genuine complexity" of medieval literature, and Dante as one of the *ur*-revolutionaries of language with his "synthetic" judgment and vernacular both in practice (*Commedia*, *Vita nuova*) and in theory.

These conceptions were part of the intellectual paradigm of the literary circles of Samuel Beckett's youth and his juvenile manifesto "Dante...Bruno. Vico..Joyce."[7] The remarks about Dante's *De vulgari eloquentia* in this manifesto serve as elements of difficult and obscure poetics related to James Joyce's *Work in Progress*. While Beckett's text, on the one hand, relies on the received general avant-garde ideas of Dante as roughly sketched out above, it is also a modern manifesto proclaiming the principles of the present and even the future vernacular writing (and Beckett's own, rather than Joyce's writing). Also at this level, Beckett may thus be claimed to subscribe to the Dantean project in the *De vulgari eloquentia* which has been described as "a self-commentary in which the author tends to analyze his own methods of artistic production, which he implicitly identifies as the exemplar of every poetic discourse." (Eco 1999, 30)

What, then, does Beckett's self-commentary (as projected on Dante and Joyce) promote? If by 'medievalism' we understand the recognition of a certain identity between the medieval period and a later period (Bloch and Nichols 1996, 3), Beckett's Dante can be seen as a projection of modernist identities onto the medieval author. For Beckett, "Dante is proof of Joyce's artistic importance" (Caselli 2005, 11). The Dante depicted in the "Dante...Bruno. Vico..Joyce" epitomises a liter-

---

[7] See the manifestos published in the 1920s in the Parisian magazine *Transition* (founded by Eugene Jolas) and signed by its famous cast of international contributors (Beckett, Joyce, Jolas, Kafka, Klee, Tzara) in *Transition. A Paris Anthology*.

ary and linguistic experimentation that has more to do with the poetic paradigms of the 1920s than the medieval emergence of vernacular poetry. Precisely this feature, however, makes Beckett's manifesto an important articulation of the question which haunted both the medieval and modern writer. While celebrating the analogy between Dante and Joyce as ingenious creators of vernacular languages, Beckett also tackles some problems of literary language that continued to bother him throughout his own writing career. The one explored in this article is multilingualism: could it be seen – as Beckett's manifesto seems to suggest – as an elementary part of poetics in the same sense as style, figures or meters? Instead of being a changeable medium, multilingualism could thus become a device or a desire that actually *produces* modern literariness, and its *forma locutionis,* in a fundamental way.

The synthetic language and mighty vindication of the "vulgar"

> For in that whole area that extends from the mouth of the Danube (or the Meotide marshes) to the westernmost shores of England, [...] only one language prevailed, although later it was split up into many vernaculars by the Slavs, the Hungarians, the Teutons, the Saxons, the English, and several other nations.
> (Dante 1999, 17)

In the search for new modes of representation, the issue of multilingualism has been a lasting one in the history of the literary movements (Rasula and McCaffery 1998). The avant-garde 'value' of Dante in the early 1900s must be understood in the context of a new language-oriented era that cherished the attempts "to break free of [his] mother-tongue" (Dante 1999, 35, of Aldobrandino dei Mezzabati). The Italian futurist Filippo Marinetti had already realised and utilised in the early 1910s the *revolutionary possibilities of literary bilingualism,* as was aptly phrased by Paolo Valesio. Marinetti used his bilingualism both as a lyrical tool (as he wrote in both Italian and French) but also as the symbol of a new historical climate, as "Futurism once again launched Italian discourse on the international scene as an alternative to French linguistic imperialism [...] but in close collaboration with the latter imperial language" (Valesio 2002, 150). An avant-garde language based on the languages that had dominated modern discourse from the Enlightenment onwards would – according to Valesio (150) – not have been credible.

This is an important observation when considering both Dante's Italian and Beckett's English. For the purposes of his manifesto, Beckett clearly needed and used the antagonism between the anterior "abstract" (in terms of expressivity) and imperialist (in terms of power relations) language and the new, free language of particularism. This antagonism is stronger in Beckett's "Dante…Bruno. Vico..Joyce" than it is in Dante's *De vulgari eloquentia*.

> They both [Dante, Joyce] saw how worn out and threadbare was the conventional language of cunning literary artificers, both rejected an approximation to a universal language. If English is not yet so definitely a polite necessity as Latin was in the Middle Ages, at least one is justified in declaring that its position in relation to other European languages is to a great extent that of mediaeval Latin to the Italian dialects.
> (Beckett 1972, 17–18)

It has been claimed recently in the context of medieval literary criticism that in the *De vulgari eloquentia* Dante is in fact not primarily concerned with the traditional relationship between Classical and vernacular literature. According to Zygmunt G. Barański, "[Dante's] aim was to establish a new 'modern' literary hierarchy by exploring the respective artistic merits and achievement of French, Provençal and Italian" (Barański 2005, 571). Beckett, for his part, is less interested in the multitude of modern vernaculars than in the antagonism between old and new, an idea (allegedly) also shared by Dante.

Moreover, regarding the 'vernaculars' of Dante and Marinetti, we find there another analogy between the status of Italian in the early fourteenth century and its status in the early twentieth. Medieval Italian literature was a latecomer to the Romance vernaculars and, as claimed by Barański, the variety of different regional languages which could be heard on the peninsula inevitably called into doubt the very existence of an Italian literary language (571). Dante turned these "potential weaknesses […] to his own advantage and to that of Italian" (571) by transcending the dialectical fragmentation and creating his multilingual style – not unlike, we may add, Marinetti seven centuries later.

If this is true regarding Italian, the status of English to Beckett and his fellow avant-gardists was quite different – almost the opposite to the merely local interest of Italian. The English writer had confronted the (allegedly) abstract, universal and global nature of the tongue, as becomes obvious in "Dante...Bruno. Vico..Joyce" and in another text in the *Our Exagmination*, namely Eugene Jolas's "The Revolution of Language and James Joyce." In Jolas's essay (which is indeed a more traditional essay than Beckett's text in the same volume) the pivotal connection emerges between the quest for abstract literature and the issue of multilingualism:

> There is no logical reason why the transmutation of language in our day should not be as legitimate as it was throughout the ages. While painting, for instance, has proceeded to rid itself of the descriptive, has done away with the classical perspective, has tried more and more to attain the purity of abstract idealism, and thus led us to a world of wondrous new spaces, should the art of the word remain static?
> (Jolas 1972, 82)

This passage captures well the macrocosm of avant-garde poetics: the general quest for a non-representative (abstract) new language, a project that had already been established by the poets and theorists of futurism and dada.[8] Yet within the microcosm of a particular writer's choices, "the purity of abstract idealism" was a more controversial issue. In his manifesto "Dante...Bruno. Vico..Joyce", Beckett is almost obsessed by the terms 'abstraction' and 'abstract' in different contexts (3, 4, 6, 8, 10, 11, 12, 15, 16); with these keywords he both manifests the quest for new (non-realist) abstract art and yet, resists 'abstraction' in favour of the particular. For Beckett, the English before Joyce was "abstracted to death" until Joyce "desophisticated" it (15): there is "little or no attempt at subjectivism or abstraction, no attempt at

---

[8] This article is a part of my research project "A Quest for Abstract Literature. Avant-garde and Medievalism."

metaphysical generalisation. We are presented with a statement of the particular." (Beckett 1972, 16–17) Likewise Jolas, the writer working in three European languages, complains that the languages he had used creatively were beginning to be worn out. "There no longer exists any language for our deepest emotions about love and death" (Jolas, "Workshop" 44) – a comment that resembles the symbolist idea of the "inner word" and Dante as the master of the "synthetic judgment" required to create it (see Ivanov above). Jolas now sees the English language as fit for a re-birth due to its universality (90) and Joyce as an exemplary vanguard writer in his attempt to amalgamate not only the languages of the British Isles (Manx, English, Irish, Gaelic, Welsh) but also the languages spoken in the British Empire, even "modern American, so fertile in astonishing anarchic properties" (90; also 83).

While Jolas was interested in multilingualism as a broader cultural politics, in Beckett's manifesto we may detect the idea of multilingualism as a poetic device. It is crystallised in Beckett's idea of a *synthetic language*, or the possibility of such a language:

> [Dante's] conclusion is that the corruption common to all the dialects makes it impossible to select one rather than another as an adequate literary form, and that he who would write in the vulgar must assemble the purest elements from each dialect and construct a synthetic language that would at least possess more than a circumscribed local interest: which is precisely what he did. He did not write in Florentine any more than in Neapolitan. He wrote a vulgar that *could* have been spoken by an ideal Italian who had assimilated what was best in all the dialects of his country, but which in fact was certainly not spoken nor even had been.
> (Beckett 1972, 18)

In this passage the multitude of languages seems to serve – for Dante according to Beckett – as a basis for the reduction of the purest elements in the dialects. Dante, for his part, was first excited by the sheer quantity and *materia* of the dialects. "Italy alone presents a range of at least fourteen different vernaculars", internal variation within these vernaculars and, ultimately, "even in this tiny corner of the world, the count would take us not only to a thousand different types of speech, but well beyond that figure" (Dante 1999, 25). This numeral joy of multilingualism almost resembles an *ars combinatoria* which multiplies the number of alternatives (in terms of lexis, syntax, and all other imaginable features of languages) and combinatory possibilities. However, it is not the multiplication of combinations that Dante and Beckett's poetics seek, but abstraction – or in Dante's words (27), "clearing the tangled bushes and brambles out of the wood," "pruning away," "rooting out," or "sieving" the dialects.

This vindication of the vulgar established Beckett's own poetics – or prosaics – as he later, in the 1940s and 1950s, would write his major prose works primarily in French and only then translate his work into his mother tongue. He, too, was writing "neither in Florentine nor in Neapolitan" but instead cherished stylistically the (Dantean) synthetic language or genuine vulgar which was the result of not writing directly in one's own native tongue.

These remarks are the basis for a language issue which, somewhat paradoxically, results in both "a synthetic language" – Beckett's French and English as alienated from the idiomatic ways of using these languages as mother tongues – and in a vernacular vulgar style: Beckett's domestic and unadorned style which *could* have been spoken by an ideal Frenchman or Englishman, but never was. Here we should recall Beckett's often-quoted later comment about the reasons for choosing to write in French; his desire was to "write without style", to "impoverish" himself further (e.g. Wolosky 1995, 57).

A poetics of reduction

> And I hold that what can be said of things that have quantity and quality is also true of any predicate whatever, and even of substances: in short, that everything can be measured, in so far as it belongs to a genus, by comparison with the simplest individual [*signum*] found in that genus.
> (Dante 1999, 39)

Beckett's analogy between Dante and Joyce is thus clearly limp as far as the theory of language as an abstract *versus* particular element is concerned. If we read Dante without Beckett's avant-gardist mediation, Dante seems to collect elements from each Italian dialect to, in fact, *abstract* the noble vernacular from the particular dialects – just as Aristotle in his *Poetics* induced the features of the ideal tragedy from the multitude of existing particulars.[9] Although Beckett rejected the general idea of abstract language, his idea of a synthetic language and its specific *particularism* nevertheless produced, in his own prose works, linguistic literature which was free from the burden of uncomplicated mimesis and which made visible the textures of language. Regarding Beckett's bilingualism, it is worth mentioning that one of the Danteesque characters who often features in Beckett's works is Sordello. The relations between the Sordello of the *Divine Comedy* and Beckett's prose have been explored (Caselli 2005, 50–53, 134–135) but the Sordello of the *De vulgari eloquentia* is less known and more important here. Not unlike Beckett the writer, this Sordello "abandoned the vernacular of his home town" (Dante 1999, 35). In this respect Dante was an eminent proto-avant-gardist in manifesting the possibility of more or less abstract literary language – and indeed he did it quite as controversially and paradoxically as did the early twentieth-century avant-gardists themselves.

---

9 For the problematic concepts of and controversies around Dante's *gramatica* and noble vernacular, see Eco 1999, 30–50.

Petrarch in the footsteps of Dante

Unn Falkeid

Dante and Petrarch have been portrayed as rivals in the history of literature since the time of Petrarch himself. Early on, Boccaccio suggested that Petrarch was envious of Dante since the former gave the impression of avoiding the latter's name and books. In modern critiques we can find similar explanations of Petrarch's seemingly complex attitude towards Dante. John Freccero, for instance, has suggested that Petrarch's reservation represented "possibly the first example in the west of [...] the 'anxiety' of influence" (Freccero 1975, 39). Despite the many traces of Dante in Petrarch's texts, Dante is seldom if ever referred to. However, as far as other authors or literary models are concerned, Petrarch did not try to hide his sources and this may be considered to be a literary and ideological programme to him. Petrarch not only imitated and emulated his models; he continually confirmed his bookish erudition through the prominent use of other voices in his own texts. Thus his personal, individual style appears to result from an exclusive process of transforming fragments written by others.

In his three letters on imitation (*Fam.* I, 8; XXII, 2; XXIII, 19), Petrarch clearly explains the mechanism of this form of literary transformation. In an original way, though also strongly linked to the Classical metaphor of digesting, he stresses the importance of a conscious process of *assimilation* of the past to learn from it, and a process of *dissimilation* to create our own individuality. An author needs to know the words that have wandered through history, the relative meaning of the words and the different sources of the sentences and expressions. In an imitative process, an author has either to visualize his sources – *alienis dictis* – or to transform them so they become something radically different. As he explains to Boccaccio, "I grant that I like to embellish my life with sayings and admonitions of others, but not my writing unless

I acknowledge the author or make some significant change [...].¹ Most important for an author is developing his individuality and forming his own style. But this articulation requires a historical consciousness, a familiarity with tradition, so that the author is able to distinguish his own voice from those of others. Without this fundamental historical knowledge the poet's self will fragment – as Rome was a fragmented city, "fracte urbis", according to Petrarch (*Fam.* VI, 2). In a letter to his friend Giovanni Colonna he complains about the Romans' ignorance. The citizens of Rome, he argues, have forgotten their own past so that the city is now physically and morally ruined:

> Sadly do I say that nowhere is Rome less known than in Rome. I do not deplore only the ignorance involved (although what is worse than ignorance?) but the disappearance and exile of many virtues. For who can doubt that Rome would rise again instantly if she began to know herself?"²

In other words, to avoid a fragmentation of the self we have to remember our past, to be aware of the notion that "the self is literally the persona through whom the fragments of the past resound", as Giuseppe Mazzotta writes in his important monograph on Petrarch (1993b, 97). Only through the Socratic advice of self-knowledge are we able to articulate our own individuality as human beings.

As an author, Petrarch was well aware of this advice. He always seems to clarify his sources or his debts – or he transforms them so they appear to be something quite different. He recalled his manuscripts repeatedly just to make some minor changes and corrections and constantly polished his songs and poems to elaborate on his dialogue with

---

1 *Fam.* XXII, 2, 16: "Vitam michi alienis dictis ac monitus ornare, fateor, est animus, non stilum; nisi vel prolato auctore vel mutatione insigni [...]". All the English quotations from Petrarch's letters are taken from Aldo Bernardo's translation.
2 *Fam.* VI, 2, 14: "Qui enim hodie magis ignari rerum romanorum sunt, quam romani cives? invitus dico: nusquam minus Roma cognoscitur quam Rome. Qua in re non ignorantiam solam fleo – quanquam quid ignorantia peius est? – sed virtutum fugam exilium multarum. Quis enim dubitare potest quin illico surrectura sit, se ceperit se Roma cognoscere?"

Petrarch in the footsteps of Dante

other authors and perfect his own authorial voice.[3] In accordance with his own theories of imitation, this is how he avoids the risk of being an ape that just repeats the words and phrases of others. But what happens with Dante? Why does Petrarch almost never mention his Florentine colleague by name? As many scholars have indicated, Petrarch's texts are full of references to Dante.[4] Indeed, there are so many evident traces of the *Comedy* in his literary works that even modern readers are struck by them, as was the fourteenth-century Italian public. Yet Petrarch avoids naming Dante.

In his answer to Boccaccio, Petrarch refutes all speculations that he is jealous of Dante. He maintains that the reason he has never owned a copy of Dante is a fear of becoming immersed in his writings: he did not want to become an unwitting imitator. So any possible similarity between them cannot in any way be explained by theft or imitation, according to Petrarch:

> This one thing I wish to make clear, for if any of my vernacular writings resembles, or is identical to, anything of his or anyone else's, it cannot be attributed to theft or imitation, which I have avoided like reefs, especially in vernacular works, but to pure chance or similarity of mind, as Tullius calls it, which caused me unwittingly to follow in another's footsteps.[5]

Petrarch claims that any possible resemblance to Dante might be due to the fact that he, by ignorance, has followed in his footsteps. Like Rome, he has ignored himself and his own literary tradition. Consequently he follows in the footsteps and repeats the words of others, something

---

3 As is well known, Petrarch never finished his texts. He constantly corrected, polished and improved them, something that of course has been extremely interesting to philologists and biographers, such as Giuseppe Billanovich, Ernest Hatch Wilkins, Francisco Rico, Hans Baron, Nicholas Mann etc.
4 A classical study of the extant use of Dante in *Canzoniere* is Paolo Trovato, *Dante in Petrarca. Per un inventario dei dantismi nei "Rerum vulgarium fragmenta"*, Firenze, 1979.
5 *Fam.* XXI, 15, 12: "Hoc unum non dissimulo, quoniam siquid in eo sermone a me dictum illius aut alterius cuiusquam dicto simile, sive idem forte cum aliquo sit inventum, non id furtim aut imitandi proposito, que duo semper in his maxime vulgaribus ut scopulos declinavi, sed vel casu fortuito factum esse, vel similitudine ingeniorum, ut Tullio videtur, iisdem vestigiis ab ignorante concursum."

that a poet who wants to develop his own individual style should avoid like reefs.

In Petrarch's famous letter about his ascent of Mont Ventoux (*Fam.* IV, 1), the resemblance to Dante's *Comedy* is again very conspicuous – and again Dante's name is not mentioned. However, rather then interpreting the ascent as a failed imitation, as Robert M. Durling (1977) and Thomas M. Greene (1982) have proposed, and rather than interpreting the exclusion of Dante's name as a sign of Petrarch's envy or 'anxiety' of influence, as John Freccero has done, in my opinion Petrarch's project is of another character: the letter is, in a sense, a demonstration of colliding on the very reefs which Petrarch said he always tried to avoid. The wanderer seems unwittingly to follow in Dante's footsteps, resulting dramatically in a fragmented self and the corruption of his model.

The letter of Mont Ventoux is dated 26 April 1336, and it was apparently written the same day as he climbed the mountain. The 2000-meter high Mont Ventoux is situated nearby Avignon where Petrarch grew up with his family. With his younger brother Gherardo and a copy of St Augustin's *Book of Confessions* under his arm – a book that Petrarch maintained he always had with him – he sets out. However, his brother's ways of climbing the mountain soon appears quite different: he who will later become a monk marches straight to the top. But for Francesco the ascent is much more difficult, both physically and morally. He wanders in the valleys, stumbles, and tries to find short cuts which prove to be circuitous. But when he finally reaches the summit, he receives payment for his struggle: from Mont Ventoux the view is overwhelming, and the wanderer admires what he sees.

From the summit the wanderer considers the world underneath and around him – and is pleased by the view. Yet his pleasure is not complete. Having looked around, the wanderer opens Augustine's *Book of Confessions* and reads by chance the following sentences by the Church Father:

And they go to admire the summits of mountains and the vast billows of the sea and the broadest rivers and the expanses of the ocean and the revolutions of the stars and they overlook themselves.[6]

Petrarch explains that he was astonished by these words. He closed the book enraged with himself because he was even then admiring earthly things after having been long taught by pagan philosophers that he ought to consider nothing wonderful except the human mind compared to whose greatness nothing is great. With a trembling and restless heart and unaware of the stony pathway, Petrarch then returns to the cottage from which he had set out the same morning. Night has fallen, and the pilgrim wanders in the light of the full moon. When he arrives, he goes alone to a corner of the house to write to his friend, the Augustinian monk and professor of theology at the University of Paris, Dionigi da Borgo San Sepolcro, to whom the letter is dedicated.

The letter seems to belong to the Christian meditative tradition of St Augustine. In addition to being the climbing of a real mountain, the ascent of Mont Ventoux is also a memorial journey, a pilgrimage inwards and upwards to God. The pilgrim himself provides several allegorical interpretations of his journey, for instance by comparing it to the ascent to the blessed life. As Albert Russell Ascoli indicates, the wanderer's aim, the summit of the mountain, is described as the Trinity (Ascoli 1991, 21). The highest top is called the "Son", but instead it seems more like the "father", he explains. But it has been given its real name, "The Windy Mountain", for obvious reasons. The allusions to the Trinity – to the Father, Son and Holy Spirit – should then be clear enough.

As we can see, readers are offered two ways of interpreting the ascent – both allegorical and literal – of which the one does not exclude the other. However, not only the wanderer's own allegorizing of the journey, but also the many intertextual references of the letter link the ascent to the Christian mystical tradition – to St Augustine's *Book of Confessions*, to Bonaventura's *Itinerarium mentis in Deum*, to St Francis' stigmata at the mountain of La Verna in Tuscany (described in

---

[6] *Fam.* IV, 1, 27: "Et eunt homines admirari alta montium et ingentes fluctus maris et latissimos lapsus fluminum et occeani ambitum et giros siderum, et relinquunt se ipsos."

Bonaventure's biography *Legenda major*), to the biblical story of the transfiguration of Christ – and, of course, to Dante's *Comedy*.[7]

The most explicit intertextual reference in the letter is, of course, to St Augustine's *Book of Confessions*. The wanderer takes the Augustinian text with him and quotes it frequently during the journey, and the letter itself is dedicated to an Augustinian monk who has given him the book by the Church Father. However, the most contemporary intertextual reference is Dante's *Comedy*, which is not mentioned at all in the letter. Nevertheless, we can find several traces of the poem in the letter, something that is profoundly examined by Roberto Mercuri (1987). Let me briefly dwell on some of these traces or similarities discussed by him (Mercuri 1987, 344–349): first of all the allusions to the *Comedy* are visible in the strategy of constructing an epic of the self, which has obviously been developed in emulation with Dante. There are also macro-structural allusions, such as the symbolism of the number three: the journey lasts three days, the wanderer stumbles and falls three times, desire has three forms and there are three levels of contemplation. Although the symbolism of the number three has long traditions in mystical literature, it certainly also has great relevance in Dante's texts, both in *Vita nuova*, where it is connected to the myth of Beatrice, and in the basic structure of the *Comedy*.

In addition to these macro-structural allusions, Mercuri also mentions other similarities to Dante's text: for instance, Petrarch establishes the date of his journey to be 26 April 1336, which is precisely ten years after he left Bologna, the city where he had spent his young days as a student. In other words the wanderer is somewhere in between youth and maturity, like Dante starts his journey "nel mezzo del cammin di nostra vita". Moreover, 26 April 1336 is Good Friday, the selected moment of redemption and penance. Dante started his journey on the same day, Good Friday 1300. Like Dante, Petrarch sets out early in the morning. He is conflicted by tedium ("cum iam tedio confectum perplexi pigeret erroris") as Dante is, who is accused by Vergil for his empty erring ("perché ritorni a tanta noia?": *Inf*, I, 76). Finally the

---

[7] In a forthcoming article I elaborate a more thorough analysis of Petrarch's imitational strategies of St Augustine and his radical critique of the Church Father's conversional ideology: "Petrarch and the modern self. A Reading of the Mont Ventoux letter", *Forum Italicum* (forthcoming).

Petrarchan wanderer decides to try to climb the mountain, as Dante is encouraged to climb the mountain by Virgil ("perché non sali il dilettoso monte") (*Inf*. I, 77).

We can find these and many other similarities on different levels – literal, thematic and figural – between Petrarch's letter and Dante's *Comedy*. But despite all these similarities, there is much that separates the two journeys. One striking difference is the descent that follows the Petrarchan ascent, a descent that leaves the wanderer exactly where he began, in the valley of Vaucluse.[8] Contrary to Dante's description of the successive journey towards God, Petrarch narrates a circular journey on which the pilgrim both physically and spiritually ends where he started. He never obtains any affirmation of his earlier allegorizing from where he started the climb of the mountain, and he never reaches the mystical aim at the summit – the inner self or the image of God. Unlike Dante, who caught a glimpse of his own self at the profound of the Trinity, in the fountain of the Truth and the eternal Light, the only experience that the Petrarchan pilgrim has is that he has forgotten himself.

The payment for his allegorizing, for his memorial exercises and journey inwards and upwards to God, is the Augustinian admonition that he has overlooked himself (*Fam.* IV, 1, 27). The memorial journey transforms into a journey of *oblivion*. The wandering towards God becomes a wandering *away* from God. Instead of gaining knowledge ("intelligentia"), the pilgrim is thrown into confusion and anger ("iratus"). Rather than a *vita nuova*, the expected conversion at the summit of Mont Ventoux, he experiences a kind of death: he is petrified by St Augustin's words: "Obstupui, fateor" (*Fam.* IV, 1 28). That the pilgrimage is a journey away from God is clearly demonstrated at the end of the letter. The wanderer is descending the mountain instead of climbing upwards. His heart is still restless. And the light of the moon involves night and an absence of the sun, the fountain of light and life. In contrast to Dante's pilgrimage towards knowledge, light, peace and truth, the Petrarchan ascent ends in confusion, darkness and a restless emptiness.

As we have seen, Petrarch explained to his friend Boccaccio that any similarities to Dante in his texts were probably due to the fact

---

8 A. R. Ascoli (1991) strongly emphasizes this difference between Dante and Petrarch. According to him such a descent was extraordinary in the Christian literary tradition.

that Petrarch, ignorantly, had wandered in his footsteps. In my view, the consequence of this is serious enough for the wanderer in the letter of Mont Ventoux: the unwitting repetition of Dante's journey, physically as well as spiritually, is followed by a fragmentation of the self. The pilgrim does not receive any affirmation of or guarantee for his allegorical interpretations of the journey. The ascent of Mont Ventoux appears to be only the climbing of an earthly mountain – and nothing more. The journey cannot be interpreted as a conversion in a dramatic narrative about the wandering of a human being towards God, and therefore neither as a chapter in the book of God, in God's universal salvational plans. In contrast to Dante, the acknowledging subject in the Petrarchan text, the self, does not acknowledge his existence in God or Logos. As a result, and this is something that becomes very clear at the end of the letter, the self belongs to the uncertain, ever-changing world. According to Petrarch, he has to hurry to write the letter when he returns from his journey:

> [...] while the duties of preparing the meal occupy the servants, I have gone alone to a hidden portion of the inn in order to write this to you hastily and extemporaneously lest with delay my determination to write might subside with the change of place or our feelings.[9]

In other words, if he delays writing, the narrative might alter. The self, or the portrait of the self, may disappear or be transformed by the changing of time and space ("raptim et ex tempore"). Time and space, then, seem to direct his mind as well as his body.[10]

This wandering in Dante's footsteps, however, does not only result in a fragmentation of the self. It also affects Petrarch's model – unwittingly or not – namely Dante's *Comedy*. By repeating Dante's journey,

---

[9] *Fam.* IV, 1, 35–36: "Interim ergo, dum famulos apparande cene studium exercet, solus ego in partem domus abditam perrexi, hec tibi, raptim et ex tempore, scripturus; ne, si distulissem, pro varietate locorum mutatis forsan affectibus, scribendi propositum deferveret."

[10] In a forthcoming article I shall examine Petrarch's complex theories on the relationship between writing and life, style and self: "Style, the Muscle of the Soul. Theories on reading and writing in Petrarch's texts", *Quaderni d'Italianistica* (vol. 29, issue 1, 2008).

the letter articulates a critique of a certain conversional ideology and reading practice. The ascent of Mont Ventoux demonstrates the collapse of the Christian *allegorese*, which was fundamental in the *Comedy*. The universe in the Petrarchan letter does not appear to be a logical *ordo* anymore, as it was for the converted mind of the pilgrim of the *Comedy*.

On his way down the mountain, the pilgrim's contemplations may be interpreted as a rather serious critique of the epistemology of the *Comedy*. The wanderer explains that he often, upon returning home that day, turned back to look at the summit of the mountain. But the summit no longer appeared to be the blessed life. Rather, it reminded him of the pride of his earlier allegorizing and of the human *hybris* in every attempt to reach the truth. He himself had certainly failed. But he wonders if anyone at all exists who has managed to conquer the extremes of insolence and mortal destiny. With a quotation from Virgil he maintains that "happy is he who could know the causes of things and submitted his fears an inexorable fate and the rumblings of greedy Acheron to his scorn".[11] Yes, he must be happy, comments Petrarch, if he exists at all – "siquis usquam est" (*Fam.* IV, 1, 34). The quotation from Virgil implies a serious critique of Dante: Dante's pilgrimage went through the world of Acheron, through the very kingdoms of the dead, and his guide to earthly paradise was, ironically enough, Virgil. In the context of Petrarch, Virgil is again brought in, but now as a sage that reproves the human *hybris*, the insolent belief that we may cross the underworld, overcome death and gain certain knowledge in the circle of God.

According to Petrarch's own explanation, the resemblance to Dante might be caused by the fact that he unwittingly has followed in his footsteps. In the letter of Mont Ventoux he seems to have repeated, ignorantly, Dante's journey resulting in a fragmentized self and the collapse of Dante's encyclopaedic order. However, this ignorance, which as we have seen is the worst of all sins according to Petrarch, also appears, strangely, to be a peculiar technique to celebrate the *Comedy*: as the ascent of Mont Ventoux is demystified or "detheologized" and emerges only as the climbing of a real mountain rather than a journey

---

11 *Fam.* IV, 1, 34: "Felix qui potuit rerum cognoscere causas / Atque metus omnes et inexorabile fatum / Subiecit pedibus strepitumque Acherontis avari!" Petrarch cites here Vergil, *Georg.*, II 490–92.

towards God, the *Comedy* is also "detheologized" in Petrarch's extraordinary reading. The *Comedy* does not represent a vision of God anymore, but rather the poetic construction of a human being.

Vandringsmandens identitet
i Den guddommelige komedie

Jørn Moestrup

Hovedformålet med nærværende indlæg er at gå lidt nærmere ind på visse fortælletekniske problemer i *Den guddommelige komedie*, først og fremmest forholdet mellem det indlagte fortællerjeg og vandringsmanden, "l'io narrante" og "itinerante". Man kan selvfølgelig interessere sig for flere narrative niveauer ud over de to nævnte, og i det mindste et af dem er uomgængelig nødvendigt, såfremt analysen rettes mod tekstheldeden: forfatterjeget, den implicitte forfatter eller hvilken terminologi, man nu benytter sig af. Følgende klassiske parametre må man i dette tilfælde anvende i en strukturbeskrivelse af teksten og inden for denne redegøre for brugen af fortællerjeget – det vil så gøre det muligt at isolere en række tekststeder, hvor det overordnede niveau tydeligvis styrer fremstillingen, hvor forfatteren høres bag fortælleren. Det er ikke så simpelt, som det lyder, men helt galt bliver det, hvis man prøver en fremgangsmåde, der er naturlig i behandlingen af et nyere forfatterskab med adskillige titler og gerne med forskellige genrer. Her ville man først søge efter den samlede tekstmasses fællesnævnerkompleks, derefter gentage søgningen for hver titel og til sidst applicere begge resultater på det relevante værks jegfortæller, hvis en sådan findes – man prøver, så at sige, at lytte til to overordnede stemmer i forhold til jeget. Kompleksiteten i denne måde at angribe tingene på varierer stærkt, og i Dantes tilfælde er det nok kun en teoretisk mulighed – jeg er i hvert fald ikke bekendt med forsøg af lignende art. Det hænger sammen med flere ting. *Den guddommelige komedie* er godt nok ikke det eneste fiktionsværk i forfatterskabet, men indtager en så dominerende position i sammenhængen, at de øvrige profiler, man kan hente i lyrikken eller i *Vita nova*, nærmest bliver suget op af hovedværket. Det er vanskeligt at finde sådanne strukturelementer i dem, at de i tilstrækkeligt omfang kan siges at bidrage til helheden. Naturligvis er der tale om selvstændige og kunstnerisk meget værdifulde enheder, og vist findes 'stil novo'-elementerne ikke i tilsvarende omfang eller form i Komedien, men der er langt herfra og så til at beskrive en Dante med ungdomsværkerne og en markant anden manifesteret alene i Divina Commedia. Komedien er ikke en sten på vejen: den genoptager og transformerer ungdomsværkerne i en meget omfattende syntese, som det vil være nærmest umuligt at udskille fra det samlede forfatterskab på en måde, der kan bruges til noget – den fylder for meget.

Vigtigt i denne forbindelse er også, at vi er så dårligt informerede om Komediens tilblivelseshistorie. Den er skrevet over et langt tidsrum, omkring femten år ser det ud til, og der skete mange afgørende ting i verden omkring ham, og med Dante selv, mellem 1306 og 1321. Paverne kom til at sidde fast i Avignon; Europas mest magtfulde ridderorden, Tempelherrerne, blev slagtet af Philip Le Bel; Henrik den VII's togt til Italien blev en kæmpefiasko, hvilket fjernede ethvert håb hos Dante om at få bragt politisk orden i tingene, men ikke hans overbevisning om kejserdømmets guddommelige oprindelse. Han blev en kendt person, og dele af værket begyndte at cirkulere i afskrifter, men det forhindrede ikke en supplerende dødsdom fra regimet i Firenze, så den sidste rest af håb om en tilbagevenden forsvandt – det håb, der formodentlig i sin tid bidrog til planen om det store værk. Desuden er det nok i denne periode, at den kommende voldsomme forværring i Europas almentilstand, socialt og sundhedsmæssigt, markeret af pesten 1347, begynder at tage fart. Alt dette har uundgåeligt sat spor i Dantes sind og dermed i *Den guddommelige komedie*, selv om det er vanskeligt direkte at påvise dem. Det er langt fra usandsynligt, og det skal jeg prøve at komme lidt nærmere, at visse ændringer i fortællestrukturen, der specielt berører vandringsmanden og fortælleren i Paradiset, skal relateres til de store begivenheder, der havde fundet sted, af personlig og almen karakter. I modsætning til Petrarca og Boccaccio har vi ikke bevaret forfattermanuskripter af Dante, så vi har ingen mulighed for at kaste os over eventuelle tekstrettelser. At de har været der, ved vi som bekendt, fordi der i teksten forekommer årstal vedrørende bestemte personer og begivenheder, som må ligge efter affattelsestidspunktet for den pågældende passus. Omfanget kan vi kun gisne om.

Vandringsmandens identitet i Den guddommelige komedie

Inden vi forlader oversigten over de narrative niveauer, vandreren, fortælleren og forfatteren, skal det lige tilføjes, at en selvbiografisk stemme undertiden, om end sjældent, lader sig høre på en helt speciel måde – jeg skal blot citere et enkelt eksempel. Det skal naturligvis understreges, at et selvbiografisk niveau konstant er indlagt i fortællingen, i profetierne til vandringsmanden om det kommende eksil, i dialogen med Bonagiunta i 24. sang af Purgatoriet, i mødet med tipoldefaderen Cacciagiunta i Paradiset og flere andre steder, f.eks. hvor vigtigheden af vandringsmandens kommende rejseberetning fremhæves. Disse tekststeder indgår så at sige i vandringsmandens og jegfortællerens fælles profil, som i vid udstrækning er baseret på selvbiografisk stof – men når det personlige truer med at tage overhånd og løsrive sig fra sammenhængen, som i det eksempel vi kommer til, sørger Dante for, at der alligevel etableres en relevant forbindelse, således i scenen i første girone i Purgatoriet, hvor de hovmodige, i superbi er anbragt, mødet med miniaturemaleren, Oderisi da Gubbio, XI sang, linie 96–98: "Così ha tolto l'uno all'altro Guido / la gloria della lingua; e forse è nato / chi l'uno e l'altro caccerà del nido" – der er ikke megen tvivl om, hvem der hentydes til, men i de følgende linier gøres der afbigt for denne selvbevidste passus: "Non è il mondan romore altro ch'un fiato / di vento, ch'or vien quinci e or vien quindi, / e muta nome perchè muta lato" – så blev det passet ind i den lutringsproces af de hovmodige, der finder sted der, hvor vandringsmanden befinder sig

I Purgatoriet, XXVI, 121. sgg, forholder det sig helt anderledes. Her er vandringsmanden kommet til syvende og sidste kreds, i lussuriosi, og taler med den store provencalske lyriker, Giraut de Bornelh, som præsenterer ham for den mest fremtrædende af alle kollegerne, Arnaut Daniel, og samtidig harcelerer over de tåber, stolti, som ikke begriber, at han er den største. Om dem bliver det sagt: "A voce più ch'al ver drizzan li volti, / e così ferman sua oppinione / prima ch'arte o ragion per loro s'ascolti" – Allerede her, i diskussionen om, hvem af de provencalske lyrikere, der er den vigtigste, er vi ude i en fjern digression, og det tangerer det absurde i de følgende linier: "Così fer molti antichi di Guittone, / di grido in grido pur lui dando pregio, / fin che l'ha vinto il ver con più persone". At Giraut de Bornelh skulle have den ringeste anelse om den ikke voldsomt betydningsfulde toskanske digter Guittone d'Arezzos eksistens, er mildt sagt usandsynligt. Dante bærer åbenbart rundt på en god portion irritation over, at man lokalt – i hvert fald i Arezzo og omegn – bliver ved med at tro, at Guittone var noget. Han får et æselspark, og så fik sjælen ro, men denne udladning er helt uden sammenhæng med, hvad der i øvrigt foregår på stedet. Anna Maria Chiavacci Leonardi taler i sin udmærkede kommentar i Mondadoris Meridiani-udgave om Dantes "interesse polemico" i sagen (Chiavacci 1994, 783), og det er meget pænt sagt. Her har vi et af de få eksempler på en selvbiografisk stemme, der ikke harmonerer med resten.

Vi vender os mod forholdet mellem fortæller og vandrer. Det har ofte været gjort til genstand for overvejelser i Dante-studierne, og der er særlig to aspekter af denne relation, som har været fremført gang på gang og stadig bliver det. For det første argumenteres der for, at der er en principiel og veltilrettelagt forskel mellem to synsvinkler, som Dante udnytter til at skabe variation og dybde i teksten – på den ene side følger vi den uforberedte rejsende og præsenteres for hans spontane reaktioner, på den anden retledes vi af en fortæller, der har oplevet det hele og nu kan kommentere sine erfaringer. – Det andet aspekt af vandrer-fortæller relationen, som her skal behandles, ligger i forlængelse af det første: forskellen mellem de to synsvinkler hypostaseres i den grad, at rejsen, og dermed vandrerens figur, behandles som et udviklingsforløb, *Den guddommelig komedie* gøres til en variant af genren Bildungsroman. Ved vejs ende er jeget et helt andet, end da det hele startede med flugten ud af la selva oscura og den mislykkede bestigning af bjerget med vilddyrene. Betragtet med indledende enfoldighed, er der noget umiddelbart overbevisende i denne måde at se tingene på – man kan vel ikke aflægge besøg, godt nok hurtige, men alligevel, i Helvede, Skærsild og Paradis uden at det sætter sine spor, og det var vel i grunden også meningen? Vandringsmanden har store problemer, da han bliver kontaktet af Vergil, hvis opgave er at redde ham fra skoven, og i første omgang skal han skræmmes godt og grundigt på turen gennem Inferno. Der er flere graverende mangler ved denne måde at angribe tingene på. For at tage det sidste først: meningen med det hele. Meget tyder på, at planen er blevet ændret undervejs, eller i det mindste, at den måde, den er blevet udfyldt på, er noget anderledes end oprindelig planlagt. Det er evident, at et værk som Divina Commedia, med en så fuldendt harmonisk struktur, må have været tænkt i hovedtræk fra begyndelsen, men det er lige så klart, at det umådeligt komplekse indhold har undergået forandringer i en 15 år lang proces. De mest interessante elementer i denne sammenhæng finder man i de erklæringer om rejsens formål, som vandrer og fortæller kommer med i fællesskab, og i tilkendegivelser fra andre om samme emne, først og fremmest Beatrice i Edens Have og Sankt Peter i Paradiset, og de harmonerer ikke særlig godt. Til en begyndelse handler det, som angivet, først og fremmest om at redde den arme vandringsmand, et initiativ, der udgår fra Maria, inspireret af ren medynk. Det virker lidt, hvis man tør udtrykke sig så uærbødigt, som en venindetjeneste over for Beatrice, og noget som helst endnu højere formål er der ikke antydning af. Man kan ikke acceptere en formulering som Michelangelo Vicones (i en i øvrigt interessant publikation fra 2001): "[...] a volere il viaggio dell'io [...] è in definitiva Dio stesso, la cui volontà è intuita dalla Vergine Maria, che la comunica a Lucia, che la rende nota a Virgilio, che finalmente la trasmette al diritto interessato Dante" – den er der faktisk ikke noget belæg for. I stedet kunne meget tale for, at Dante på dette indledende stade slet ikke havde tænkt sig, inden for den grandiose struktur, som rejsen giver ham mulighed for at skildre, at pilgrimmen skulle have den afgørende rolle, han senere fik, specielt i Paradiset. Først på toppen af Purgatoriebjerget, da Beatrice har taget ham til nåde igen, understreger hun, i 32. og endnu grundigere i 33. sang (henholdsvis vv. 103–5 og 52–57), at et hovedformål med rejsen er den beretning, han skal levere til sine syndefulde samtidige, når han kommer tilbage til jorden. Denne linie fortsættes efter bestået eksamen med Sankt Peter i Paradiset, (XXVII, 63–5), og det gælder i det hele taget, at opstigningen til Paradiset medfører en vægtforskydning til fordel for pilgrimmen – han er på en ganske anden måde end tidligere på rejsen placeret i centrum, han er aktiv deltager og ikke blot den iagttager, han primært var i de første to cantiche. Det er vanskeligt at se, at det nye rejsemål i sig selv skulle motivere denne ændrede rolle, som må have andre og væsentlige årsager. Her er vi naturligvis på hypotesernes vidtstrakte overdrev, men det er ikke urimeligt at se bevægelsen fra synder til profet, fra skarp til nådesløs kritik, af institutioner snarere end personer, alt inden for samme katedralbygning – som en reaktion på en stærkt forværret situation, både for Dante selv (dødsdømt og uden det ringeste håb om at kunne vende tilbage) og for de magtstrukturer, han anså for indstiftet af Gud, imperiet og pavemagten: kejseren Henrik den 7. død, nærmest under flugt fra Italien, Sankt Peters efterfølgere bosat fjernt fra Rom og underkastet det franske monarki.

Opfattelsen af forholdet mellem fortæller og vandrer hænger nøje sammen med synet på teksten som udviklingsroman, og den klassiske tekst på dette område er Francis Fergussons nu mere end halvtreds år gamle afhandling, *Dante's Drama of the Mind* med undertitlen *A Modern Reading of the Purgatorio*[1]. Den har langtfra mistet sin aktualitet, og er mig bekendt aldrig blevet systematisk modsagt. Den har spillet en stor rolle for den mest kendte bog, der er skrevet i Skandinavien om Dante, Lagerkrantz' *Från helvetet till paradiset*, men parallelle synspunkter støder man ofte på, f.eks. i Lene Waage Petersens artikel fra 1995, "Odysseus sidste rejse", hvor det bl.a. hedder:

> Vi har allerede sagt, at personen Dante i digtet er spaltet i to: pilgrimmen Dante, der oplever første gang, og taler direkte til Vergil og sjælene; og fortælleren Dante, som *har* oplevet rejsen og hvis projekt er at beskrive den. Dante udnytter denne fundamentale modsætning sådan som det sker i erindringsfortællinger, der har karakter af dannelsesromaner; det yngre jeg oplever, reagerer, fejler; det ældre korrigerer, forklarer.
> (Waage Petersen 1995, 79)

– Jeg skal understrege, at der ikke er noget grundlag for at polemisere med Petersen, hvis undersøgelse handler om noget helt andet, men netop det forhold, at emnet blot strejfes og at den skitserede holdning nærmest fremstilles som en selvfølgelighed, er et godt vidnesbyrd om, hvor aktuel denne problemstilling stadig er.

Lagerkrantz citerer Fergusson langstrakt i sin kommenterede bibliografi (214–15) og er stærkt påvirket af hans synsmåde. Det hedder således:

> Det er [...] mange steder svært at se, hvor grænsen mellem pilgrimmen og fortælleren går. De lever på forskellige planer og tilhører forskellige generationer, men gnister springer ustandseligt imellem dem. Den ældres ansigtstræk, mærket af politiske

---

[1] Ny udgave Greenwood Press Reprint, 1981.

og religiøse lidenskaber, træder frem bag den yngres ufærdige ansigt. Den unge ledes – ofte som et barn ført af en far eller en mor – mod paradiset af Vergil og Beatrice. Den ældre driver med kraft og kundskab sit digt frem mod samme mål under samme personers beskyttelse. Mens fortælleren Dante har tidens højeste dannelse, ejer pilgrimmen Dante kun ufuldstændige kundskaber. Pilgrimmen er helt i en udviklingsroman. Han udvikles gennem de lektioner i moral, politik og religion, som livet, vandringen giver ham. Det varer længe, inden han kommer til klarhed. Hans udviklingskamp er et af Komediens store temaer. (Lagerkrantz 1965, 13-14)

Der er valgt et langt citat, der dels ligger fuldstændig på linie med Fergusson, dels med et maksimum af klarhed skitserer en bestemt holdning til tingene, som jeg gerne vil prøve at gøre op med. Den citerede passus starter med at fastslå, at det er vanskeligt at skelne mellem vandringsmand og fortæller, og det kan man kun være enig i. Resten er stort set en fremstilling i fiktionsform af, hvordan vandrer og fortæller kunne have været, hvis de i stedet for litterære personer havde været levende mennesker. Hvordan i alverden finder man ud af, f.eks., at fortælleren har sin tids højeste dannelse, mens vandreren kun har ufuldstændige kundskaber? I den citerede passus af Oderisi (*Purg.* XI, 97-9) er der som omtalt ikke meget at diskutere – ingen ældre og kun få, overfølsomme Dante-kommentatorer har tvivlet på, at forfatteren taler om sig selv, og det gør han med samme selvfølelse længere fremme i Purgatorio, da han – og det er stadigvæk den 35-årige det drejer sig om, og som her har ordet – retleder Bonagiunta: "I' mi son un che, quando / amor mi spira, noto [...]" – der som fremstående repræsentant for en ny digtning på et helt andet niveau da også behandles med skyldig ærbødighed af sin ældre forgænger. Der er ikke i teksten noget grundlag for den fremsatte påstand om niveauforskel mellem vandrer og fortæller. Naturligvis har fortælleren oplevet det hele, men han fremstår ikke af den grund som klogere. Når han forklarer noget, siger han det, vandreren allerede har forstået; han korrigerer aldrig, og når vandreren dummer sig, irettesættes han af Vergil eller Beatrice, under ingen omstændigheder af fortælleren, der begrænser sig til at referere reprimanden, som vandreren naturligvis forstår og accepterer og fortælleren med ham. Divina Commedia er rig på situationer, der viser en genial digters utrolige indsigt i den menneskelig psyke, men den bliver aldrig brugt til at etablere en forskel på vandrer og fortæller.

Hvorfor sådan?
Om Komedien på italiensk og andre sprog

Ole Meyer

> all without mistaking
> any thing
> for what it may not be
> (Lawrence Ferlinghetti)

Vilkårene for oversættelsen og oversætteren

Opgaven med at overføre *La (Divina) Com(m)edia* til dansk, svensk eller norsk er en anden end på engelsk, tysk eller fransk, og ikke kun fordi sprogene er forskellige. På store sprog er der allerede et stort antal oversættelser at vælge mellem, og flere kommer hele tiden til: mange af dem gode, men såre forskellige. På nordisk er friheden både større og mindre: man er ikke lige så nødt til at rydde sig plads og finde sin egen form, forskellig fra de andres; til gengæld må man levere en disciplineret tekst der kan stå alene i lang tid som en adækvat gengivelse af kildeteksten på målsproget. Der kommer jo næppe andre foreløbig.

De mål jeg har sat mig for den danske Komedie (2000, 3. udg. 2004), har foruden filologisk, semantisk og metrisk teksttroskab været hensynet til læselighed, frasering og flerstemmighed. Det er hensyn der går fra det mere til det mindre entydige, men dog ikke vilkårlige. De kan naturligvis komme i indbyrdes konflikt, og må da prioriteres. Flerstemmighed indebærer bl.a. temposkift i personernes diktion, og differentiering i og mellem fortæller- og personstemmer – ligesom hos Dante selv. Jeg læser m.a.o. Komedien som en proto-roman, der også kan regnes for den første europæiske jeg-roman: det er i hvert fald et synspunkt der har hjulpet med til oversættelsen.

Det er selvfølgelig ikke den eneste mulige læsemåde, og nogle vil sikkert protestere mildt. Argumenterne kan læses andetsteds og skal ikke gentages her.[1] Imidlertid: teksten tilhører på et tidspunkt læseren, ikke den der har skrevet den, og hvis nogen ikke bryder sig om fraseringer og stilfarvninger der afviger fra hvad man forventer som litterært normalsprog eller lignende, tilkommer det ikke mig at kommentere det.

Hvis således en læser hellere ville høre Beatrice sige kontant og hurtigt til Vergil i *Helv.* II 72:

Jeg kom af kærlighed, der bød mig tale.

fremfor det mere dvælende og markerede:

Af kærlighed, der bød mig tale, kom jeg.

– kan og vil jeg ikke modsige det. Begge dele er korrekte 11-stavelsesvers, og mulige gengivelser af den lidt sære sætning *amor mi mosse, che mi fa parlare* (ikke den mulige og mere ligefremme **amor mi mosse e mi fa parlare*) [2]. Jævnfør de forskellige nutidsfraseringer i f.eks. Scialoms *amour m'a incitée, me fait parler*; eller Durling & Martinez' *love has moved me and makes me speak* over for Carsons *as love moved me, I speak because of love* eller Peter Dales *Love moved me. Love has made me speak*. Hurtigere vs. langsommere, et eller to åndedrag.

Kildeteksten og dens sprogform

La Comedias editionsfilologiske historie er lang, kompleks og vel næppe afsluttet. Også jeg følger Petrocchis Vulgata-udgave fra tresserne eller sekstiåra, men har i tredje udgave indsuppleret et par steder fra Sanguinetis tekst (2001); det er der redegjort for i noterne. I løbet

---

1 "Dante's Divine Comedy – Epic or Novel?", i: *Letteratura Italiana Antica* V, ed. Antonio Lanza, Roma 2004, eller den omtrent tilsvarende artikel i *Perspektiv på Dante I*, udg. Christian Kaatmann & Ole Meyer, København 2001.
2 ** Mi mosse amore, che mi fa parlare* forekommer nærliggende, men er vistnok ikke sproghistorisk mulig.

af den sidste menneskealder er udgiverne formentlig kommet tættere og tættere på hvad man kan regne for Dantes egen ru og variable sprogform (her skal også nævnes Lanzas florentinske udgave fra halvfemserne eller nittiårene). Hvilket dog ikke betyder at det der står, står der på samme måde som Dante selv har skrevet eller dikteret det, og her er der flere fælder for den der ikke kender en smule til middelalderlige håndskrifter i forhold til trykte bøger.

Hvis man f.eks. tror man ved at Dante i Inferno XI, 80-101 skrev alle tre begrebsord *Fysik, Filosofi* og *Etik* med stort, som senere udgaver gør, og undrer sig over at oversættelsen ikke gør det, har man uforvarende læst forkert i originalteksten. Distributionen af store/små bogstaver blev først fastlagt i nyere tid, ligesom regler for gængs tegnsætning: begge dele skyldes i det væsentlige 1500-tallets venetianske bogtrykkere, hvem vi jo forresten også skylder markedsføringen af *La Comedía* som *Divina*. Hvis Dante eller hans skriver eventuelt, i en for længst tabt autograf eller diktat, skulle have skrevet *Filosofia* (v. 97) med stort (men formentlig *etica*, v. 80, og *fisica*, v. 101), har det været fordi ordet hos ham står versinitialt. Når også trykte udgaver skriver *Filosofia*, foruden *Etica* og *Fisica*, er det fordi ordet indleder en replik og dermed følger efter (senere tiders!) punktum og anførselstegn – blot altså ikke i den danske oversættelse. *Etik* og *Fysik* er imidlertid titler på værker af Aristoteles – som dog ikke har efterladt sig noget skrift med titlen *Filosofi*, så lidt som Duke Ellington har skrevet et stykke der hedder *Jazz* ... For nu at undgå en måske nærliggende misforståelse, kan man i oversættelse bytte om på ledfølgen i Vergils replik: en idé jeg fik fra Ingvar Björkesons svenske *Komedi*. Den får her ordet over for teksten i Bosco & Reggios udgave (vv. 97-100; man kan forresten bemærke sig den let arkaisk-poetiske adverbialordstilling som Björkeson stedvis tillader sig, her dog i Vergils fortalte personsprog):

Filosofia, mi disse, a chi
la 'ntende
nota, non pure in una
sola parte
come natura lo suo
corso prende

Han svarade: På flera ställen
visar
filosofin, för alla som förstår
den
hur från gudomlig skaparkraft
och vishet

dal divino 'ntelletto e	hela naturen härleder sitt
da sua arte	ursprung
e se tu ben la tua Fisica	och om du läser uppmärksamt
note [...]	Fysiken [...]

Om navne og ordformer i øvrigt gælder det at navnepraksis i oversættelsen ikke kan være lige så konsekvent dansk som Dantes er italiensk. Hans konsekvens må dog ikke forveksles med stringens: navne og andre ord kan skifte form efter kontekst og behov, så *virtù* også kan hedde *virtude* (jf. nedenfor), pronominet *me* blir dialekt-toskansk til *me-e*, det grove ord *introcque* fortrænger et bestemt sted *frattanto* el. lign. (*Helv.* XX, 130), *Thomas Aquinas* el. *Tommaso* (*Purg.* XX, 69) *d'Aquino* omtaler sig selv som *Thomas* (*Pd.* X 99: nogle udgivere antager her en fransk udtale og skriver *Thomàs*), men kaldes snart efter af Bonaventura for *Tomma* (*Pd.* XII 110: mon nogen oversætter turde skrive *Tommy*?), og Paulus (*Paolo*) lyder i en fransk paves mund som *Polo* (*Pd.* XVII 136 – på dansk *Povl*), osv. osv. Det kan man ikke følge hver gang, men i oversættelsen kaldes f.eks. Frederik II's sønnedatter *Costanza* (Constance) for *Konstanza* på jorden (*Purg.* III), mens hendes oldemor hedder *Konstantia* i Himlen, hvor den kvalitet ved hende, og ved hendes navn, er i fokus (*Pd.* III). Og fortællerstemmen siger *vores vandring gennem livet*, mens Vergil til Beatrice siger *vor menneskehed* (*Helv.* II, 77). Og så videre.

Dette er et af flere felter hvor en oversættelse ikke kan tage sig så mange friheder som Dante selv. Dem er der jo skrevet en del om, fra Bembo i 1500-tallet og fremefter. Skellet går mellem dem der i renæssance- eller klassicistisk ånd fordrer højstemt egalitet – som i et epos eller en klassisk tragedie – og dem der indrømmer forskelligheder, herunder lavsprog – som i en roman eller en komedie. Litteraturhistorisk forventeligt forholder oversættelser til forskellige tider sig uens til dette spørgsmål, men forskellene kan også ses mellem næsten samtidige, moderne oversættelser, på fransk f.eks. mellem Vegliante og Scialom. Blandt de indledende citater har jeg markeret forskellige gengivelser – konkrete, allegoriske eller vidtløftige – af nogle centrale ord i Komediens første terzin. Her er en bred vifte af stil, fra fransk preciøsitet, tysk og guldalderdansk idealisme til engelsk klassicisme, akademisk omstændelighed, med mere. Gmelins klare nøgternhed, Scialoms ekspressive musikalitet og Musas fortælle-energi kan kun antydes i uddraget. Det samme gælder Belfast-digteren Ciaran [udt. kieran] Carsons herlige gadesprog med tone af irsk ballade: den slags er der kun plads til på større sprog, og dog har jeg tilladt mig at låne et par steder fra ham, og fra landsmanden Seamus Heaney, til min tredje udgave. Hans forord slutter:

[...]When I began looking into the *Inferno*, it occurred to me that the measures and assonances of the Hiberno-English ballad might provide a model for translation. It would allow for sometimes extravagant alliteration, for periphrasis and inversion to accomodate the rhyme, and for occasional assonance instead of rhyme; it could accomodate rapid shifts of register. So I tried to write a *terza rima* crossed with ballad.

[...] in fact the Italian or the Florentine of the *Inferno*, so far as I can read it, has a relentless, peripatetic, ballad-like energy, going to a music which is by turns mellifluous and rough, taking in both formal discourse and the language of the street. It moves from place to place, as Dante walked through Italy, as he walked through the Inferno.

As I walked the streets of Belfast, I wanted to get something of that music.

Lidt om Dantes syntaks: den veksler jo mellem det skriftlige – på et skriftsprog som endnu ikke har fundet sin senere form, og som han selv leder i retninger hvor det ikke havde været før – og det mundtlige, som optræder i replikker og andet, dog ikke nødvendigvis hver gang en fortalt person har ordet. Mundtlighed er som bekendt ikke altid lig enkelhed: der kan være lag af underforståethed, f.eks. med hensyn til hvad den talende forudsætter bekendt eller præsent for modtageren, og hvor meget samtalepartnere medtænker eller indlever sig i hinandens tanker. Vi er inde på det komplicerede begreb tekstlig polyfoni, som Michel Olsen diskuterede på Stockholm-seminaret (Cullhed red. 2006). Det kan her være interessant at se på hvordan sammenhængen mellem sætningerne etableres, logisk og narrativt. Et belysende eksempel er en logisk forbinder som konjunktionen *se*, der hos Dante synes at dække varierende betydninger som på senere sprogtrin varetages af flere forskellige konjunktioner og forbindelser. (Siger jeg uden at være sproghistoriker.)

Alle kommentatorer osv. er naturligvis enige om den simple betydning *hvis*, altså betingelse eller antagelse: *Se tu segui la tua stella*, osv. (*Inf*. XV, 55), samt om betydningen *om*, i indirekte spørgsmål: *saprai se m'ha offeso* (*Inf*. XXXIII, 21). Slige tilfælde er entydige. Betydningen *selvom* eller *skønt*, er oftest også klart : [...] *ei non peccaro; e s'elli hanno mercedi non basta, perché non ebber battesmo*, siger Vergil om indvånerne i Limbo (*Inf*. IV, 34–35). Men umiddelbart efter siger han *e se furon dinanzi al cristianesmo, non adorar debitamente a Dio*, og hvad mener han mon her? Taler han om dem alle, udøbte børn, ædle hedninger og prækristne voksne under et, eller kun om den sidste kategori?

Der er vist tre muligheder, men ingen af dem synes nu at passe helt på passagens indhold:

1. *hvis*, dvs.: "de af dem (de voksne) der blev født før dåben indstiftedes, og derfor ikke er historiske kristne". Indholdsmæssigt og logisk synes det i orden, og de fleste oversættere har vistnok forstået det således: *And if they lived before Christianity* (Durling & Martinez), med flere. Men en sådan læsning støder mod *e se*, som synes at etablere en parallel opad i teksten, til det før nævnte *s'elli hanno mercedi*, og dermed pege på:

2. *(anche) se*, selvom.[3] Hvilket dog her gir en meget indviklet læsning, som implicerer en række underforståede udsagn i retning af "Og [*selvom du kan indvende at*] de [, *altså nogle af dem, jo*] var fra før kristendommen [*og dermed burde være lovligt undskyldt*], er dét ikke nok, fordi [*det væsentlige er at heller ikke*] de besad kristendom". Således tolker faktisk *Enciclopedia Dantesca* stedet, men kun få oversættere har valgt en sådan læsning: *Wenn sie auf Erden wandelten vor Christus* (Reinhold Schoener) åbner vel i hvert fald for muligheden. Der kan være flere grunde til oversætternes tilbageholdenhed: sådan underforstået, nærmest folkeligt-jovialt plejer den ellers nøje skanderende Vergil ikke at udtrykke sig. Og mon vi kan regne med en så ud- og indviklet grad af dialogisk polyfoni, i betydningen implicit formulering af samtalepartnerens (her Dante-personens) tanker, i en

---

3   *Enciclopedia Dantesca*, V, 1984 (1972), artiklen *Se*, pkt. 7, der citerer denne passage.

så tidlig tekst? Måske, måske ikke, men det ville i en oversættelse nok kræve en længere og trættende note til at forklare hvad meningen egentlig skulle være. Og derfor, eller også derfor:

3. *Og da de* [dvs. de fleste af dem] *leved inden kristendommen, tilbad de ikke Gud på rette måde*, er vel hvad sagen grundlæggende drejer sig om, og således har jeg oversat. Således vist også Marc Scialom: *Ayant vécu avant le christianisme*, foruden Zoozmann: *Weil sie vor* [fremhævet ved spatiering] *Christo lebten*, ellers vistnok ingen. Giorgio Siebzehner-Vivanti regner dog blandt andet med en betydning *con valore causativo* = *siccome*. [4] (En bedre term end *causativo* ville her nok være *implicativo* el. lign., altså for betydningen *eftersom, idet, siden* – eller *da*. På fransk *puisque* snarere end *parce que*; på moderne italiensk *poiché, dato ché, siccome*, eller *giacché* (jf. nedenfor), i rækkefølge fra det formelle til det mere kollokviale. Det drejer sig kort sagt om 'det vi går ud fra' som fælles præmis for diskursen mellem samtalepartnere).

Helt går det vist ikke op, men jeg har valgt hvad man kunne kalde en *translatio facilior*. Interessant er det at Dante tilsyneladende har færre, mindre differentierede ord på dette felt end man finder senere, på mere udviklede trin af italiensk skriftsprog: han bruger *se* (få gange) og *perché* (hyppigt, med varierende betydninger: kausalt eller kausativt = *fordi* og implikativt = *eftersom, idet*). Et interessant sted desuden, i en refereret replik, det folkelige *da che*: [...] *Padre, da che tu mi lavi* (*Inf.* XXVII, 108, jf. Olsen s. 258): det svarer vel til moderne *giacché*. Her oversætter for eksempel Björkeson med det skriftsproglige *eftersom*, mens jeg fra og med tredje udgave har valgt det mundtlige *når nu*.

Målteksten tone og sigte

Vi er allerede på vej ind i det mindre entydige, nemlig hvordan målteksten skal lyde og virke, dog stadig ud fra en analyse af kildeteksten.

Om prosodi og versstil har jeg skrevet mere udførligt andetsteds, med den hovedpointe at der omkring 1960 er sket et fundamentalt skift i poetisk diktion, på dansk som i andre vestlige litteraturer: fra skrift- til talesprog, hos os anskueliggjort i eksempelvis forskellen mellem

---

4 *Dizionario della Divina Commedia*, 1989 (1953), artiklen "Se", § 8, der dog ikke bruger dette eksempel.

lyden hos Ole Sarvig og Frank Jæger over for Klaus Rifbjerg og Ivan Malinovski.[5] Det stiller andre betingelser og muligheder for en klassikeroversættelse, især af en forfatter som Dante der netop ikke skrev glatte petrarkiske eller klassicistiske vers som den senere tradition krævede. Skellet mellem italiensk middelalder (omkring 1200-tallet, inkl. Dante) og renæssance (fra Petrarca til Bembo) svarer her til forskellen mellem nordeuropæisk renæssance-barok (eksempel Shakespeare), og den senere klassicisme (eksemplerne legio).

Komediens fortællerstemme går hos mig ud fra moderne talesprog der leverer fortællingens ligefremme og energiske grundtone, forskellig fra de danske forgængeres 1800-talsdiktion. Sidste vers i Helv. I kan dermed enkelt oversættes som *Så gik han foran, og jeg fulgte efter* – *Allor si mosse, e io li tenni dietro* – over for Molbechs *Da gik han forud og jeg fulgte trolig* (1851, med rim på *Bolig* to linier før) og Hee Andersens endnu mere stampende jambiske: *Da gik han frem, og jeg ham fulgte efter* (1963).

Men der er også andre stemmer, heriblandt den fortalte jeg-persons mere eller mindre autoritative røst, med lån fra religiøs, filosofisk og andre slags mere langsom sprogbrug. Alt sammen har det sin mere eller mindre entydige modsvarighed hos Dante, uden altid at kunne overføres i en 1:1-relation.

Arkaismer har jeg søgt at undgå, undtagen hvor de enkelte steder har en funktion: *ved hiin Oldings Kalden* (*Purg.* XXX, 16, kursiveret) for det latinske *ad vocem tanti senis* (17). Et herligt ord som *miskundhed* (*Pd.* XXXIII, 19, for Dantes *misericordia*) optræder 30–35 gange i den danske salmebog, alt efter hvilke former og afledninger man regner med (iflg. Holger Bennikes *Salmeordbog*). Björkeson har her *misskund*, Ulleland *misskundsemd*. Det kan vist ikke helt erstattes af noget andet ord, ikke engang af *barmhjertighed*; men hvis nogen studser over det, kan det måske illustrere det forhold at religiøst sprog næppe har været produktivt på dansk i generationer, hvorved der for nogle vel er sket et ordtab. Skønt ordet fortsat findes og bruges.

Tilsvarende kan, på et syntaktisk plan, gælde for en salmevending som den jeg har lagt Dante i munden i hans taksigelse til Beatrice (*Pd.*

---

5 "Syllabiske vers på dansk", i: *Metrik & Musik*, red. Christian Kock, Rhetor Förlag 2002 (= *Skrifter utgivna av Centrum för Metriska Studier*, 13).

XXX, 86–87): [...] *med alle midler som du besad og vidste ret at bruge*. Adverbiet og dets placering sender en diskret hilsen til Brorsons *Op al den Ting* (i den norske salmebog *Opp, alle ting*) som der også refereres til i *Helv.* XXVIII; andre steder er der forbindelse til Grundtvig og Kingo. (Her er ikke tale om såkaldt 'omvendt ordstilling'[6], der ikke forekommer i teksten). Komedien selv er som bekendt fuld af den slags intertekstuelle referencer, men kun få kan overføres direkte, i det mindste ikke uden at overbelaste noteapparatet.

Her kunne så interessant diskuteres hvorledes en moderne oversættelse fra en sekulær tid kan forholde sig til en tekst, et sprog og en tid der er gennemvævet af religion på måder der er fremmed for de fleste, oversætteren indbefattet. Til den anglokatolske *Komedie*-oversætter (og krimiforfatter) Dorothy L. Sayers' udsagn om sig selv som en af et *we who share Dante's basic assumptions*, bemærkede nogle årtier senere den lærde og klarsynede Kenelm Foster, O.P.: *One wonders if she ever thought about just how many of his assumptions she really did share* [...] Det er et problem der endnu i 1963 næppe havde meldt sig på noget subjektivt plan for fhv. stiftsprovst Knud Hee Andersen, fra den daværende danske kirkes yderste højrefløj. Hans *Komedie* kan betegnes som den sidste danske guldaldertekst, narrativt, stilistisk og ideologisk; jf. Georg Brandes' kritik hundrede år tidligere i Shakespeare-essayet om det *Uendeligt Smaa* og det *Uendeligt Store*. Brandes fremhæver som bekendt Shakespeares ligefremme realisme, ligesom Erich Auerbach hundrede år senere pegede på Dante som *Dichter der irdischen Welt*.

Med hensyn til filosofisk begrebsrethed er det et selvfølgeligt vilkår at et givet begreb hos Dante ikke hver gang kan gengives med ét og samme ord – men som regel gør det dog, og den almindelige læser blir ikke snydt. At derimod en forsker bør kontrollere i originalteksten, eventuelt med støtte i en f.eks. fransk eller engelsk paralleloversættelse, er vel en selvfølge.

---

6 Begrebet er vist ikke lingvistisk veldefineret da det ikke drejer sig om et fænomen der optræder i naturligt sprog. Men almindeligvis bruges det vist om ugrammatisk placering af subjekt eller objekt: *Endnu den* (skoven) *vækker angst i mine tanker* (Hee Andersen, 1963); *Hvor enkelte af Nattens skjønne Terner / Jeg alt igjennem Kløften kunde kjende* (Molbech, 1851), eller faktisk endnu Björkeson, 1983: [...] *ropade Minos då han mig blev varse*. Ikke at forveksle med (grammatisk) inversion.

Til anskueliggørelse kan man her overveje det ovenfor citerede eksempel fra ellevte helvedssang hvor Björkeson oversætter *arte* med (*skapar*) *kraft*, jeg og Magnus Ulleland derimod med *kunst* (Mark Musa: *artistic workmanship*, Marc Scialom: *art*, Peter Dale og Ciaran Carson: *Art*) – og det ene er næppe i sig selv rigtigere end det andet. Tilsvarende for *intelletto*: *vishet* (Björkeson), (*guddoms*)*tanken* (Meyer), *Intellekt* (Ulleland), *intellect* (Musa og Dale), *pensée* (Scialom), *Intellect Sublime* (Carson).

Filosofiske knudesteder og -termer har jeg efter evne kommenteret formuleringen af undervejs, jf. også Forord s. 38. Jeg kan her bruge anledningen til at uddybe det lidt, hvilket ikke er sket før:

En ét-ord-til-ét-ord-gengivelse er ikke i sig selv mere retvisende end en flerords (selvom 1:1-strategien vistnok almindeligvis og med rette gennemføres i oversættelse af egentlige filosofiske fagtekster, enten ved at vælge et indfødt ord eller ved at overføre det fremmede ord til målsproget). De få steder hvor *Komedie*-oversættelsen bruger flere ord for ét begreb, skyldes det mindre versnød end hensynet til – netop – præcision hvor ét ord ikke ville dække (jf. fra en anden klassiker det græske *logos* som Faust i første akt hos Goethe har sin famøse kval med at gengive på tysk: *Wort? Sinn ? Kraft? Tat?*).

Begrebet *pietà/pio* berøres kort i Kommentaren (*Helv*. V, 117 med videre henvisning til VI 2–3; henvisningen kunne også udvides til V 140). Det kommer jo fra det klassisk-latinske *pietas*, som i sig selv er et ganske komplekst begreb; også i adjektivformen, der kendes fra Vergils gentagne omtale af sin helt som *pius Aeneas*: her udtrykkes en sum af forestillinger som kun meget ufuldstændigt dækkes af *dyd(ig)* eller lignende, nemlig trofasthed, ærbødighed, fromhed, pligtopfyldelse, offerberedthed, traditions- og skæbnebevidsthed og mere til: samlet det augustæiske ideal af den gode romerske borger. Skulle alt det rummes i ét dansk ord, måtte Æneidens hovedperson vel finde sig i at hedde *den piøse Æneas [...] Med kristendommen kommer endnu mere til, ikke mindst psykologisk. Når således Dante-personen føler *pietà* over for Paolo og Francesca, dækker det som et minimum dels kristen og human medynk på deres vegne, dels anfægtelse på egne vegne. Dertil et strejf af fromhed, m.m.: *pitié-piété* på fransk eller på engelsk *pity* + *piety* (med en undertone af *anxiety*?).

Tilsvarende for det antikke *virtus*, eller Dantes *virtù/virtude*. Når Odysseus i Inferno XXVI, 120 slutter sin berømte tale med en appel til skibsfællerne om at stræbe efter *virtude e canoscenza*, dækkes summen af de to ord næppe helt af kun to danske: *dyd* (omtrent i Oplysningsbetydning)+ *kløgt* + *kundskab* synes at være et (måske pedantisk?) minimum for at sige det han vil have sagt (plus måske endda *kraft*, *evne*, *mod* for så vidt angår *virtude*). Jeg afviger her fra Björkeson (og tilsvarende Ulleland på norsk), der nøjes med *dygd och kunskap*, og dem om det. På engelsk kan man nøjes med *virtue* (i ordets flerfoldige betydning) + *knowledge*, i det mindste hvis man vil ramme bredt. Det gør såvel Durling & Martinez som andre, hvorimod f.eks. Musa har *excellence and knowledge*, Carson *knowledge and the good*, mens Scialom på fransk fravælger *vertu* for *vaillance* (*et connaissance*), vistnok et pletskud. Dette blot for at nævne nogle gode, ganske forskellige, nyere oversættere til både prosa og vers. Måske fornemmer man dog at få om nogen af deres løsninger direkte ville gå på dansk, dersom talen skal have den tilsigtede virkning på Odysseus' kammerater.

Samme art problemer ville vel melde sig også for en prosaoversættelse, i hvert fald til dansk. Om det i øvrigt tynger eller snarere letter læsningen at indføre enkelte oplysninger i teksten der ellers ville have stået andetsteds, kan jo hverken bevises eller modbevises i relation til den enkelte læser. Det sker i sagens natur i få tilfælde, vel en snes steder i de 4–5000 terziner. F.eks. i Purgatorio V, 24: salmen *Miserere* blev vistnok sunget antifonisk, som vekselsang, og jeg har indlagt ordet som tolkning af *a verso a verso*, vers for vers. Jeg har ikke opfattet sådant som egentlige tilføjelser til hvad der allerede stod implicit hos Dante, som evident for hans samtidige læsere, men ikke for os i dag – men det kan gerne diskuteres. Eksempelvis Magnus Ullelands *Gudomlege Komedie* har en anden, mere stramt filologisk-leksikalsk strategi på flere steder: *eg har vilja seie det Dante seier, korkje meir eller mindre* (*Etterord*, s. 656), hvad han gennemgående realiserer som ordrethed, hvilket må respekteres, men vel også kan diskuteres.

Hvorom alting er: oversættelsesetisk er det klart mere ubehageligt at tilføje end at udelade, og jeg har kun gjort det sparsomt og nødtvungent (*Purg*. XVI, 6–7 er et sjældent eksempel på en egentlig tilføjelse). Udeladelser kan ikke altid undgås, f.eks. i gengivelsen af Dantes lange opremsninger af sammenligninger (*Inf*. XXII, 1–12, XXV, 85–90): her gælder det om at ramme helheden snarere end detaljen, hvis begge dele ikke kan lade sig gøre.

Tolkninger er det alt sammen, hvad enten målsprogsforfatteren kalder sit produkt for oversættelse, *übertragungen* el. *umguß* (Stefan George-krukkeri) eller gendigtning (et ord jeg helst undgår). Skulle en oversættelse på ethvert punkt svare til originalen, ville der jo ikke være tale om en oversættelse, men simpelthen om originalen – som nogle nok vil foretrække at læse. Tosprogede udgaver som Jacqueline Rissets til fransk (*vers libres*) eller Durling & Martinez' til amerikansk engelsk (let rytmiseret prosa, inddelt i terziner) kan her være en god hjælp, blot man gør sig det selvfølgelige klart at heller ikke de undslipper tolkningsvilkåret; ej heller er de nødvendigvis i sig selv de bedste oversættelser til de sprog. Om der er brug for lignende på nordisk, velsagtens med en prosa- eller friere versoversættelse, skal jeg ikke kunne sige. (Afdøde professor Ingemar Boström var i gang med en svensk interlinear-oversættelse til studiebrug, men jeg ved ikke hvad der blev af den).

Til slut: to steder i Komedien på dansk er jeg stadig ikke tilfreds med, og Paradiso XXV, 1 er det ene: det havde været godt at få plads til adjektivet *il poema sacro* (det hellige digt, eller helligdigtet), såvel som til Ugolinos *fiero pasto* (grumme måltid, *Inf.* XXXIII, 1). I begge tilfælde havde jeg metrisk korrekte løsninger der inkluderede ordene, men som jeg endte med at fravælge fordi de lød urent og presset, ligesom 'oversatte' i frasering og tone, hvilket er prekært hvor teksten taler med stor stemme; jeg skal ikke belemre med eksemplerne. Kloge sangere transponerer også hellere musikken lidt ned, end risikerer knæk på høje, eksponerede toner. I begge tilfælde ræsonnerede jeg til trøst (måske mest for mig selv?) at betydningselementet dog var til stede andetsteds i terzinen, i første tilfælde med Himlens hånd der sammen med Jordens har skrevet med på digtet. Helt tilfredsstillende er det ikke. Hvis nogen har gode forslag – der både lyder rent og bevarer Paradiso XXV's markerede *mai*: "no-gen-sind-e", såvel som *ha posto mano*: "(hvis) hånd har skrevet med på", foruden simultan-langsomheden i Ugolinos *forbendola*: "alt imens han tørrede (mun)den" (Seamus Heaney, uovertruffet: *That sinner eased his mouth up off his meal* [7]), alt sammen under hensyn til balancen i terzinerne – skal æren ikke være min. I forvejen skylder jeg 2–3 % af versene til andre, som er takket med glæde i første og senere udgaver.

---

7 "Ugolino", i: *Field Work*, 1979.

Hvorfor sådan? Om Komedien på italiensk og andre sprog

Tekstbilag

Nel mezzo del **cammin** di nostra vita
 mi ritrovai per **una selv(a)** oscura,
 che **la diritta via** (e)ra smarrita.
Ahi /E quant(o) a dir qual er(a) è cosa dura,
 (qu)esta selva selvaggia e aspr(a) e forte
 che nel pensier rinova la paura!
Tant'è amara che poc(o) è più morte;
 ma per tratter del ben ch'i'vi trovai
 dirò de l'altre cose ch'i v'ho scorte.
Io non so ben ridir com' i' v'intrai...

Paa Midten af vor **Bane** gjennem Livet
 Jeg fandt mig i **en Skovs bælgmørke Sale**,
 Forvildet fra **den Vej, som var mig givet**.
Ak, hvilken Byrde haard det er at tale
 Om hvordan Skoven var, den vilde, øde!
 Min Skræk ved Tanken kaldes op af Dvale.
Knap mere besk det var mig, om jeg døde;
 Dog vil jeg for det Held, jeg fandt, tillige
 Alt andet nævne, som mig der gav Møde.
Hvordan jeg kom derind, jeg kan ej sige...
Christian K.F. Molbech , 1851 (optrykt senest 1967–68)

På midten av vår **valfart** gjennem livet
 omklamret mig **en skog, den mørke, store**,
 for bort fra **rette sti** jeg lot mig drive.
Å, hvor det er mig hårdt å ta til orde
 om denne skog — vild, tett og tornet står den
 for tanken, som på ny lar angsten bore.
Så vond, så vond!—Knapt døden overgår den!
 Men for det godes skyld jeg òg har funnet,
 vil jeg fortelle alt i tur og orden.
Et slør av slummer for mitt syn var spunnet...
Kristen Gundelach ,1965

IN **the midway** of this our mortal life,
 I found me in **a gloomy wood**, astray
 Gone from **the path direct** : and e'en to tell,
It were no easy task, how savage wild
 That forest, how robust and rough its growth,
 Which to remember only, my dismay
Renews, in bitterness not far from death.
 Yet, to discourse of what there good befell,
 All else will I relate discovered there.
 How first I entered it I scarce can say,
Such sleepy dullness in that instant weighed
 My senses down, when the true path I left; ...
Henry Francis Cary, The Vision [sic] , 1805

Midtvejs paa livets **sti, som vi skal træde**,
 jeg fandt mig inde i **en dunkel skov**,
 fordi jeg fra **den rette vej** var veget.
Knud Hee Andersen ,1963

Auf halbem **Wege** unsers Erdenlebens
 Mußt ich **in Waldesnacht** veirrt mich shauen,
 Weil ich **den Pfad** verlor **des rechten Strebens**.
Richard Zoozmann, o. 1910

Es war inmitten unsres **wegs** im leben ·
 Ich wandelte dahin durch **finstre bäume**
 Da ich **die rechte strasse** aufgegeben.
Stefan George, 1903

À mi-chemin des jours que notre vie augure,
 Ayant quitté **la route** où j'avais marché droit,
 J'atteignis certain soir **une forêt obscure**.
Martin Saint-René, 1935 (19698)

Grad in der Mitte unsrer **Lebensreise**
 Befand ich mich in **einem dunklen Walde**,
 Weil ich **den rechten Weg** verloren hatte.
Hermann Gmelin, 1949

Midway along **the journey** of our life
 I woke to find myself in **a dark wood**,
 for I had wandered off from **the straight path**.
Mark Musa (US), 1972

Half way along **the road we have to go**
 I found myself **obscured** in a **great forest**,
 Bewildered, and I knew I had lost **the way**.
C.H. Sisson (UK), 1983

Till mitten hunnen på vår levnads **vandring**
 hade jag i **en dunkel skog** gått vilse
 och irrat bort mig från **den rätta vägen**.
Ingvar Björkeson , 1983

Midtveges fram i **gonga** gjennom livet
 eg fann meg att i **tjukke, svarte skogen**,
 i vilska fór eg langt frå **rette vegen**.
Magnus Ulleland, 1993

Au milieu du chemin de notre vie,
 je me trouvai dans **une forêt sombre**,
 la juste direction étant perdue.
Marc Scialom, 1996

À la moitié du chemin de notre vie
 je me retrouvai par **une sylve obscure**,
 où **la voie droite** avait été perdue.
Jean-Charles Vegliante, 1996

Halfway through the **story** of my life
 I came to in **a gloomy wood**, because
 I'd wandered off **the path**, away from the light.
It's hard to put words to what that wood was:
 I shudder even now to think of it,
 so wild and rough and tortured were its ways...
Ciaran Carson (Ulster), 2002

Melodien der blev væk. Dante på dansk

Conni-Kay Jørgensen

Der findes på dansk tre fuldstændige oversættelser af Dantes guddommelige komedie. Den første stod Christian Molbech for, og den udkom i perioden 1851-62. Molbech bibeholder Dantes versemål og anvender kun kvindelige rim, men han bruger femfodsjamber, og det giver jo unægtelig en anden og mindre fri rytme end Dantes 11-stavelsesvers. Men det, man især har kritiseret Molbech for, er hans overdrevne brug af udtryk fra ældre dansk digtning. En af de mere barske kritikere mente, at sproget "bliver vredet indtil det gyselige"[1], og det er vanskeligt at benægte. Man har også kritiseret de mange omskrivninger, som går ud over præcisionen. Omskrivningerne var nødvendige på grund af rimtvangen, som stiller store krav til oversætteren. Begge de efterfølgende danske oversættere har ganske enkelt droppet rimene, og det er et forståeligt valg.

Det, Molbech derimod roses for, er den, nå ja, søde stil: klangfylden, musikken, poesien. Det er disse faktorer, der får flere anmeldere til at karakterisere værket som et kunstnerisk mesterstykke, og det er også dem, der har bevirket, at man har læst Dante på dansk igennem tiderne. Oversættelsen er blevet genoptrykt talrige gange, og i en udgave fra 1929 skrev Valdemar Vedel: "At indlemme de fremmede Litteraturers Mesterværker i sin egen ved virkeligt digteriske Overførelser er noget, som maa være ethvert Folk, men især et lille, magtpaaliggende."[2] Til disse virkelig digteriske overførelser regner Vedel Molbechs, og det er helt igennem rimeligt, men ændrer naturligvis intet ved den kendsgerning, at bogen i dag virker gammeldags og kan være svær at læse – der er jo gået halvandet hundrede år, siden den udkom.

---

1 Foss, Otto. "Dante paa dansk." *Aarhus Stiftstidende*, 8/2 1963.
2 Vedel, Valdemar. Forord til Molbechs oversættelse, G. E. C. Gads forlag, 1929:9.

Og der gik hundrede, inden den næste danske oversættelse kom, nemlig i 1963, og denne gang hed oversætteren Knud Hee Andersen. Han anvender urimede femfodsjamber, som er blevet kaldt "lidt vaklende"[3]. Det kan være rigtigt nok, og man kan også, som flere gjorde, ærgre sig over de mange antikverede ord og udtryk; en anmelder blev så skuffet, at han spurgte "jamen, hvor er da fornyelsen, hvor er friskheden?"[4] Denne kritiker tøver ikke med at påpege, at han klart foretrækker Molbechs ældre oversættelse. Det er han ikke ene om, men de fleste anmeldere roser dog Hee Andersen for den langt større præcision, og hans oversættelse er unægteligt meget tættere på originalteksten. Desuden har han forsynet hver enkelt sang med et relativt langt forord samt med kommentarer og – noget der letter læsningen meget – marginbemærkninger, der angiver, hvem der taler.

Jeg mener, at Hee Andersens oversættelse havde fortjent en langt større udbredelse, end den fik, men forlaget (G. E. C. Gad) har sovet i timen. Bogen kom i flot udstyr, tre illustrerede bind i fin kassette, den var og er dyr, og forlaget burde i anledning af 700-årsdagen for Dantes fødsel have udsendt en billigudgave, som uden tvivl ville være blevet solgt i mange eksemplarer i årenes løb. Men denne undladelsessynd har så til gengæld skabt plads for endnu en dansk oversættelse, Ole Meyers, der kom i år 2000 og allerede er optrykt i en tredje udgave. Med forsvindende få undtagelser har anmelderne været ovenud begejstrede, så jeg regner med, at den kritik, jeg vil fremføre i det følgende, vil blive opfattet som et konstruktivt supplement til en ellers overvejende positiv modtagelse. Og da det i dag er Meyers oversættelse, der læses, finder jeg det naturligt at koncentrere mig om den, idet jeg vil give en række eksempler på forskellige problemer, den er behæftet med, efter først at have opridset mere principielle indvendinger.

Meyer bevarer Dantes 11-stavelsesvers, og hvis Molbechs rimtvang havde uheldige konsekvenser, så gælder det samme for Meyers insisteren på at bevare metrikken. Et eksempel kan være, at hele sætninger enten udelades eller tilføjes, som nu i Helvedes 1. sang, hvor Dante (for nemheds skyld siger jeg blot "Dante" om både pilgrimmen, fortælleren og forfatteren) møder en løve så frygtindgydende, at *parea che l'aere ne*

---

3 Frederiksen, Emil. *Dante*. København, Gyldendal, 1965:146.
4 Kruuse, Jens. "En dansk Guddommelig Komedie fra vore Dage." *Jyllands-Posten*, 13/12 1963.

tremesse, hvilket bliver til "så selve luften rundt omkring den skælved og syntes lammet, ramt af gru og rædsel" (*Inf.* I, 47–48).

Der tilføjes hyppigt karakteriserende adjektiver, og der indføjes oplysninger, som ikke findes i originalteksten:

Guiglielmo > "Vilhelm af Oranien" (*Par.* XVIII, 46)
Fotin > "FOTINOS; DIAKONEN" (*Inf.* XI, 9)
Sigieri > "Siger[] [...] den filosof" (*Par.* X, 136)
il castello > "Engelsborg" (*Inf.* XVIII, 31)
la lunga guerra > "krige [...] mod Hannibal" (*Inf.* XXVIII, 9–10)
'l fosso tristo > "floden hvis vand er blod" (*Inf.* XIV, 11–12)
beato serto > "rosenkrans af lærde" (*Par.* X, 102)
la santa mola > "møllehjulet af vise tænkere" (*Par.* XII, 2–3)
mesta selva > "selvmorderskov" (*Inf.* XIII, 107)
La dolorosa selva > "Selvmorderskoven" (*Inf.* XIV, 10)
al grande officio eletto > "udvalgt til Marias søn og værge" (*Par.* XXV, 114)

og mere af samme skuffe. Faktisk så meget mere, at man uden overdrivelse kan sige, at oversætteren har indarbejdet et noteapparat i teksten, vel at mærke uden at gøre opmærksom på det. En diskutabel strategi, der har konsekvenser såvel for nøjagtigheden som for poesien. Det bliver pædagogisk, pedantisk og prosaisk.

Eksempel: når Dante forventer, at læseren ved, hvad der menes med *Quel che Timeo de l'anime argomenta* – så finder oversætteren det opportunt at skrive "det som Platon i dialogen om Timaios påstår om sjælen" (*Par.* IV 49–51).Og når Dante nævner Æsops fabel *dov' el parlò de la rana e del topo*, så bliver det til fablen "om frøen der ved list vil drukne musen" (*Inf.* XXIII, 6). Et tredje eksempel: Vi hører om *quel Donato ch'a la prim' arte degnò porre mano*, det vil sige den Ælius Donatus, der satte sig ned og skrev en bog om den første af de syv artes liberales, nemlig grammatikken, hvilket Dante forventer, at læseren ved. Den danske oversætter derimod tilføjer en bogtitel samt en helt ny oplysning – på bekostning af den oprindelige:

Donatus, hvis Ars Grammatica endnu studeres.
(*Par.* XII, 137–138)

Et fjerde eksempel. Odysseus beretter: *L'un lito e l'altro vidi infin la Spagna, / fin nel Morrocco, e l'isola d'i Sardi, / e l'altre che quel mare intorno bagna.*

> Kyst efter kyst så jeg: mod vest lå Spanien,
> mod syd Marokko, og mod nord Sardinien
> og andre øer det hav skyller rundt om.
> (*Inf.* XXVI, 103-105)

Som var vi midt i en geografitime og ikke i et digterværk.

I de opregnede eksempler er oversætterens tilføjelser ikke forkerte, de hører bare ikke hjemme i teksten, mens man i andre tilfælde må spørge sig selv, hvor oversætteren har sine oplysninger fra. Det gælder eksempelvis, når Dante i Helvede genkender Venedico Caccianemico og konstaterer *Già di veder costui non son digiuno*. På dansk bliver det til "Ham der, ham kender jeg da fra Bologna!" (*Inf.* XVIII, 42) Det står der jo ikke, og det er faktisk usikkert, hvor de to mødtes; måske var det i Bologna, måske var det et andet sted. Man har lov til at have en mening om den slags, men det er ret uortodokst at sætte ens egen prosaiske tolkning i stedet for originalens poetiske udsagn.

Der findes også andre former for tilføjelser, som hverken er diskutable eller korrekte (om end malplacerede), de er simpelt hen forkerte. Eksempel: I Helvedes 2. sang hører vi, at Dante alligevel ikke rigtig har hverken mod på eller kræfter til den forestående vandring. Men det lykkes Vergil at overbevise ham om, at han har både Maria, Lucia og Beatrice med sig, hvilket får ham til at rette sig op som en blomst efter nattefrosten. Dine ord får mig til at længes, siger han til Vergil, så lad os gå: jeg vender tilbage til mit første forsæt – altså det om at påbegynde vandringen. Her tilføjer oversætteren for egen regning et "uforandret" (*Inf.* II, 138), og det giver unægtelig en anden mening. Bevægelsen går også den anden vej, når Meyer springer adjektiver over, som i følgende eksempler ud af en meget lang række:

> *fatale andare* > "vandring" (*Inf.* V, 22)
> *Stige, questo tristo ruscel* > "Styx" (*Inf.* VII, 107)
> *anime distrutte* > "sjæle" (*Inf.* IX, 79)

Og når Dante to gange kalder sit digt for helligt, er det påfaldende, at oversætteren ganske enkelt udelader adjektivet. Det er jo ikke uden betydning, at digteren vælger så stærkt et ord.

Eksemplerne er talrige, og man kan vanskeligt tale om en forbedring i forhold til de to tidligere danske oversættelser. Om dem mener Meyer, at de er "holdt i en fiktivt middelalderligt-romantisk sprogtone"[5]. Det er ikke let at forstå, hvad der menes med "middelalderligt-romantisk", men under alle omstændigheder skydes der langt over målet, og man kan passende påpege, at Meyers egen oversættelse ikke alene er i høj grad genfortællende og prosaisk, den er også gammeldags, og det af flere grunde.

Blandt grundene er dobbeltbestemte konstruktioner, hyppig brug af omvendt ordstilling og af passivkonstruktioner:

"Og allerede bar min isse kronen" (*Par.* VIII, 64)
"hvor endnu de pompejanske stridstrompeter gjalded"
(*Par.* VI, 71–72)
"Firenzes hele stridsmagt" (*Purg.* XIII, 116)
"lad os begge glædes ved din tale" (*Purg.* XXIV, 42)
"alle syntes glade ved at nævnes" (*Purg.* XXIV, 26)
"blikket droges" (*Par.* II, 25)
"dér frydedes jeg ved dig." (*Par.* XVI, 6)

Hertil kommer en lang række ikke just nudanske ord og udtryk som eksempelvis *slig, sligt, han fatted mig ved hånden, bedre farne, fredsæl, ætling, tilforn, silde, en unse, ingensinde, synes mig, kærte, huld, jordsmon, han gør deraf et stempel, jordelivet, til vé for, til kummer for, uspurgt, den ganske himmel, avindsyge, forskertse, frille, og lod sig derpå kure ned på ryggen*, eller hvad med *fordi han ikke ville bie lyset* (*Par.* XIX, 48)? En oversættelse, der er mere gammeldags end Molbechs, *som ej vented efter Lysets Straale*. Teksten får hos Meyer ind imellem netop den patina, den ikke burde have, hvilket også følgende eksempel viser.

I Helvedes 3. sang er vi nået til forgården, og her kommer, da Vergil præsenterer de lunkne for Dante, nogle af Komediens bedst kendte

---

[5] Meyer, Ole. "Den middelalderlige og den moderne Dante." *Humaniora. Et magasin om humanistisk forskning*, IV:11, 1997:6.

vers, *Fama di loro il mondo esser non lassa; / misericordia e giustizia li sdegna: / non ragioniam di lor, ma guarda e passa*. Hos Meyer lyder det i en påfaldende blanding af gammeldags ord og moderne talesprog:

> De efterlader intet ry i verden,
> foragtede af miskundhed og retfærd.
> Men nok om dem: se på dem og gå videre.
> (*Inf.* III, 49–51)

Meyer har i en avisartikel erklæret, at man skal oversætte *La divina commedia* "flerstemmigt, mangefarvet og talesprogsnært, ikke homogent, højtideligt og skriftsprogligt som tidligere oversættere har gjort på deres tids præmisser."[6] Men det lykkes kun delvist for ham, og ofte må han ty til distraherende, hjemmestrikkede udtryk:

> "mit sind løb fuldt af begær" (*Purg.* XXIX, 32–33)
> "blomster steg og faldt fra deres hænder" (*Purg.* XXX, 21)
> "en blandt dem, hvis hoved bar tre øjne" (*Purg.* XXIX, 132)
> "alle dem hvis øjnes evne ikke er vokset op i kærlighedens flamme" (*Par.* VII, 59–60)
> "Til faderen, til sønnen og til ånden" (*Par.* XXVII, 1)
> "derfor regner, hagler, sner her ikke" (*Purg.* XXI, 46)

På italiensk kan en person godt være *distruggitor di sé* (*Inf.* XXII, 50), men på dansk kan man vanskeligt bortødsle sig selv, sådan som Meyer har oversat det.

Et sidste eksempel: det blæste ikke mere end at fuglene "stadig øved deres sangkunst" (*Purg.* XXVIII, 15). Molbech kunne ikke have gjort det bedre.

Hertil kommer regulære neologismer og sammensatte ord, der vanskeliggør læsningen: *monstruøse, ubelønnet, rustningklædt, tvillingguder, Malebranchekompagniet, tyveilden, lyshvidt, stjernekroppe*, og så *longobardertanden* der "snapped efter Guds sande kirke" (*Par.* VI, 94–95).

---

6 Meyer, Ole. "Dante på dansk – for tredje gang." *Jyllands-Posten*, 13/12 2000.

Som sagt vil Meyer oversætte flerstemmigt, men han respekterer ikke den for Dante så vigtige niveauforskel mellem fører og vandringsmand, som nu for eksempel i Helvedes 1. sang, hvor denne henvender sig til hin med et ærbødigt *Poeta*, jeg beder dig om at vise vej. Det bliver på dansk til "Min digterven", hvilket ikke ligefrem er ramt på kornet. Tilfældet er langt fra enestående; eksempelvis oversættes senere *'l mio duca* med "min ven og fører" (*Inf.* XXI, 98). Hos Dante findes der ikke ansats til denne form for familiaritet.

Lignende stilbrud ses også, når [*il*] *poverel di Dio*, den hellige Frans, kaldes for "Guds lille tigger" (*Par.* XIII, 33), og Domenicus, der som bekendt hjælper Kristus med urtehaven, får stillingsbetegnelsen "arbejdsmand" (*Par.* XII, 71)!

Over for sin egen oversættelse fremsætter Meyer i en artikel fra 1998 (altså ikke i bogen) følgende bemærkelsesværdige forbehold: "Selv med umage kan en metrisk oversættelse nok ikke love at være helt begrebsret, og en filosof eller idéhistoriker vil formentlig skulle supplere med en prosaoversættelse."[7] Som man kan se, er forbeholdet dog – om jeg så må sige – forbeholdent: det er *muligt*, at filosoffer og idéhistorikere får en utilstrækkelig service. Imidlertid viser det sig, at den manglende terminologiske stringens er et væsentligt svaghedspunkt, og selvom oversætteren åbenbart mener, at det er mindre vigtigt at yde Dante retfærdighed på dette område, må man konstatere, at det faktisk er et stort problem, at han ikke gør det. Et problem, som naturligvis ikke angår filosoffer og idéhistorikere alene; komediens idé-indhold er jo ikke uvæsentligt. Men da oversætteren selv er opmærksom på problemet, vil jeg ikke gøre ret meget ud af det, blot lige antyde, at det viser sig helt ned i minusklerne.

I Helvedes 11. sang skriver Dante *Etica*, *Fisica* og *Filosofia*, men på dansk optræder filosofien i modsætning til de to andre med et degraderende lille begyndelsesbogstav. Hvorfor? Fordi oversætteren åbenbart mener, at Dantes skrivemåde alene er begrundet i den kendsgerning, at filosofien indleder en sætning. Om de filosofiske fagtermini kan bemærkes, at de nærmest konsekvent omskrives i stedet for at blive oversat. I modsætning til Dante omgås Meyer letsindigt med begreber som stof

---

7 Meyer, Ole. "At oversætte Dante i dag." *Litteraturmagasinet Standart*, XII:1, 1998: 19.

og form, mål, grænse, foranderlighed, upåvirkelighed, skabelse, ånd, sjæl, intellekt, væsen, substans, skæbne og forsyn, og den usikre terminologi gør det rent faktisk umuligt at følge med i Dantes udredninger.

Der er flere faktorer end de allerede nævnte, der bidrager til at gøre oversættelsen unøjagtig, det gælder for eksempel omformninger som den følgende, hvor en hensigtskonstruktion erstattes med en betingelseskonstruktion. Dante møder Bertrand de Born, der bærer sit eget hoved i hånden. For at du kan fortælle om mig, når du kommer hjem, siger han til Dante, skal jeg nu sige dig, hvem jeg er: *E perché tu di me novella porti*, hvilket på dansk bliver til "Og hvis du ønsker at fortælle om mig." (*Inf.* XXVIII, 133) Og det er jo noget helt andet.

En anden diskutabel strategi er at springe over direkte tale, som oversætteren ofte gør. Og når den ikke springes over, er den gerne meget lidt talesprogsnær, som for eksempel når Vergil i Helvedes 1. sang svarer Dante *Non omo, omo già fui* > "Mand var jeg før [...] for sekler siden" (*Inf.* I, 67). Det er det rene fyld, og Vergil kommer til at fremstå som en skolelærer over for en lidt tungnem elev. Og når Vergil få linjer efter fortsætter *Poeta fui*, så bliver det på dansk til det prosaiske "Dér blev jeg digter", som således kommer til at stå uden sammenhæng med *omo già fui*.

I oversættelsen findes endvidere personificeringer, som i selv er uheldige, og som ikke er i harmoni med Dantes egne udtryksformer, eksempelvis *che se pigrizia fosse sua serocchia* > "som var fru Doven selv hans søster" (*Purg.* IV, 111). Fru Doven?!

Hertil kommer et væld af angliserende udtryk som for eksempel "luk dine ører op" (*Inf.* XXIV, 142), "plages af sin tørst" (*Inf.* XXX, 56), "navarreseren var ikke sen til at samle sine ben" (*Inf.* XXII, 121–122) – som var der tale om skelettet.

Endelig kan nævnes mere eller mindre forvirrende inkonsekvens, som nogle gange *Rom*, andre gange *Roma*, nogle gange *Konstanza*, andre gange *Konstantia*, nogle gange fordanskes italienske sted- og egennavne (når de da ikke ganske enkelt springes over), andre gange gør de ikke, og det virker helt tilfældigt, når Pier Pettinaio bliver til Peter Kammageren, og Federico Tignoso forbliver Federico Tignoso. Men lad os nu se nærmere på teksten.

Vi er i starten af Helvede, hvor Dante møder Beatrice, der præsenterer sig som følger:

I' son Beatrice che ti faccio andare;
vegno del loco ove tornar disio;
amor mi mosse, che mi fa parlare.
(*Inf.* II, 70-72)

Vid: jeg som sender dig, er Beatrice;
jeg længes atter mod det sted jeg kom fra;
af kærlighed, som bød mig tale, kom jeg.

Eksemplet viser, hvorledes sætningerne bliver brudt op på en måde, som går ud over læsbarheden, og hvorledes Meyer bruger ét og samme ord, når Dante ikke gør det: *jeg kom, kom jeg*. Endvidere kan man mene, at *jeg som sender dig er* ikke blot er uheldigt i sig selv, men også fordi pilgrimmen kommer til at fremstå som en pakke, der afleveres på posthuset. Eksemplet viser også den i hele oversættelsen udbredte brug af imperativ: *vid*, det er hverken poetisk eller talesprogsnært. I det hele taget skurrer imperativerne fælt: "Lad ikke foden glide" (*Purg.* IV, 37), "Oprejs dem og hjælp dem!" (*Purg.* VI, 110), "undres ikke ved hvad jeg fortæller" (*Par.* XVI, 85).

Vi er nu i slutningen af 5. sang, Francesca har just afsluttet sin beretning, og Dante siger:

Mentre che l'uno spirto questo disse,
l'altro piangëa; sì che di pietade
io venni men così com' io morisse.
(*Inf.* V, 139-141)

Imens den ene talte, græd den anden
ved hendes ord, så jeg af angst og medynk
blev bleg og vakled, raved som en døende.

Det turde være overflødigt med kommentarer til dette voldsomme stilbrud i Komediens vel berømteste sang, *raved som en døende!*, men man kan mærke sig dobbeltkonfekten *talte – ord*, og dobbeltoversættelsen af *pietade*, der bliver til både angst og medynk.

Et andet nøglested har vi i 7. sang, fjerde kreds, hvor de gerrige og ødsle hører til. Dante og Vergil ser, hvordan der stiger bobler op fra vandet, som skjuler nogle af synderne, der siger

> Tristi fummo
> ne l'aere dolce che dal sol s'allegra,
> portando dentro accidïoso fummo
> (*Inf.* VII, 121–123)

> Vi besudled
> med vores sure dunst den luft der elskes
> og kærtegnes af solen

Meyer springer over den uundværlige oplysning, at synderne var *tristi*, og han misforstår terzinen: at de besudlede luften, savner belæg i originalteksten. Og man kan mene, at det er lige meget nok at lade solen elske og kærtegne luften, så stærkt er *allegrare* ikke. Prøv at sammenligne med Hee Andersens korrekte og poetiske oversættelse:

> Uglade var vi
> i jordens milde luft, hvor solen spiller,
> med bitre dunster gemt i vore hjerter

Heller ikke følgende oversættelse af Meyer kan siges at være en forbedring af forgængernes. Vergil forlader Dante et øjeblik, og denne bliver frygteligt bange for, at han ikke kommer tilbage

> Così sen va, e quivi m'abbandona
> lo dolce padre, e io rimagno in forse,
> che sì e no nel capo mi tenciona.
> (*Inf.* VIII, 109–111)

> Han går, den milde fader, og tilbage
> står jeg i uvished, forladt, alene,
> mens 'ja' slås i min sjæl med 'nej', og omvendt.

Peter slås med Poul, og omvendt? Molbech har "Ja og Nej stærkt i mit Hoved stride", Hee Andersen "med ja og nej det svirrer i mit hoved."

Dante og Vergil møder nu, i ottende kreds, Odysseus og Diomedes, og Dante vil gerne tale med dem, men Vergil mener, at det er bedst at lade ham føre ordet:

> Lascia parlare a me, ch'i' ho concetto
> ciò che tu vuoi; ch'ei sarebbero schivi,
> perch' e' fuor greci, forse del tuo detto.
> (*Inf.* XXVI, 73–75)

Meyer flytter usikkerhedsmomentet og tilføjer igen noget for egen regning:

> Lad mig, som nok har gættet hvad du ønsker,
> tage ordet, for det sprog som du benytter
> er fremmed og forkert i græske øren.

Der bliver i originalteksten kun sagt, at grækerne, fordi de er grækere, næppe gider svare Dante, ikke andet.

I samme sang har vi endnu et nøglested. Odysseus opfordrer sit mandskab til ikke at give op, men fortsætte rejsen:

> Considerate la vostra semenza:
> fatti non foste a viver come bruti,
> ma per seguir virtute e canoscenza.
> (*Inf.* XXVI, 118–120)

> Betænk det frø af hvilket I er spiret!
> For I blev ikke skabt som stumme bæster,
> men til at søge dyd og kløgt og kundskab.

Dantes tekst er klar og letforståelig, mens den danske volder visse vanskeligheder: det er ikke nemt hverken at søge dyd eller at betænke et frø. Og vi blev da faktisk skabt som stumme bæster. Igen falder sammenligningen med de tidligere danske oversættelser ud til deres fordel.

Betænk, af hvilken stamme I er rundet;
I blev ej skabte til som dyr at leve,
men til at følge dyd og vinde kundskab.
(Hee Andersen)

Lad Eders ædle Udspring ej sig dølge!
I skabtes ikke for som Dyr at leve,
men at I Dyd og Kundskab skulle følge.
(Molbech)

Vi er stadig i ottende kreds, nu i tiende slugt, hvor vi finder blandt andre Sinon (som lokkede trojanerne til at lukke hesten ind i deres by). Han og falskmøntneren Adam udveksler høfligheder:

'E te sia rea la sete onde ti crepa',
disse 'l Greco, 'la lingua, e l'acqua marcia
che 'l ventre innanzi a li occhi sì t'assiepa!'
(*Inf.* XXX, 121–123)

Og Grækeren: 'Men du af tørst skal pines,
saa tungen revner, og af raaddent vand,
der spænder ud din bug for dine øjne!'
(Hee Andersen)

'Dig pine skal din Tørst, der Huller brænder
i Tungen,' vedblev *Grækeren* at smæde,
'og raaddent Vand som dig din Bug udspænder.'
(Molbech)

Igen må man konstatere, at Meyers oversættelse ikke er nogen forbedring:

- 'Og må du plages fælt af tørst,' sagde Sinon,
'til tungen sprækker! Og gid spildevandet
gør maven til et bjerg for dine øjne!'

Melodien der blev væk

Det er ikke bare uheldigt, *spildevand!*, det er også forkert. Der er hos Dante intet ønske om, at vandet skal udspile Adams mave, men kun om, at han må plages af det vand, der de facto gør det.

En tilsvarende uheldig formulering finder vi i et sidste eksempel fra Helvede, vi er i niende kreds, nærmere bestemt i området Antenora, hvor landsforræderne straffes ved nedfrysning. Her kommer Dante til at give Bocca degli Abbati et spark i hovedet, og denne klager:

'Or tu chi se' che vai per l'Antenora,
percotendo', rispuose, 'altrui le gote'
(*Inf.* XXXII, 88–89)

Og hvem er du, der her i Antenora
går rundt og sparker frit til godtfolks kinder?

Det er ufrivilligt morsomt, og Dante ville ikke være fornøjet.

Følgende to, klart forståelige terziner bliver til volapyk hos Meyer. Vi er i Purgatoriets første kreds, hvor Dante og Virgil ser en marmorklippe med relieffer. Dante beskriver det, hvor ærkeenglen Gabriel er indhugget.

L'angel che venne in terra col decreto
de la molt' anni lagrimata pace,
ch'aperse il ciel del suo lungo divieto,
dinanzi a noi pareva sì verace
quivi intagliato in un atto soave,
che non sembiava imagine che tace.
(*Purg.* X, 34–39)

Den engel der nedsteg med fredens budskab,
den fred vi havde bedt for gennem lange
og kummerfyldte år, den fred der åbned
de længe stængte paradisets porte -
dér stod han, ligesom åndet ind i klippen,
så at man skulle tro han ville tale.

Dante har *pace* én gang i den første terzine, Meyer har hele tre gange *fred*. Og vi får et par for hele oversættelsen typiske eksempler på en upoetisk gentagelse *den engel ... dér stod han, den fred, den fred*. Derudover distraheres man af neologismen *kummerfyldt* og af det gammeldags *længe stængte* (helt identisk med Hee Andersen), der står i uheldig kontrast til den sidste, udprægede prosaiske linje. For øvrigt er også de lange, kummerfulde år fri fantasi; der står blot *mange*.

Prøv igen at sammenligne med Hee Andersens mere korrekte, præcise og poetiske oversættelse:

> Hin engel, der til jorden kom med budskab
> om freden, mange aar med taarer ventet,
> som aabned Himlens længe stængte døre,
> for vore øjne fremstod saa livagtig,
> i stenen hugget, med saa mild en mine,
> som var det ej et billed uden mæle.

I sjette kreds møder Dante Forese Donati, der spørger ham, hvornår de mon skal ses igen – et lidt foruroligende spørgsmål fra en afdød – og Dante svarer, at han jo ikke ved, hvor lang tid, der kommer til at gå, men at han allerede længes, for livet i Firenze er ikke spændende:

> però che 'l loco u' fui a viver posto,
> di giorno in giorno più di ben si spolpa,
> e a trista ruina par disposto.
> (*Purg.* XXIV, 79-81)

Hos Molbech lyder det:

> Thi Byen, som jeg lever i derhenne,
> fra Dag til Dag mer blotter sig for Dyder,
> og er bestemt til sørgelig at ende.

Hos Meyer:

> For der hvor jeg blev sat og nu må leve,
> hensygner godhed hver dag stadig mere,
> og dør nok inden længe helt af tæring.

Lad os gå hastigt videre til Paradiset, hvis 2. sang indledes med en advarsel:

> O voi che siete in piccioletta barca
> desiderosi d'ascoltar, seguiti
> dietro al mio legno che cantando varca,
> tornate a riveder li vostri liti
> (*Par.* II, 1-4)

> I læsere, som i et lille fartøj,
> har fulgt mig ivrigt og med åbne øren
> imens mit skib med sang er stævnet udad:
> vend om mod jeres egne, kendte kyster

Vel læser man ikke med ørerne, men i poesi er meget jo tilladt, og jeg nævner denne manglende omsorg for metaforens kohærens, dels fordi den manifesteres ofte, dels fordi eksemplets eksplicitte læserhenvendelse, som er uden belæg i originalen, ikke står alene: et sted bliver et enkelt *qua* til "hér hvor dette skrives" (*Par.* I, 45), og et andet sted bliver et enkelt *qui* til "her hvor dette læses" (*Purg.* XV, 6).

Vi bliver i Paradisets 2. sang, hvor det nu forklares, hvorledes mennesket i himlen spontant vil forstå sandheder, som det på jorden blot tror på. Sandhederne vil fremstå akkurat ligesom bestemte selvindlysende sandheder fremstår på jorden:

> Lì si vedrà ciò che tenem per fede,
> non dimostrato, ma fia per sé noto
> a guisa del ver primo che l'uom crede.
> (*Par.* II, 43-45)

Det betyder, i Hee Andersens perfekte oversættelse,

> Hist skal det ses, hvad her ved tro vi griber,
> ikke bevist, men givet os til kende
> lig det, vi tror paa som den første sandhed.

Som jeg startede med at påpege, er Meyers oversættelse, når det angår mere filosofiske områder, ikke altid pålidelig, og denne passus er ganske enkelt blevet misforstået:

> Dér får vi det at se som hér vi tror på,
> dog ikke som abstrakt bevis, men víst os
> ud fra den første sandhed som vi kender.

Meningen forvanskes, og udsagnet bliver uforståeligt. Der er på ingen måde tale om et årsagsforhold mellem den første sandhed og så det, mennesket kommer til at forstå i himlen. Der er alene tale om en sammenligning, der angår det epistemologiske aspekt.

Beatrice forklarer nu, i Paradisets 4. sang, at man nogle gange ser sig tvunget til at vælge mellem to onder og således nødsages til at gøre noget, som i og for sig er forkert.

> Molte fiate già, frate, addivenne
> che, per fuggir periglio, contra grato
> si fé di quel che far non si convenne
> (*Par.* IV, 100–102)

> Min ven, på flugt fra fare sker det ofte
> at man imod sin vilje handler ilde
> og tanketomt

Tanketomt er oversætterens indskud, og det forvrider meningen til ukendelighed. Igen er Hee Andersen at foretrække:

> Alt mange gange er det sket, min broder,
> at nogen mod sin vilje, for at undfly
> en fare, gjorde, hvad han ikke burde.

Justinian beretter, i Paradisets 6. sang, om sit liv og fortæller blandt andet, at pave Agapetus hjalp ham med at finde den rette tro. En tro, der nu – akkurat som vi hørte i 2. sang – i himlen forekommer ham så indlysende og klar, som det på jorden forekommer ethvert menneske klart, at af to modstridende sætninger, må den ene være sand, den anden falsk.

> Io li credetti; e ciò che 'n sua fede era,
> vegg' io or chiaro sì, come tu vedi
> ogne contradizione e falsa e vera.
> (*Par.* VI, 19–22)

> Hvad hans tro viste, ser jeg ligeså klart som
> enhver kan se hvordan det er umuligt
> at 'A' og 'ikke-A' kan tænkes sammen.

Oversætteren springer den afgørende første sætning over: jeg troede på ham! hvorved udsagnet svækkes betydeligt, og kontradiktionsprincippet fremstilles ved hjælp af tekniske termini, som ikke hører hjemme i poesi. Eksemplet er ikke ekstremt; i Paradisets 13. sang (139–142) bydes man følgende pinligt prosaiske udredning:

> Selvom hr. A blir enig med fru B om
> at X er en bandit, men Y en from mand, [så...]

Dante befinder sig nu i Venushimlen, hvor han taler med sin gamle ven Karl Martel. Martel beretter om sin slægt og kommer også med en længere teologisk redegørelse for forholdet mellem Guds skaberværk og de onde kræfter. På et tidspunkt påpeger han over for Dante, at dennes selskab behager ham, og derfor vil han gerne tilføje yderligere forklaring; han siger, at Dante nu vel må have forstået,

> ma perché sappi che di te mi giova,
> un corollario voglio che t'ammanti.
> (*Par.* VIII, 137–138)

men for at du skal se, at du mig glæder,
vil jeg endnu tilføje en forklaring.
(Hee Andersen)

Hos Meyer ser vi et mislykket forsøg på at overføre det metaforiserende verbum til dansk:

men som et tegn på glæden du bereder mig,
får du en ekstra kappe som foræring.

Thomas Aquinas beretter om den hellige Frans, der allerede som meget ung trodsede sin far for en kvindes skyld, dvs. fattigdommen, som alle holder døren lukket og låst for, som var det for døden:

ché per tal donna, giovinetto, in guerra
del padre corse, a cui, come a la morte,
la porta del piacer nessun diserra
(*Par.* XI, 58–60)

idet han, endnu ung, trodsed sin fader
og valgte én til brud der ligesom døden
er uvelkommen *i de fleste huse* (min kursivering)

Hvem mon byder døden indenfor?
I Marshimlen forklarer Cacciaguida, at der ikke er noget mærkeligt i, at slægter går til grunde, i betragtning af, at også byer gør det.

udir come le schiatte si disfanno
non ti parrà nova cosa né forte,
poscia che le cittadi termine hanno.
(*Par.* XVI, 76–78)

I oversættelsen vendes der op og ned på det hele, og udsagnet mister enhver mening:

og hør hvorledes slægter går til grunde,
så vil du ikke længer undres over
at heller ikke byer lever evigt.

Dertil kommer, at forsikringen om, at det ikke vil virke hverken mærkeligt eller svært at forstå, ganske enkelt springes over og erstattes med *så vil du ikke længer undres*, hvilket er noget af en afsvækning.

Apropos afsvækning kan vi tage et sidste eksempel. Eksemplet er ét ud af en lang række, hvor oversætteren bruger ét og samme ord, når Dante bruger flere. En strategi, der ikke just højner det poetiske niveau. Vi er i Paradisets 33. sang:

Oh quanto è corto il dire e come fioco
al mio concetto! e questo, a quel ch'i' vidi,
è tanto, che non basta a dicer 'poco'.
(*Par.* XXXIII, 121-123)

Hvor svagt er sproget her, hvor blegt mod tanken,
og denne i sig selv så svag mod synet
at 'svag' er alt for svagt et ord at bruge!

En firdobbelt gentagelse, der ikke er basis for i teksten.

På et tidspunkt i Paradiset hører Dante en melodi så smuk, at uanset, hvor meget man havde gjort sig fortjent til, så ville den være en fuldt ud tilstrækkelig belønning: "tal melodia, ch'ad ogne merto saria giusto muno" (*Par.* XIV, 32-33). Nu kræver det jo som bekendt en vis anstrengelse at læse *La divina commedia*, om det så er på italiensk eller i en oversættelse, og den melodi, man som belønning får at høre hos Dante, får man et godt indtryk af i de to ældre danske oversættelser. Molbech og Hee Andersen er gammeldags, ja, men de er ikke forældede, for de gør det, Meyer ikke gør: de slår tonen an. Kald dem gammeldags, kald dem upræcise, kald dem omskrivende, kald dem for frie – tilbage står, at det svinger. Det gør det sjældent i Meyers oversættelse.

Contributors

Asbjørn Bjornes
Publishing editor, Lunde Forlag, Oslo. Holds an advanced degree in theology from Fjellhaug Academy, Oslo. Master of Arts in comparative literature, University of Oslo. Special interests: Dante, Tuscan poetry of the Duecento, The Metaphysical Poets, and John Milton.

Leonardo Cecchini
Lecturer in Italian at the University of Aarhus. He has published on Dante, Tommaso Landolfi, Giorgio Caproni and on literary theory in the 20th century.

Anders Cullhed
Professor in General and Comparative Literature at Stockholm University. He has published books and articles in three main areas: Swedish lyrical modernism, Spanish baroque poetry and late antique and medieval literary theory. He is the Swedish co-ordinator of the Nordic Dante Network.

Trond Berg Eriksen
Professor at the Department of History of Ideas, University of Oslo. Editor of anthologies, journals and encyclopaedias. Published works on Aristotle, Augustine, Dante and Machiavelli.

Unn Falkeid
Postdoctoral fellow in Italian literature at the University of Oslo. She has published articles and a monograph on Petrarch (2007), essays on and translations of modern Italian literature, and is currently working on a postdoctoral project about the cultures of Avignon in the 14th century. She has previously been the chief-editor of modern fictional

literature in the Norwegian publishing house, Gyldendal. She is the Norwegian co-ordinator of the Nordic Dante Network.

Espen Grønlie
Works as a literary critic in the weekly Norwegian journal *Morgenbladet*. His MA in comparative literature compared Dante's ideas on poetry with those of Guido Cavalcanti and Ezra Pound. His translation into Norwegian of Dante's *De vulgari eloquentia* has been published under the title *Om diktning på folkespråket*.

Jesper Hede
Ph.D. in European Studies and an MA in Italian and Medieval Studies. He is the author of *Reading Dante: The Pursuit of Meaning* (Maryland, Md.: Lexington Books, 2007), and is currently writing a book on the hermeneutics of rhetoric, on a grant from the Carlsberg Foundation.

Conni-Kay Jørgensen
Ph.D., writes about Italian literature and philosophy.

Giuseppe Mazzotta
Sterling Professor in the Humanities for Italian at Yale University and the current president of the Dante Society of America. He has written numerous essays about each century of Italian literary history. His books include: *Dante, Poet of the Desert: History and Allegory in the Divine Comedy* (1979); *The World at Play in Boccaccio's Decameron* (1986); *Dante's Vision and the Circle of Knowledge* (1993); *The Worlds of Petrarch* (1993); *The New Map of the World: the Poetic Philosophy of Giambattista Vico* (1999); *Cosmopoiesis: The Renaissance Experiment* (2001).

P.M. Mehtonen
Adjunct Professor of Comparative Literature at the Universities of Tampere and Helsinki, Finland. Amongst other publications, Mehtonen is the author and editor of *Illuminating Darkness. Approaches to Obscurity and Nothingness in Literature* (2007) and *Obscure Language, Unclear Literature. Theory and Practice from Quintilian to the Enlightenment* (2003).

Contributors

Ole Meyer
M.A. in Scandinavian Studies & English, author of the most recent Danish translation of Dante's *Commedia* (2000, 3. ed. 2004). Lecturer in Danish at Florence University 2003–06. He has published essays and books on Scandinavian literature and on Dante; co-founder and, together with Christian Kaatmann, Danish coorodinator of the Nordisk Dante-Netværk / Nordic Dante Network, 1998; member of the editorial board of *Letteratura Italiana Antica*, ed. Antonio Lanza.

Jørn Moestrup
Professor Emeritus, University of Southern Denmark. Publications on Pirandello *The Structural Patterns of Pirandello's Work* (Odense 1973), articles on Italian literature of the 19th centuries. Editor of Christian Molbech's translation of Dante's *Comedy* into Danish (1966).

Ülar Ploom
Professor at the Institute of Germanic and Romance Languages and Cultures of the University of Tallinn. Main fields of interest: late medieval and Renaissance studies, theory and poetics of translation, poetry. Works: *Petrarca. Secretum. Commented translation and essay* (Tallinn 1995). *Quest and Fulfilment in the 13th century Italian Love Lyric* (Tallinn 2000). *Dante. Inferno. Commentaries and preface to the 1st full Estonian translation* (Tallinn 2008 *in spe*). Two collections of poetry (2002, 2006).

Hanne Roer
Associate Professor of Rhetoric, University of Copenhagen. Ph.D. thesis: *Dante Impositor. On the Origins of Poetry and Language in Dante and the Modistae*, University of Aarhus 2000. Translations with a commentary of Dante's *De vulgari eloquentia* (with C. Høgel) and *The Letter to Cangrande* are published this year: *Dante om sprog og poesi.* (Syddansk Universitetsforlag 2008). Next year a book titled *Beatrice og det universelle sprog* will be published by Aarhus Universitetsforlag.

Literature

Agamben, Giorgio 1999. *The End of the Poem. Studies in Poetics*, Translated by Daniel Heller-Roazen. Stanford, California, Stanford University Press

Aquinas, Thomas 1952. *The Summa Theologica of Saint Thomas Aquinas*. Translated by Fathers of the English Dominican Province. Revised by Daniel J. Sullivan. Vol. 1. In William Benton (Publisher). Chicago, Encyclopaedia Britannica 1952–59, 30th printing 1988

Aquinas, Thomas 1952–54. *The Disputed Questions on Truth. Questiones Disputatae de Veritate*. Translated by Robert W. Mulligan, S.J., James V. McGlynn, S.J. and Robert W. Schmidt. S.J. Chicago, Henry Regnery Company. HTML edition By Joseph Kenny, O.P. *Quaestiones Disputatae de Veritate. Truth by Thomas Aquinas.*

Aquinas, Thomas 1975. *Summa Contra Gentiles. Books I–IV*. 1975. Translated with an Introduction and Notes by Anton C. Pegis, F.R.S.C., James F. Anderson, Vernon J. Bourke and Charles J. O'Neil. Notre Dame, London, University of Notre Dame Press

Aquinas, Thomas 1993. *Commentary on Aristotle' s De Memoria et reminiscentiae*. In Aquinas, Thomas: *Selected Writings*. Selected and translated by Timothy McDermott. Oxford, Oxford University Press

Aristotle 1986. *De Anima* [On the Soul]. Translated, with an introduction and notes, by Hugh Lawson-Tancred. Harmondsworth, Penguin

Arp, Hans (Jean) & Samuel Beckett et al. 2001. "Poetry is Vertical" (1941). Caws, Mary Ann ed.: *Manifesto: A Century of Isms*. Lincoln, University of Nebraska Press, 529

Ascoli, Albert Russell 1990. "'Neminem ante nos': Historicity and Authority in the *De vulgari eloquentia*". *Annali d'Italianistica* VIII, 186–231

Ascoli, Albert Russell 1991. "Petrarch's Middle Ages: Memory, Imagination, History, and the 'Ascent of Mont Ventoux'". *Stanford Italian Review* 10, 5–44

Ascoli, Albert Russell 1993. "The Unfinished Author: Dante's Rhetoric of Authority in *Convivio* and *De Vulgari Eloquentia*". Rachel Jacoff ed.: *The Cambridge Companion to Dante*. Cambridge and New York, Cambridge University Press, 45–66

Ascoli, Albert Russell 2008. *Dante and the Making of a Modern Author*. Cambridge University Press, Cambridge

Auerbach, Erich 1993. *Literary Language & its Public in Late Latin Antiquity and in the Middle Ages*, tr. Ralph Manheim. Princeton, Princeton University Press

Barański, Zygmunt G. 1995. "Dante's Signs: An Introduction to Medieval Semiotics and Dante". Barnes, John C. & Cormac Ó Cuilleanáin ed.: *Dante and the Middle Ages. Literary and Historical Essays*. Dublin, Irish Academic Press, 139–80 (Publications of the Foundation for Italian Studies, University College, Dublin)

Barański, Zygmunt G. 2005. "Dante Alighieri: experimentation and (self-)exegesis". In Minnis, Alastair & Ian Johnson ed.: *The Cambridge History of Literary Criticism*. Cambridge, Cambridge University Press, 561–82 (Vol. 2: The Middle Ages)

Barnes, John C. & Cormac Ó Cuilleanáin ed. 1995. *Dante and the Middle Ages. Literary and Historical Essays*. Dublin, Irish Academic Press (Publications of the Foundation for Italian Studies, University College, Dublin)

Barolini, Teodolinda 1984. *Dante's poets: Textuality and Truth in the Comedy*. Princeton, Princeton University Press

Barolini, Teodolinda 1992. *The Undivine Comedy. Detheologizing Dante*. Princeton University Press, Princeton New Jersey

Barolini, Teodolinda 1993. "Dante and the Lyric Past". In Rachel Jacoff ed.: *The Cambridge Companion to Dante*. Cambridge, Cambridge University Press

Barolini, Teodolinda 2000. "Dante and Francesca da Rimini: Realpolitik, Romance, Gender". *Speculum* 75, 1–28

Baudelaire, Charles 1961. *Œuvres complètes*. Yves Gerard Le Dantec & Claude Pichois ed. Paris, Gallimard (Bibliothèque de la Pléiade)

Beckett, Samuel 1972. "Dante...Bruno. Vico.. Joyce". Beckett, Samuel et al.: *Our Exagmination Round His Factification for Incamination of Work In Progress*. London, Faber and Faber, 1–22

Beckett, Samuel et al. 1972. *Our Exagmination Round His Factification for Incamination of Work In Progress*. London, Faber and Faber

Beckett, Samuel 1993. *Dream of Fair to Middling Women*. London, Calder Publications

Literature

Bible, the Holy 1984, New International version

Biblia Sacra Vulgata 1994. Stuttgart, Deutsche Bibelgesellschaft

Bjornes, Asbjørn 2002. *Selvfokusering, lovprisning og erkjennelse i Dantes* Vita nuova. Hovedfagsoppgave i allmenn litteraturvitenskap, Institutt for nordistikk og litteraturvitenskap ved Universitetet i Oslo

Bloch, R. Howard & Stephen G. Nichols ed. 1996. *Medievalism and the Modernist Temper*. Baltimore, The Johns Hopkins University Press

Bloom, Allan 1991. "Interpretive Essay." In *The Republic of Plato*. Translated, with notes and an interpretive essay by Allan Bloom. Second ed. New York, Basic Books

Boldrini, Lucia 2001. *Joyce, Dante, and the Poetics of Literary Relations. Language and Meaning in* Finnegans Wake. Cambridge University Press, eBrary Academic Complete. University of Tampere Lib. [31 Jan. 2008]. <http://site.ebrary.com>

Bonaventura da Bagnoregio 1994. *Itinerario della mente verso Dio*. Trans. Massimo Parodi & Marco Rossini. Milano, Rizzoli

Botterill, Steven 1996. "Introduction". Dante Alighieri: *De vulgari eloquentia*. Cambridge, Cambridge University Press (Cambridge medieval classics, 5)

Boyde, Patrick 1971. *Dante's Style in his Lyric Poetry*. Cambridge, Cambridge University Press

Calvino, Italo 1988. *Lezioni americane. Sei proposte per il prossimo millennio*. Milano, Garzanti

Cary, H.F. 1871. *The Vision: or Hell, Purgatory, and Paradise of Dante Alighieri*. London, [s.n.]

Caselli, Daniela 2005. *Beckett's Dantes. Intertextuality in the Fiction and Criticism*. Manchester, University Press

Caws, Mary Ann ed. 2001. *Manifesto. A Century of Isms*. Lincoln, University of Nebraska Press

Cestaro, Gary P. 2003. *Dante and the Grammar of the Nursing Body*. Notre Dame, Indiana University of Notre Dame Press

Chiavacci Leonardi, Anna Maria 1994. *Noter til Dante Alighieri, Commedia, Purgatorio*. Milano, Mondadori

Cohn, Ruby 2001. *A Beckett Canon*. Ann Arbor, University of Michigan Press

Collins, James J. 1989. *Dante: Layman. Prophet. Mystic*. New York, Alba House (Society of St. Paul)

Contini, Gianfranco 1976. "Dante come personaggio-poeta della Commedia" (1957). In *Un'idea di Dante: Saggi danteschi*. Torino, Einaudi, 33–63

Corti, Maria 1982. *Dante a un nuovo crocevia*. Firenze, Sansori

Cullhed, Anders (ed.) 2006. "Dante og polyfoni". *Perspektiv på Dante II*. København, Multivers

Cullhed, Anders (forthcoming). "'Sermo stupescit': Figurations of Ineffability in High Medieval Poetry (Alan of Lille, Dante, Petrarch)". Andrée, Alexander & Erika Kihlman ed.: *Hortus troporum. Florilegium in honorem Gunillae Iversen*. Stockholm, Almqvist & Wiksell International (Acta Universitatis Stockholmiensis. Studia Latina Stockholmiensia)

Curtius, Ernst Robert 1993. *Europäische Literatur und lateinisches Mittelalter*. Tübingen, Franke

Dante Alighieri 1912. *Göttliche Komödie, In deutsche Terzinen übertragen von* Richard Zoozmann, in *Dantes Poetische Werke*, vols. 1–4, Freiburg im Breisgau

Dante Alighieri 1929. *Dante Alighieris guddommelige komedie*. Overs. af Christian K. F. Molbech. København, Gad

Dante Alighieri 1929. *Göttliche Komödie. In reimlosen Terzinen treu ins Deutsche übersetzt von* Reinhold Schoener. Leipzig, [s.n.]

Dante Alighieri 1949. *The Comedy of Hell*. Translated by Dorothy L. Sayers. Harmondsworth, Penguin

Dante Alighieri 1949–57. *Die Göttliche Komödie. Übersetzt von* Hermann Gmelin, 1–3 + *Kommentar* 4–6. Stuttgart, [s.n.]

Dante Alighieri 1963. *Den guddommelige Komedie*. På dansk ved Knud Hee Andersen. København, Gad. 3 b.

Dante Alighieri 1965. *Dante og Beatrice. Et utvalg fra Dantes ungdomsdiktning og Divina Commedia*. Gjendiktning ved Kristen Gundelach. Oslo, Dreyer

Dante Alighieri 1968. *Den Guddommelige Komedie*. Paa Dansk ved Christian K. F. Molbech. København, Thaning & Appell. 3 b

Dante Alighieri 1970. *The Divine Comedy. Inferno*. Translated, with a Commentary, by Charles S. Singleton. Vol. 1: Text. Bollingen Series LXXX. Princeton, Princeton University Press

Dante Alighieri 1973. *The Divine Comedy. Purgatorio*. Translated, with a Commentary, by Charles S. Singleton. Vol. 2, Commentary. Bollingen Series LXXX. Princeton, Princeton University Press

Literature

Dante Alighieri 1975. *The Divine Comedy. Paradiso.* Translated, with a Commentary, by Charles S. Singleton. Vol. 1: Text. Bollingen Series LXXX. Princeton, Princeton University Press

Dante Alighieri 1979. *Opere minori,* vol. II. Riccardo Ricciardi. Milano–Napoli

Dante Alighieri 1984–86. *The Divine Comedy.* Translated with an introduction, notes and commentary by Mark Musa [1971–84], 1–3. London, Penguin (Penguin Classics)

Dante Alighieri 1985. *La Divina Commedia. Paradiso.* Ed. Natalino Sapegno. Firenze, La Nuova Italia

Dante Alighieri 1987. *La Divina Commedia, 1–3.* A cura di Umberto Bosco e Giovanni Reggio. Firenze, Le Monnier

Dante Alighieri 1988. *La Divina Commedia.* Testo critico della Società Dantesca Italiana. Riveduto, col commento scartazziano rifatto da Giuseppe Vandelli. Milano, Ulriko Hoepli Editore

Dante Alighieri 1990. *Il Convivio (The Banquet).* Translated by Richard H. Lansing. New York, Garland

Dante Alighieri 1990. *La Divina Commedia.* Vol. I-III: *Inferno, Purgatorio, Paradiso.* ed. by N. Sapegno. Firenze, La Nuova Italia

Dante Alighieri 1991–97. *Commedia.* Milano, Arnoldo Mondadori

Dante Alighieri 1992. *La Divine Comédie.* Texte original, Traduction, introduction et notes de Jacqueline Risset, 1–3. Paris, Flammarion

Dante Alighieri 1993. *Convivio.* In *Tutte le opere. Divina Commedia, Vita Nuova, Rime, Convivio, De vulgari eloquentia, Monarchia, Egloghe, Epistole, Quaestio de aqua et de terra.* Introduzione di Italo Borzi. Commenti a cura di Giovanni Fallani, Nicola Maggi e Silvio Zennaro. Roma, Newton Compton Editori

Dante Alighieri 1993. *The Divine Comedy.* Translated by C.H. Sisson, with an introduction and notes by David H. Higgins. Oxford University Press

Dante Alighieri 1993–96. *Den guddommelege komedie.* Til norsk ved Magnus Ulleland. Oslo, Gyldendal. 3 b.

Dante Alighieri 1994. *La commedia secondo l'antica vulgata.* Edited by Giorgio Petrocchi. Firenze, Le Lettere. 4 vols.

Dante Alighieri 1995. *Convivio.* Prefazione, note e commenti di Piero Cudini. Garzanti Editore s.p.a.

Dante Alighieri 1995. *La Comédie. Traduction* Jean-Charles Vegliante. Paris, *Enfer* (La salamandre /Imprimerie nationale)

Dante Alighieri 1995. *La commedia: nuovo testo critico secondo i più antichi manoscritti fiorentini*. A cura di Antonio Lanza. Roma, De Rubeis Editore

Dante Alighieri 1995. *The Divine Comedy*. Translated by Allen Mandelbaum with an Introduction by Eugenio Montale and Notes by Peter Armour. London, Everyman's Library

Dante Alighieri 1995. *Vita Nuova*. Italian Text with Facing English Translation by Dino S. Cervigni and Edward Vasta. Notre Dame and London, University of Notre Dame Press

Dante Alighieri 1996. *De vulgari eloquentia*. Translated by Steven Botterill. Cambridge, Cambridge University Press

Dante Alighieri 1996. *Monarchy*. Translated by Prue Shaw. Cambridge, Cambridge University Press

Dante Alighieri 1996. *Œuvres complètes. Traduction nouvelle sous la direction de Christian* Bec. Traductions et notes de Christian Bec, Roberto Barbone, François Livi, Marc Scialom [*Divine Comédie*] et Antonio Stäuble. Paris, Le Livre de Poche

Dante Alighieri 1996. *The Divine Comedy of Dante Alighieri*. Edited and translated by Robert M. Durling. Introduction and Notes by Ronald L. Martinez and Robert M. Durling, Vol. 1: Inferno. Oxford University Press

Dante Alighieri 1997. *Den gudomliga komedin*. Översatt och kommenterad av Ingvar Björkeson. Stockholm, Natur & Kultur

Dante Alighieri 1997–98. *Commedia. Con il commento di Anna Maria Chiavacci Leonardi*. 3 vols: 1. *Inferno*. 1998, 2. *Purgatorio*. 1998, 3. *Paradiso*. 1997. Milano, Arnoldo Mondadori

Dante Alighieri 1998. *The Divine Comedy: Hell, Purgatory, Heaven*. A "Terza Rima" Version by Peter Dale. London, Anvil Press

Dante Alighieri 1999. *De vulgari eloquentia*. Edited and translated by Steven Botterill. Cambridge, Cambridge University Press

Dante Alighieri 2000. *Den guddommelege komedie*. Til norsk ved Magnus Ulleland. 2. utg. Oslo, Gyldendal

Dante Alighieri 2001. *Dantis Alagherii Comedia*. Edizione critica per cura di Federico Sanguineti, Sismel

Dante Alighieri 2002. *Inferno*. A Verse Translation by Robert and Jean Hollander. New York, Anchor

Dante Alighieri 2002. *La Divina Commedia. Paradiso*. Con pagine critiche a cura di Umberto Bosco e Giovanni Reggio. Firenze, Le Monnier

Dante Alighieri 2002. *The Inferno of Dante Alighieri*. A new translation by Ciaran Carson. Great Britain, Granta Books

Dante Alighieri 2004. *Dantes guddommelige komedie*. Overs. af Ole Meyer. [København], Multivers

Dante Alighieri 2007. *Epistle to Can Grande*. Translated by James Marchand (University of Illinois). The text was prepared for the web on 26–27 June 1996 by Jim Dean. [Accessed December 10, 2007]. <http://www.english.udel.edu/dean/cangrand.html>

Dante Alighieri 2007. *Paradiso*. A Verse Translation by Robert and Jean Hollander. New York, Doubleday

De Sanctis, Francesco 1957. "Francesca da Rimini" (1869). Now in *Saggi critici*, Bari, Laterza

Del Corno Branca, Daniela 1998. *Tristano e Lancillotto in Italia*. Ravenna, Longo

Dronke, Peter 1975. "Francesca and Héloïse". *Comparative Literature* 26, 2, 113–135

Durling, Robert M. 1974 "The Ascent of Mt. Ventoux and the Crisis of Allegory", *Italian Quarterly* 18, 7–28

Eco, Umberto 1988. *The Aesthetics of Thomas Aquinas*. Translated by Hugh Bredin. Cambridge, Harvard University Press

Eco, Umberto 1995. *The Search for the Perfect Language*. Translated by James Fentress. Blackwell, Oxford

Eco, Umberto 1999. *Serendipities. Language and Lunacy*. Translated by William Weaver. San Diego, Harvest Book

Eliot, T.S. 1963. *Collected Poems 1909–1962*. London, Faber and Faber

Falkeid, Unn (forthcoming). "Petrarch and the Modern Self. A Reading of the Mont Ventoux letter", *Forum Italicum*

Falkeid, Unn 2008. "Style, the Muscle of the Soul. Theories on Reading and Writing in Petrarch's texts". *Quaderni d'Italianistica*, 29, 1

Ferrante, Joan M. 1985. *Woman as Image in Medieval Literature*. Durham, The Labyrinth Press

Fineman, Joel 1986. *Shakespeare's Perjured Eye. The Invention of Poetic Subjectivity in the Sonnets*. Berkeley, University of California Press

Fitch, Noel Riley 1990. *In transition: A Paris Anthology: Writing and Art from transition Magazine 1927–30*. With an Introdustion by Noel Riley Fitch. New York, Anchor Books

Franke, William 1994. "Dante's Address to the Reader and its Ontological Significance". *Modern Language Notes* vol. 109, no. 1, 117–127 (Italian Issue, January)

Freccero, John 1975. "The Fig Tree and the Laurel: Petrarch's Poetics". *Diacretics* 5, 34–40

Genette, Gerald 1982. *Palimpsestes. La littérature a second degré.* Paris, Editions du Seuil

George, Stefan 1988. *Dante: Die Göttliche Komödie. Übertragungen* [1904–25]. Stuttgart, Klett-Cotta Verlag (*Sämtliche Werke*, Band X/XI)

Ginsberg, Warren 1999. *Dante's Aesthetics of Being*. Michigan, University of Michigan Press

Greene, Thomas M. 1982. *The Light in Troy: Imitation and Discovery in Renaissance Poetry*. New Haven, Yale University Press

Greimas, Algirdas Julien & Joseph Courtés 1988. *Semiotik. Sprogteoretisk ordbog*. Aarhus, Aarhus Universitetsforlag

Harrison, Robert Pogue 1988. *The Body of Beatrice*. Baltimore, The Johns Hopkins University Press

Hatcher, Anna & Mark Musa 1968. "The Kiss: *Inferno* V and the Old French Prose Lancelot". *Comparative Literature* 20, 97–109

Hawkins, Peter 1984. "Dante's 'Paradiso' and the Dialectic of Ineffability". Hawkins, Peter S. & Anne Howland Schotter ed. *Ineffability: Naming the Unnamable from Dante to Beckett*, New York, AMS Press, 5–21 (AMS Ars poetica, 2)

Hawkins, Peter S. 1993. "Dante and the Bible". *The Cambridge Companion to Dante.* ed. Rachel Jacoff. Cambridge, Cambridge University Press, 120–35

Hawkins, Peter S. 1999. *Dante's Testaments. Essays in Scriptural Imagination*. Stanford, Stanford University Press

Hede, Jesper 2007. *Reading Dante: The Pursuit of Meaning*. Lanham, Lexington Books

Ivanov, Vyacheslav 2001. "Thoughts about Symbolism" (1912). Translated by Ronald E. Peterson. Caws, Mary Ann ed.: *Manifesto: A Century of Ism*, 63–70

Jacomuzzi, Angelo 1995. "Il "topos" dell'ineffabile nel "Paradiso". In *L'Imago al Cerchio e altri studi sulla "Divina Commedia"*. Milano, Franco Angeli

Jaeger, Stephen C. 1999. *Ennobling Love: In Search of a Lost Sensibility*. Philadelphia, University of Pennsylvania Press

Jolas, Eugene 1972. "The Revolution of Language and James Joyce". Beckett, Samuel et al.: *Our Exagmination Round His Factification for Incamination of Work In Progress*, 79–92

Kennedy, F. ed. 1980. *Lancelot du Lac: the Non-Cyclic Old French Prose Romance*. Oxford, Clarendon Press

Kleinhenz, Christopher 1986. "Dante and the Bible: Intertextual Approaches to the *Divine Comedy*". *Italica*. ed. Robert J. Rodini. Published by the American Association of Teachers of Italian. Vol. 63, No. 3, 225–36

Kleinhenz, Christopher 1997. "Dante and the Bible: Biblical Citation in the '*Divine Comedy*'". *Dante. Contemporary Perspectives*. Ed. Amilcare A. Iannucci. Toronto, University of Toronto Press, 74–93

Lagerkrantz, Olof 1965. *Fra helvede til paradis. En bog om Dante og hans guddommelige komedie*. København, Schønberske

Luzzi, Joseph 1998. "Literary History and Individuality in the De vulgari eloquentia". *Dante Studies*, 161–88

Mallette, Karla 2005. *The Kingdom of Sicily, 1100–1250. A Literary History*. Philadelphia, University of Pennsylvania Press.

Manetti, Aldo 1984. "Dante e la Bibbia". *Bollettino della Civica Biblioteca* (Bergamo)

Marigo, Aristide 1957. *Notes to Dante Alghieri: De vulgari eloquentia*, ed. Marigo, Felice LeMonnier. Firenze

Mastrobuono, Antonio C. 1990. *Dante's Journey of Sanctification*. Washington DC, Regnery Gateway

Mazzaro, Jerome 1981. *The Figure of Dante. An Essay on the* Vita Nuova. Princeton, Princeton University Press

Mazzotta, Giuseppe 1979. *Dante, Poet of the Desert. History and Allegory in the Divine Comedy*. Princeton, Princeton University Press.

Mazzotta, Giuseppe 1993a. *Dante's Vision and the Circle of Knowledge*, Princeton, Princeton University Press

Mazzotta, Giuseppe 1993b. *The Worlds of Petrarch*. Durham, Duke University Press

Mengaldo, Pier Vincenzo 1978. *Linguistica e retorica di Dante*. Pisa, Nistri–Lischi (Saggi di varia umantià, 21)

Menocal, María Rosa 1991. *Writing in Dante's Cult of Truth: From Borges to Boccaccio*. Durham and London, Duke University Press

Mercuri, Roberto 1987. "Un' 'ascesione' altamente simbolica: la Familiare IV, 1". In the chapter "Genesi della tradizione letteraria italiana in Dante, Petrarca e Boccaccio", in *Letteratura italiana, Storia e geografia*. Vol. I. *L'età medievale*, Torino, Giulio Einaudi Editore, 344–353

Minnis, A. J. 1984. *Medieval Theory of Authorship. Scholastic Literary Attitudes in the Later Middle Ages.* London, Scolar Press

Minnis, Alastair & Ian Johnson ed. 2005. *The Middle Ages.* Cambridge, Cambridge University Press (The Cambridge History of Literary Criticism, 2)

Moréas, Jean 2001. "The Symbolist Manifesto" Translated by Mary Ann Caws. Caws, Mary Ann ed.: *Manifesto: A Century of Isms*, 50–51

Musa, Mark 1973. *Dante's Vita nuova: A Translation and an Essay.* Bloomington, Indiana University Press

Myhre, Klara 1985. "Salmenes bok – betydning og bruk." And: "Hymner." *Bibelverket. Fortolkning til Salmenes bok*. Vol. I. By Klara Myhre, Jens Olav Mæland, Karsten Valen. Oslo, Luther Forlag og Lunde Forlag

Najemy, John M. 1982. *Corporatism and Consensus in Florentine Electoral Politics, 1280–1400.* Chapel Hill, The University of North Carolina Press.

Nichols, Stephen G. 2005. "Writing the New Middle Ages." *PMLA* 120.2, 422–41

Noakes, Susan 1983. "The Double Misreading of Paolo and Francesca". *Philological Quarterly* 62, 2, 221–39

Ovid 1985. *Metamorphoses*. Translated by Mary M. Innes. Harmondsworth, Penguin (Penguin classics)

Ovid 1991. *Le metamorfosi*. Translated by Enrico Oddone. Milano, Bompiani

Patrologiae cursus completus. Series Latina. 1–217. Ed. J.-P. Migne. Paris, apud J.-P. Migne editorem, 1844–55 [abbreviated *PL*]

Pazzaglia, Mario 1967. *Il verso e l'arte della canzone nel* De vulgari eloquentia. Firenze, Pubblicazioni della Facoltà di Magistero dell'Università degli studi di Bologna.

Petrarca, Francesco 1933–42. *Epistolae familiares*, 4 vols. Edited by Vittorio Rossi and Umberto Bosco: *Le Familiari di Francesco Petrarca*. Edizione nazionale delle opere di Francesco Petrarca. Vols. 10–13. Florence, Sansoni

Petrarch, Francesco 1975–85, *Rerum Familiarum Libri*. Translated by Bernardo, Aldo: Letters on Familiar Matters, 3 vols. Albany, N.Y. State, University of New York Press.

Popper, Karl 1995. *The Open Society and Its Enemies. Volume One: The Spell of Plato*. Fifth ed. London, Routledge

Pound, Ezra 2001. "Dante". Hawkins, Peter S. & Rachel Jacoff: *The Poet's Dante: Twentieth Century Responses*. New York, Farrar, Straus, and Giroux

Pseudo-Dionysius 1987. *The Complete Works*. New Jersey, The Paulist Press

Rabaté, Jean-Michel 2008. "Joyce and Jolas: Late Modernism and Early Babelism" *Journal of Modern Literature* 22.2. [1999], 245–52. ProjectMuse, University of Tampere Lib. [Read 31 Jan]. <http://muse.jhu.edu>

Rasula, Jed & Steve McCaffery ed. 1998. *Imagining Language: An Anthology*. Cambridge, The MIT Press

Reynolds, Barbara 2006. *Dante. The Poet, the Political Thinker, the Man*. London, I.B. Tauris & Co. Ltd

Ryan, Christopher 1993. "The theology of Dante." *The Cambridge Companion to Dante*. ed. Rachel Jacoff. Cambridge, Cambridge University Press. 136–52

Saint-René, Martin, 1966. *La Divine Comédie de Dante, traduite littéralement entièrement en terza rima françaises*, 1935–38, Paris, Bibliothèque des études poéthiques

Sanguineti, Edoardo 1980. *Il realismo di Dante*. Firenze, Sansoni

Scipio, G.C. & A. Scaglione ed. 1988. *The Divine Comedy and the Encyclopedia of Arts and Sciences*. Amsterdam, John Benjamins Publishing Co

Scorrano, Luigi 1998. "Inferno XIII: Un orizzonte di negazione". In *Deutsches Dante-Jahrbuch*, 73. band. Köln-Weimar-Wien, Böhlau Verlag

Seung, T.K. 1962. *The Fragile Leaves of the Sibyl: Dante's Master Plan*. Westminster, Newman Press

Seung, T.K. 1976. *Cultural Thematics: The Formation of the Faustian Ethos*. New Haven, Yale University Press

Seung, T.K. 1982. *Semiotics and Thematics in Hermeneutics*. New York, Columbia University Press

Seung, T.K. 1988. "The Metaphysics of the *Commedia*". Scipio, G.C. & A. Scaglione ed.: *The Divine Comedy and the Encyclopedia of Arts and Sciences*. Amsterdam, John Benjamin's Publishing Co, 181–122.

Shapiro, Marianne 1990. *Dante's Book of Exile: The* De vulgari eloquentia. Lincoln, University of Nebraska Press.

Shaw, J.E. 1965. *Essays on the Vita Nuova*. Reprinted with the permission of the Princeton University Press. New York, Kraus Reprint Corporation

Singleton, Charles S. 1954. *Dante Studies I: Elements of Structure*. Cambridge, Harvard University Press

Singleton, Charles S. 1958. *Dante Studies II: Journey to Beatrice*. Cambridge, Harvard University Press

Singleton, Charles S. 1970–75. *Dante Alighieri: The Divine Comedy*. Translated with a commentary. Princeton University. 3. vols.

Singleton, Charles S. 1983. *An Essay on the* Vita Nuova. Baltimore, The Johns Hopkins University Press

Smalley, Beryl 1964. *The Study of the Bible in the Middle Ages*. Notre Dame, Indiana, University of Notre Dame Press

Spitzer, Leo 1955. "The Addresses to the Reader in the 'Commedia'". *Italica*, vol. 32, No. 3 (Sep.), 143–65

Strauss, Leo. "On Plato's Republic". In *The City and Man*. Chicago, Rand McMally, 1964

The Holy Bible 1984. New International Version. Grand Rapids. Michigan, Zondervan Bible Publishers (Twelfth printing)

Trovato, Paolo 1979. *Dante in Petrarch. Per un inventario dei dantismi nei "Rerum vulgarium fragmenta"*. Firenze, Leo S. Olscchki Editore

Valesio, Paolo 1998. "*Inferno V*: the Fierce Dove."*Lectura Dantis*", 14–15, 3–25

Valesio, Paolo 2002. "'The Most Enduring and Most Honored Name.' Marinetti as Poet" Marinetti, F. T.: *Selected Poems and Related Prose*. ed. Luce Marinetti, translated by Elizabeth R. Napier & Barbara R. Studholme, with an essay by Paolo Valesio. New Haven, Yale University Press. 149–65

Waage Petersen, Lene 1995. "Odyssevs' siste rejse". *Romanske rejser. En tematisk rundfart i de romanske litteraturer*. København, Museum Tusculanum

Wolosky, Shira 1995. *Language Mysticism. The Negative Way of Language in Eliot, Beckett and Celan.* Stanford, Stanford University Press

Wood, Diana 2002. *Medieval Economic Thought*, Cambridge, Cambridge University Press.